(NOT) GETTING PAID TO DO WHAT YOU LOVE

GENDER, SOCIAL MEDIA, AND ASPIRATIONAL WORK

BROOKE ERIN DUFFY

Yale

UNIVERSITY PRESS

New Haven and London

Published with assistance from the Mary Cady Tew Memorial Fund.

Yale University Press books may be purchased in quantity for educational, business, or promotional use. For information, please e-mail sales. press@yale.edu (U.S. office) or sales@yaleup.co.uk (U.K. office).

Set in Adobe Garamond type by IDS Infotech, Ltd.
Printed in the United States of America.

ISBN 978-0-300-21817-6 (hardcover : alk. paper)

Library of Congress Control Number: 2016961763

A catalogue record for this book is available from the British Library.

This paper meets the requirements of ANSI/NISO Z39.48-1992 (Permanence of Paper).

10 9 8 7 6 5 4 3 2 1

In Loving Memory of
My Dad
Daniel Lee Pilszak
(1949–2015)

Contents

Preface

Popular rhetoric suggests that social media platforms like Facebook, Twitter, and YouTube have opened the sluice gates of creative expression. The idea is seductive, and it helps to explain the appeal of social media for the legions of young aspirants hoping to break into the creative industries. As a scholar of cultural production, I was intrigued by the promise of self-made careers fashioned online. I had just finished a book on the women's magazine industry, which chronicled producers' efforts to contain the impending threat of fashion bloggers and other independent voices. Could these social media creators really bypass the legacy companies or, alternatively, harness the currency of their networked "audiences" to land coveted positions in the industry's ranks? I was curious about the *experiences* of the (mostly) young women writing the blogs, uploading the videos, and posting to Instagram. Rhetoric aside, I wanted to know how they managed their enterprising ventures, behind the glossy filters and curated life-sharing. To what extent were their passion projects *paying off*?

I decided to ask them. Over a span of three years, I interviewed dozens of social media producers to make sense of their experiences and aspirations. What I found is that the narrative of creative self-expression—touted by the press and projected by the digital aspirants themselves—conceals the unrelenting work (much of it unpaid) that takes place behind the screens. The "creative" activities of the women I interviewed were often purposeful and resolute: content was fashioned to be *on-brand*, posts were timed to coincide with spikes in platform usage, and feedback from followers was monitored with vigilance. The enterprising young women I spoke with framed their blogs and feeds in *employability* terms as much as, if not more than, self-expression. Most saw themselves—to borrow business guru Tom Peters's label—as the "CEO of Me, Inc."

These content creators, I came to realize, were motivated by the wider culture's siren call to *get paid to do what you love*. But what they experienced often fell short of the promise: only a few young women rise above the din to achieve major success. The rest are un(der)-paid, remunerated with deferred promises of "exposure" or "visibility," even as they work long hours to satisfy brands and convey authenticity to observant audiences. A grueling balancing act is required, one that I explore through the lens of "aspirational labor."

One of the goals of the book is to challenge the glowing optimism of techno-enthusiasts; it should thus be read as a rejoinder to cheering media accounts of social media entrepreneurship. Indeed, despite their buzzy headlines, articles on "Instagram Users Earn[ing] Thousands for a Single Post" or "Bloggers Turning Social Savvy into Six-Figure Incomes" fail to resonate with the lived experiences of those I studied. With this discrepancy in mind, it was important that the book allow content creators to speak in their own voices. And so I conducted fifty-six in-depth interviews with fashion and lifestyle bloggers, video bloggers (or vloggers), do-it-yourself (or DIY) fashion/jewelry designers, participants in fashion networking sites like the College Fashionista program, and street-style photographers, among others. A full list of my interviewees and other details about the interview process are available in the book's appendix.

Some of the aspirants I met over the course of this project were college students or newly minted graduates trying to stand out in an overcrowded employment market. Others were members of the "slash generation," individuals in their twenties and early thirties whose worker identities span multiple professions. For example, Danielle was a pharmaceutical sales rep/style blogger, Christie was a hairdresser/jewelry designer, Julianne was a PR representative/blogger, and so on. Some commentators, such as *New York Times* writer Sheila Marikar, argue that these hybrid professional lives are pursued for creative rather than economic reasons. But my research shows that many slashies are not merely trying to escape the banality of their "day jobs"; rather, they are trying to earn incomes from their so-called passion projects in the midst of a labor market that is rife with uncertainty.

In addition to individual interviews, I met my sources at a wide range of events—from formal industry conferences to more casual meetings of bloggers and social media pros. The former included the Women Get Social "Boot Camp" for bloggers; the annual Fashion-Forward conference; the Philly Tech Week Fashion Blogger's event; and the "Fun, Fearless, Life" weekend produced by *Cosmopolitan* magazine. Each of these events provided me with access to leaders in social media, fashion, and advertising as well as the chance to connect with those aspirants getting steeped in the culture of social media analytics, influence, and self-branding. In addition, I conducted field-work at informal events during New York Fashion Week and retail launches led by and for bloggers. To understand the ways in which digital media producers are socialized into the aspirational labor force, I drew upon a diverse series of blogger manuals and professional resources, including books (*Fashion 2.0: Blogging Your Way to The Front Row; Blog, Inc.: Blogging for Passion, Profit, and to Create Community*), thematic career manuals (*Teen Vogue Handbook: An Insider's Guide to*

Careers in Fashion), online networks and support groups (the Independent Fashion Bloggers network), and career guidance included in the blogs/vlogs themselves.

By weaving together interview data, field notes, and analyses of various texts—and drawing on writings from media studies, sociology, and gender studies—the book foregrounds the neglected dimension of gender in debates and theories of creative labor in an age of social media. And while I take seriously the "passion project" narratives of many young female content creators, I also draw out some important contradictions in their self-descriptions: between amateurism and expertise, between authenticity and strategic self-branding, and between internal drivers and external demands. Through the framework of *aspirational labor,* these women come to resemble the traditional media workers (journalists, producers, videographers) they have defined themselves against. And their roles come across as traditional in a second, gendered sense: the bloggers and social media users, I argue, end up reaffirming the already-tight bond between consumption and femininity.

In the end, I hope this book proves valuable for scholars, students, educators, and aspirational laborers themselves. And despite the book's emphasis on distinctly gendered work, it is meant to offer a lens through which to understand, anticipate, and critique larger transformations in the so-called "gig economy." Despite the rousing assurance that anyone can stand out among the inflated supply of workers, *(Not) Getting Paid to Do What You Love* pushes all of us to reconsider the stakes of social media production and promotion.

1

Entrepreneurial Wishes and Career Dreams

In spring 2014, close on the heels of toy manufacturer Mattel's controversial collaboration with *Sports Illustrated*—which featured a bathing suit–clad Barbie on the magazine's 50th Anniversary Swimsuit Issue cover-wrap—the company unveiled the latest doll in its "I Can Be" career collection: Entrepreneur Barbie. Outfitted in a modern-cut magenta dress and furnished with a diminutive tablet device and smart phone, Entrepreneur Barbie was marketed as a self-starter "ready to make a bold business move and strike out on her own to achieve her career dreams."[1] The company tapped ten prominent female entrepreneurs, including Girls Who Code founding CEO Reshma Saujani and Jennifer Fleiss, co-founder of Rent the Runway, as real-world ambassadors for Barbie's "Career of the Year." Social media figured prominently in the product launch: the hashtag "unapologetic"—originally created for the *Sports Illustrated* campaign—was repackaged as a message of female empowerment, and Barbie took to Twitter to host a virtual "Pink Power Lunch," wherein she engaged fans in 140-character dialogues about their "dream careers."[2]

Although a few public commentators lapped up Mattel's celebratory rhetoric of women's liberation, reporters and cultural critics alike mocked the company's naïve depiction of female entrepreneurship. An *Atlantic* reporter, who nodded toward Facebook COO Sheryl Sandberg with the headline "Barbie Leans In," blasted the doll's enduring penchant for pink and fetishization of unrealistic standards of female physicality.[3] *Time* reporter Jessica Roy's criticism went beyond body image censure to highlight the tension between a romanticized version of entrepreneurship and persistent gender inequalities in tech start-ups. As Roy scoffed, "Perhaps next Mattel can craft 'Silently Enduring Sexual Harassment with the Hope I Will Get a Raise' Barbie; 'Making Less Than My Male Counterparts' Barbie; 'Getting Turned Down by Investors Because I'm Pregnant' Barbie; or 'I'm Going to Die Eating This Sad Salad at My Desk Alone' Barbie."[4] While debates about the merits of Entrepreneur Barbie seemed to languish by the time the doll hit toy store shelves, muted in part by news of Mattel's precipitously declining revenues, the reactions reflect more widespread discourses of gender and self-enterprise in the aptly named "new economy."

More than ever, contemporary culture's benchmark of success is the figure of the entrepreneur; a study of young people's career aspirations revealed that roughly two-thirds of those aged eighteen to thirty-four desire to start their own business, and 37 percent want to work independently.[5] The ideal of the enterprising self feeds into and is fed by a torrent of career manuals, online articles, digital tutorials, and even college courses hyping the spirit of passion-fueled careerism. How-to books—such as *Lifestyle Entrepreneur: Live Your Dreams, Ignite Your Passions and Run Your Business from Anywhere in the World; The $100 Startup: Reinvent the Way You Make a Living, Do What You Love, and Create a New Future;* and the latest installment in John Parkin's irreverently titled series, *F**k It: Do What You Love*—provide tried and true steps for securing a career where pleasure and profit blend in perfect harmony. The affective language of "love" and "passion" is so prevalent in these employment discourses that scholar and *Jacobin* contributor Miya Tokumitsu declared "Do What You Love" the "unofficial work mantra of our time."[6]

Nowhere is this career mantra more pervasive than in the creative industries, including fashion, media, entertainment, and design. These fields are seen as idyllic professional destinations, characterized by autonomy, flexibility, and, above all, the potential for self-actualization. For young women, including those incited by what cultural theorist Angela McRobbie identifies as the "creativity *dispotif*" rampant in popular culture and the education system, "work becomes akin to a romantic relationship."[7] Yet the boundaries surrounding these industries are notoriously impermeable, especially in a "gig economy" of outsourced jobs and slashed benefits.

With other viable pathways blocked, would-be creatives are turning to social media as conduits to visibility and exposure. Silicon Valley social networks are the new audition reels for the media and culture industries—the place where stars are made, and (the hope is) paid. YouTube is frequently touted as a platform for budding musicians and comedians, and Instagram is celebrated as a public forum for modeling hopefuls.[8] Even Snapchat—with its ephemeral stories and animated face-mapping filters—has spawned a new breed of star: pithy virtual storytellers with word-of-mouth cachet.[9] The triumphant tales of the online "discovered" offer a modern-day version of screen legend Lana Turner's fabled encounter at the soda fountain. And though these celeb-bloggers and digital influencers are allegedly disrupting "the fame paradigm," they are upheld in the popular imagination as individuals *just like us.*[10]

This narrative of digital democratization is especially pronounced in the world of fashion, one of the industries I closely examine in the book. Since the mid-aughts, personal style blogs have been lauded for upending traditional hierarchies of high fashion influence and taste-making.[11] The notion that *anyone can be a fashion blogger* is an unshakable myth in popular culture, and media outlets routinely profile style influencers who lie at the margins of elite fashion's mainstream: plus-size bloggers, bloggers aged forty-plus (or alternatively those still in middle school), and hijab bloggers, as well as the more nebulous designation of "alternative fashion bloggers." The attention lavished on these and other über-stylish digital content producers is astonishing; I witnessed firsthand the frenzy that accompanies A-list fashion bloggers like Aimee Song (Song of Style) and Chiara Ferragni (The Blonde Salad) as they sashayed their way through the swarms at New York Fashion Week, preening for the cameras or snapping selfies with eager onlookers (see Figure 1). Mainstream media coverage also spotlights the economic valuation of these so-called "influencers," revealing "how style bloggers are turning social savvy into six-figure salaries" or reporting on those "paid up to $15,000 for a single Instagram post."[12]

Importantly, the high-profile activities of super-bloggers and the Insta-famous obscure the contributions of legions of other social media producers—bloggers, vloggers, DIY stylists, and more—who make nary a headline. This is a book about these enterprising, digitally networked young people and the oft-unpaid work they undertake. After all, it is the experiences of individuals *aspiring* to colonize the social media economy that give expression to what I call "aspirational labor."

Aspirational labor is a mode of (mostly) uncompensated, independent work that is propelled by the much-venerated ideal of *getting paid to do what you love*. As both a practice and a worker ideology, aspirational labor shifts content creators' focus from the present to the future, dangling the prospect of a career where labor and leisure coexist. Indeed, aspirational laborers expect that they will *one day* be compensated for their productivity—be it through material rewards

1. Chiara Ferragni, the creator of the blog The Blonde Salad, poses for a photographer outside the Michael Kors show at New York Fashion Week.
Photo Credit: Brent Luvaas.

or social capital. But in the meantime, they remain suspended in the consumption and promotion of branded commodities.

Discourses of "paying off" are central to the motivations of aspirational laborers; they expect that their investments of time, energy, and capital will yield a fulfilling, and perhaps lucrative, career. Of course, as I detail throughout this book, "paying off" is highly subjective and varies according to the interests, experiences, and ambitions of the aspirant. Some young women I interviewed seek a career in the creative industries; thus, "paying off" would mean landing a full-time position at a women's magazine, fashion house, or social media firm. Others, particularly those swept up in the infectious rhetoric of entrepreneurialism, see a high-paying blog or makeup vlog as the endgame, with income from affiliate links, brand sponsorships, and/or designer collaborations. For these individuals, the possibility of being independently employed is especially rousing.

But despite the optimism surrounding the future rewards of aspirational labor, only a fraction of content creators rises above the din to achieve major success. For the rest, the ideal of *getting paid to do what you love* remains an unfulfilled promise.

Drawing upon more than fifty in-depth interviews, participant observation, and a close analysis of professionalization resources, this book highlights a set of patterned contradictions that are essential to social media producers' own self-descriptions:

> *Authenticity vs. self-promotion:* A pervasive social media aesthetic and narrative relies on the contemporary logics of "authenticity" and "realness" but requires laborers to draw upon market logics to brand themselves.
>
> *Creativity vs. commerce:* The ideal of creative self-expression that they circulate serves to distinguish social media aspirants from

those working in cultural industries more explicitly driven by profit maximization. Yet much like the latter, individual social media producers confront commercial pressures on the path to generate income.

Hobby vs. professional status: The contrast between professional and amateur pervades the world of social media makers. Certainly, this dichotomy elides the reality that those (seemingly hobby) bloggers with the greatest number of followers have been able to parlay their digital fame into book deals, clothing lines, and designer collaborations, among others.

My use of the term *aspirational* highlights the incentive of future reward systems for present-day productive activities. This concept has important historical precedents that I trace throughout the book. In particular, I detail a significant cultural shift from *aspirational consumption*—status-induced consumerism that routes self-expression through the marketplace—to *aspirational labor,* where self-expression is articulated through a patterned set of highly individualized, value-generating productive activities.

The reference to social media activity as *labor* may initially seem puzzling, given that individuals seem to take great pleasure in their online activities. While the division between labor and leisure has always been knotty, particularly for women,[13] the ascent of digital media renders this divide doubly problematic given the myriad ways in which commonplace acts of self-expression—"liking" a brand's Instagram post, reviewing the latest gadget on Amazon, or updating one's social media profile—generate value for media and marketing institutions.[14] This conceptual slipperiness is among the reasons so many scholars have sought to delineate the borders around "free labor" in the digital economy; in the oft-quoted words of Italian scholar

Tiziana Terranova, such labor is "simultaneously voluntarily given and unwaged, enjoyed and exploited."[15] My own use of the term *labor* captures the productive, purposeful, task-oriented, and value-generating function of these activities. Moreover, as this book makes clear, these practices are quite similar to the (waged) work of traditional media producers, including journalists, video producers, advertisers, and publicists. As Jean Burgess and Joshua Green argued of the YouTube community, social media networks must be understood as "co-creative" spaces where "amateur and professional media content, identities and motivations are not so easily separated."[16]

Social and industrial constructions of gender and femininity are central to the aspirational labor system, especially in the creative industries; for this reason, most of the social media producers I interviewed were women. This is not to say that men don't engage in aspirational labor; they do. But the genres of social media production examined in this book—fashion and lifestyle blogging, beauty vlogging, DIY design—are largely populated by young women. In the popular imagination, these activities are framed through crude binaries that tend to structure conversations about gender-coded internet usage and creative expression. For instance, despite early accounts of the "masculine" blogosphere, the rapid ascension of social media has been celebrated as evidence of the internet's progressive "feminization."[17] In 2012, the Nielsen company released data that revealed a stark "gender divide" in social media habits; noteworthy among its findings was that women—especially in the eighteen to twenty-four category—were significantly more likely than men to have a blog, build social media profiles, and follow a brand online. The *Atlantic*'s Megan Garber summarized the data with a cheering assertion: "Girls may not run the world, but they dominate on the web."[18] But many of these activities are inscribed within a ubiquitous consumer landscape.

As media scholars Sarah Banet-Weiser and Inna Arzumanova argue to this end, "The idea of girls using the web more than boys . . . is already bound by conventional notions of what, and who, girls *are*—fashionistas, make-up artists, stylists, and most of all—shoppers."[19] Banet-Weiser and Arzumanova situate gendered social media praxis (they focus on shopping hauls posted on YouTube) in a historical context wherein girls and young women are seen above all as *consumers* who engage in work on the self (brand).[20]

Aspirational labor, too, relies on historically constructed notions of femininity—particularly discourses of community, affect, and commodity-based self-expression. As I show in the book, the postfeminist logics of visibility and individual expression are articulated as paths to financial empowerment. In addition, I contend that the labor of aspiration has conceptual similarities to traditional forms of "women's work" (domestic labor, reproductive labor, care labor), which have remained invisible despite their central role in servicing the engines of capitalism.[21] I thus situate aspirational labor in a cultural history of unpaid female labor with lineages traceable to systems of patriarchy and commodity capitalism.

Whether male or female, aspirational laborers are engaged in gendered practices that combine (and subsequently reproduce) both of these legacies: working, for little or no pay, to generate consumption-oriented visibility through social media/blogs. This core, gendered dimension of aspirational labor distinguishes the concept from other forms of labor that rely on the temporal deferment of wages and the normalization of risk, most notably Gina Neff's theory of "venture labor" and Kathleen Kuehn and Thomas F. Corrigan's notion of "hope labor."[22] Though these differ in important ways, they collectively address the ideologies that rationalize neoliberal workers' investments of time, capital, and labor through the promise of *eventual* capital or future success. The ideology of hope labor, Kuehn and Corrigan argue, is "positioned as a meritocratic investment in one's employment prospects" at a moment when work is evermore precarious and insecure.[23] One way to understand aspirational labor is as a particular form of hope labor, one that foregrounds participation in the consumer circuit as part of a recursive process. In addition to investing in various commodities, the work of aspirational laborers is often physically embodied in the blogger, vlogger, or Instagrammer as she models her newly purchased wares. In a reprise of the female body's visibility in twentieth-century consumer culture, the digitally networked, pixelated version not only shops but also "tags," "likes," and—most importantly—"recommends" branded goods.

The gendered social media activities I track in the book are one facet of a cultural economy marked by widespread independence. Indeed, freelancers, contract hires, and interns constitute a swelling class of workers in a "gig economy," an "on-demand economy," or perhaps least euphemistically, a "1099 economy." Though many of these individuals pursue the much-hyped ideals of flexibility and autonomy, the rapid growth of independent employment is symptomatic of what scholars and labor advocates understand as a "political economy of insecurity."[24] That is, as neoliberal ideologies and practices shift organizational risks and responsibilities onto individual citizens, workers must shoulder the burden for training, healthcare, and other benefits.

Against the backdrop of pervasive worker insecurity, it is perhaps not surprising that career-seekers are urged to identify their distinctive strengths, engage in brazen self-promotion, and spearhead "personal visibility" campaigns.[25] That is, they are to internalize the logic of personal branding. Though self-promotion is by no means a new imperative, in recent decades, structural transformations bound to the neoliberal ideologies of individuality and self-governance have instigated more self-conscious efforts to *brand the self.*[26] Increasingly, many of these practices take place across a raft of social media networks: Facebook, Twitter, Instagram, and LinkedIn. Forms of online self-branding are built into social network architectures—such as features that require users to add photos to their LinkedIn profiles or craft pithy self-descriptors to fill their Twitter bios. Other efforts to bolster one's image include practices of "micro-celebrity," which involve the calculated use of social media to "'amp up' [one's] popularity" and "gain status and attention online."[27] These and other practices command investments in time and energy: building and maintaining one's social networks; curating one's feeds with a digital cocktail of informative, thought-provoking, and witty content; and ensuring the consistency of one's self-brand across the sprawling digital ecosystem.

This book highlights the urgency of these self-promotional activities in an age of social media that hails so many of us as entrepreneurial free agents. The ideology of aspirational labor emerges amidst widespread uncertainty about the future of work and alongside technologies that promise creative fulfillment. And it's a *seductive* ideology that pairs passion with (worker) profit to glamorize labor conditions that are far less remunerative and gratifying than hyped. Aspirational labor thus romanticizes work as its conditions are becoming more precarious, time-intensive, and decidedly unromantic.

2

The Aspirational Ethos: Gender, Consumerism, and Labor

We read to dream and aspire, but also to acquire.

—*Carol Smith, publisher and chief revenue officer at* Harper's Bazaar

Hillary, a fresh-faced twenty-something hailing from coastal Virginia, had graduated college a few months prior to our interview. Though she was bringing in a steady paycheck from a job in retail, she found herself much more enthralled by the inner workings of the fashion industry. In her free time, she shared her sartorial inspirations on a personal style blog launched three years earlier; on several occasions, Hillary noted, she had overhauled the site completely. When I asked her about the current focus, she explained that it was written from the perspective of "someone making the transition from being in college and being able to get away with wearing whatever to applying for all those jobs and trying to make it in the post-grad life." She added, "It's about . . . using fashion as an outlet to be creative and express that search for a post-grad identity." Hillary's exposition about channeling *fashion for self-expression* fits rather neatly into theories of consumer culture, particularly critiques of capitalist ideologies that encourage articulations of selfhood through (women's) participation in the marketplace. Yet Hillary's blog wasn't *just* a digitally mediated

Just a Note

forum for creative expression; rather, she understood it as a potential career springboard. Indeed, she coveted a full-time career in fashion journalism and was inspired by the accounts of those who had evolved "from being independent bloggers to [those seated in] the front row of Fashion Week." She shared, "For somebody who aspires to be the next Anna Wintour [the iconic editor-in-chief of *Vogue*], that's the dream."

Hillary's ambition to break into the fashion industry is not unlike the professional aspirations of many of the young women I interviewed. And though careers in the creative industries are widely venerated in the popular imagination, the fashion sector is especially renowned for its aura of glitz, glamour, and dynamism. The seductive pull of the fashion world continues unabated—even as accounts circulate of its less-than-ideal working conditions. Fictional media portrayals offer a particularly negative caricature of the fashion and magazine industries: films like *The Devil Wears Prada* (2006) and *Intern* (2000)—and reality shows like *The Hills* (2006–2010)—depict young staffers as catty and self-serving. Meanwhile, in the news media, the magazine and fashion industries have received a spate of negative publicity for exploiting young people as unpaid interns. Though internships are understood as veritable incubators for bright-eyed college students seeking entry-level employment, positions in the so-called "glamour industries" are typically unpaid. This system inevitably aggravates existing social inequalities. After all, only those from well-heeled families can afford the myriad expenses associated with "working for free."[1]

The heated debate surrounding the shuttering of the internship program at Condé Nast, the prestigious magazine company whose titles include *Vogue, Vanity Fair, Glamour,* and *GQ,* brought these concerns into sharp relief. In October 2013, representatives for the company announced that they would be closing their coveted program, following a class-action lawsuit filed by two former Condé Nast interns. According to the plaintiffs, Condé Nast violated U.S. labor laws by failing to provide the interns with compensation through salary or educational benefits—despite the interns' role in performing value-added tasks for the corporation. One of the plaintiffs compared her *W* magazine internship to the portrayal of Andy Sachs (Anne Hathaway's character) in *The Devil Wears Prada*, except, she explained to a reporter for the *New York Times*, "we don't get any makeover in the end."[2] A number of former interns—as well as aspiring magazine editorial workers—expressed disappointment, frustration, and even outrage with Condé Nast's decision.[3] Meanwhile, critics of the unpaid internship system declared it a landmark battle in the war against economic and educational inequities in the contingent workforce.[4] Though Condé Nast eventually settled the class-action suit, former interns were reportedly hesitant to take the settlement, fearing such actions would impact their future chances of getting hired by the company.[5] Such reluctance, though disheartening, is perhaps not surprising in an era when "reputation [has] become a key commodity."[6]

Initially seen as a cause célèbre, the Condé Nast case has done little to deter creative aspirants from utilizing various channels to pursue career prospects—including these very same, oft-unpaid internships. At the same time, young people like Hillary understand social media production as an additional—or perhaps alternative—pathway to a creative career. The ideal of *getting paid to do what you love* figures prominently here. In a 2015 *Mashable* article proposing the generational label of "yuccies," a (decidedly unpalatable) acronym for *Young Urban Creatives*, author David Infante explained how the contemporary job market is engorged with college-educated twenty-somethings "infected by the conviction that not only do we deserve to pursue our dreams; we should profit from them."[7] Infante grounded his definition in a few yuccie career archetypes: "social consultants coordinating #sponsored Instagram campaigns for lifestyle brands," brogrammers (a clever portmanteau to signal the frat-boyish, "bro" culture of programming), and entrepreneurial-minded youth seduced by the potential offerings of the "internet playground."[8] The assumptions of enjoyment and leisure bolstering this "playground" narrative are not incidental: careers self-fashioned in the digital realm presumably pair pleasure and profitability.

Whether hoping to make inroads into a closed-off industry or coveting success as a digital entrepreneur, many enterprising young people are working fervently to prepare themselves for an imagined career future. But how are we to understand the productive activities of creative aspirants like Hillary in a meaningful way? To cyber-enthusiasts, digital content creators represent an emergent class of innovators empowered by technologies that upend traditional hierarchies of influence and expertise. To critics, however, these media makers are enlistees in the reserve army of the unpaid, exploited by companies paying in the always-deferred promise of "exposure." Neither of these perspectives tells the full story, in part because they almost fully disregard the significance of gendered relations and subjectivities.

"Aspirational labor" recasts the debate between digital media enthusiasts and detractors, in part by foregrounding gender and femininity. The idea refers to female content creators' belief that their (mostly) unpaid work, motivated by passion and the infectious rhetoric of entrepreneurialism, will eventually yield respectable income and rewarding careers. But aspirational labor, as a critical concept, also calls attention to the gap between this belief and the practical realities of the digital labor marketplace: just a few digital content creators reap significant material rewards from their activities. Somewhat predictably, media trend pieces tend to spotlight those who ascend to the digital economies' highest echelons: the six-figure-salary bloggers and vloggers who have achieved celebrity status. For the rest, the potential for financial success is paltry. Blogging.com's survey of 1,000 bloggers found that a mere "17% are able to sustain their lifestyle or support their family with their blogs, while 81% never make even $100 from blogging."[9] Though these statistics describe blogging activities more generally, the fashion blogger behind Grit & Glamour sought to produce more precise figures through a survey of 130 fashion, beauty, and lifestyle bloggers. She cautioned that her investigation was "not a scientific survey, by any means," but it nonetheless yielded similarly disheartening results: a mere 8 percent of bloggers make enough money to actually live on.[10]

Such findings have done little to dissuade enterprising young women from pursuing their career aspirations online.

Over the last decade, a series of social, economic, and technological shifts have thrust the ideologies and practices of aspirational labor to center stage. But an important historical precedent for this practice can be found in *aspirational consumption*—status-induced consumerism that channels self-expression through the marketplace. To understand this transformation, I turn to the traditional (and rather crude) dichotomy of male producer/female consumer. In the introduction to *The Sex of Things,* Victoria de Grazia identifies a duality that has structured cultural assumptions about femininity since at least the Victorian era: "the dichotomized relationship between Mr. Breadwinner and Mrs. Consumer."[11] Such gender-based constructions are, of course, neither natural nor neutral, yet they have created and perpetuated a close affinity between femininity and shopping that has reinforced the structures of patriarchal capitalism.[12]

At the turn of the last century, before the ideals of Victorian puritanism had fully receded into the cultural background, social theorists widely denigrated consumerism, believing that women would be unable to control themselves when confronted with a kaleidoscope of mass-manufactured wares.[13] Literary tropes about the hysteria-induced kleptomaniac owe much of their substance to this discourse; in 1883, French novelist Émile Zola described "the women with a mania for stealing, a perversion of desire, a new kind of neurosis that was classified by a mental specialist who had observed the acute result of the temptation exercised on them by the department stores."[14] Above all, then, consumerism appeared as a public expression of female amorality. Though this concern predated the internet by more than a century, it bears striking resemblance to the social fears about women and technology that emerged at the dawn of the digital age. The recent incarnation of this "moral panic" positions digitally networked girls and young women as especially vulnerable to nefarious predators, or, alternatively, stigmatizes them for their (sexual) agency.[15] Contemporary anxieties about women online can be understood as an expression of this persistent, Victorian-era moral puritanism; the internet thus represents a public space inhabited by women, much like the early department store.

A different—though not entirely inconsistent—set of cultural assumptions about "women and consumerism" gained traction in the early twentieth century, most notably the construal of the excessively emotional female consumer.[16] Indeed, as sociologist Don Slater notes, women have been described in popular culture "as whimsical and inconstant, flighty and narcissistic; they can be seduced, or their resistance overcome, by stimuli or persuasion in order to achieve market penetration."[17] This pejorative image of feminine emotive frivolity is rendered all the more potent by the stereotype of the rational male producer against which it is positioned.

Constructions of social identity manifest themselves in other ways, too. In one of the earliest writings on consumer culture—Thorstein Veblen's caustic assessment of the *nouveau riche,* first published in 1899—derogatory assumptions about gender were firmly demarcated along class lines. In explicating his notion of "conspicuous consumption," Veblen contended that among wealthy classes, it is the *man* who puts his wealth "in evidence" by ostentatiously displaying the finest drinks, weaponry, games, and living spaces. In her role of "chattel" to her "master," the wife is expected to "consume only what is necessary to her sustenance—except so far as her further consumption contributes to the comfort or the good repute of her master."[18] Yet this gender hierarchy gets disrupted among members of the lower middle class. Writes Veblen, "As we descend the social scale, the point is presently reached where the duties of vicarious leisure and consumption devolve upon the wife alone."[19] For these classes, it is the wife who consumes ceremoniously and displays such products ostentatiously.[20]

Though Veblen articulates "conspicuous consumption" as a profoundly social phenomenon—driven by class emulation and "invidious comparison" (a sense of *keeping up with the Joneses* a full five decades before this imagined family moved into the Levittown, New York, suburbs)—he failed to address the producer side of the equation, namely the role of the nascent advertising industry in cultivating a vibrant consumer marketplace. And indeed, the debate about whether power lies in *consumers' agentic desires* or *producers' ability to create demand* has largely configured contemporary consumer critique.[21] Over the last three decades or so, histories of the advertising, media, and retail systems have provided fascinating glimpses into the processes and logics of encouraging consumption.[22] As historian Stuart Ewen explains of the mushrooming marketplace for consumer goods that emerged in the wake of industrialization, "it became imperative to invest the laborer with a financial power and a psychic desire to consume."[23] The up-and-coming advertising industry rose to the task with alacrity.

Though advertisers in the late nineteenth and early twentieth centuries were charged with socializing the masses to desire newly created product categories and brands, they primarily focused on middle-class women, who had been designated as the *primary household purchasing agents.* A 1929 advertisement in *Printers' Ink,* the first U.S. trade publication dedicated to the ad industry, brought this gender division into stark relief. Reworking a line from poet Alexander Pope's "An Essay on Man," the text noted, "The proper study of mankind is man . . . but the proper study of market is women."[24] And accordingly, early advertisers worked feverishly to both guide and legitimize the shopping behaviors of "Mrs. Consumer." Ads offered prescriptions on how to be a "good" wife and mother by, for instance, maintaining a clean home, preparing hearty meals for her family, and keeping her skin soft and supple. Alternatively, dishpan hands, poor hygiene, and visible markers of age were pathologized as impediments to marriage and, ultimately, happiness. Powered by the venerable authority of these representations, such stereotypes helped to shape a limited—and limiting—ideal of domestic femininity.[25]

Of course, advertising professionals were not exclusively responsible for propagating these cultural tropes; instead, they worked closely with burgeoning media channels and, most especially, the women's magazine industry. Widely distributed and astonishingly visual, women's periodicals were seen as essential conduits to reach mothers and wives during their moments of leisure. These mass-circulation periodicals served as instruction manuals for middle-class women through their unique arsenal of content: dress patterns and recipes, images of the home, advice columns, literary fiction, and, of course, ads peddling products to improve the life of Mrs. Consumer. The *Ladies' Home Journal,* in particular, is credited with ushering in the era of the "gendered advertising forum," under the guidance of publishers Cyrus and Louisa Knapp Curtis.[26] The Curtises sought to lure prospective clients with ad placements adjacent to editorial content, a presumed assurance that readers would pay attention to the ads. Other publishers reportedly helped advertisers to create effective messages, while simultaneously publishing editorials informing their readers of the value of advertising for consumer decision-making.[27]

Even in the late nineteenth century, assumptions about class—or more accurately, the boot-strappist ideal of class mobility—steered the direction of ad messages in the United States. As media historian Nancy Walker contends, women's magazine editors were guided by the assumption that their mostly middle-class readers "aspired to improve their class standing, by improving their material surroundings."[28] Often, this ideal focused on domestic life, presenting "what the reader should want and aspire to—a larger house, more stylish clothing—and thus helping to define domestic concerns in terms of consumer culture."[29] The ideal of class ascendance continues to drive the production of imagery and messages in women's magazines and ads. When I interviewed Jason Wagenheim, who at the time was the vice president and publisher of *Teen Vogue,* about the magazine's (imagined) reader, he offered: she's the "type of young woman [who] may not be able to afford Gucci this second, but she can get the [sun]glasses for four hundred dollars . . . and she's matching them with her H&M or Topshop dress."

The evolving class consciousness captured in ads was—and remains—a response to larger transformations in cultural and economic life. Among the changes that unfurled over the first decades of the twentieth century were new understandings about the division between public and private life—a cultural barrier long structured through the binary of masculine/public and feminine/private. In fact, up through the antebellum era, it was considered unfit for middle-class women to appear alone in public spaces; after all, the city was a place for *women of the street*.[30] However, the newfangled department stores of the fin de siècle era were instrumental in overturning these cultural norms; through the coordinated efforts of store merchants like Harry Gordon Selfridge and John Wanamaker, department stores rose to prominence as "safe" spaces for women. In London, for instance, Selfridge publicized his eponymous department store as a venue that would protect women against the dangers of the city.[31] Meanwhile, U.S. department stores were constructed as retail enclaves where women could congregate with ease; hairdressers, tearooms, and nurseries were meant to facilitate leisure-time socialization.[32] As William Leach explains in his fascinating history of North American department stores, merchants strategically aimed to exploit women's class position. Fur displays, in particular, were designed "to stir up feelings of social inadequacy and envy"; merchants hoped such anxieties would prompt impulse buying.[33]

Collectively, then, these cultural histories of the advertising, media, and retail industries reveal the extent to which feminine ideals were deeply intertwined with appeals to upward mobility and *aspiration*. Indeed, just as Veblen argued that foppish members of the *nouveau riche* adorned their bodies and homes with ostentatious displays of wealth, early twentieth-century advertisers seemed to believe that female consumers could be seduced by fantasies of class ascendance.[34] Thus, ads circulating in the first decades of the twentieth century tended to depict the upper and upper-middle classes, ostensibly enticing (mostly female) consumers "to envision themselves occupying a higher rung on society's ladder than most of them in fact did."[35] Such pitches encouraged what is often described as aspirational consumption, whereby individuals purchase products or brands to imitate the consumer behavior of those occupying higher-class standing. By the 1950s, as the kitchen became a central place to demonstrate markers of (female) class status, aspirational appeals infiltrated ads for "new" models of appliances and labor-saving devices.[36]

The modern incarnations of aspirational consumption are variegated, and many of the social media producers I interviewed mentioned brands to symbolically communicate social status—be it of themselves, their fellow bloggers/Instagrammers, or their perceived readers. For example, Chanel was desirable but a brand "[not] every girl can afford"; Old Navy, by contrast, was available to the masses. A college student I spoke with coveted over-the-knee Stuart Weitzman boots but couldn't spend "half my paycheck on this pair of boots." Here, it should be noted that "class" is a sociological concept rife with interpretation; in classical social theory, it has been hitched to notions of wealth and material goods, power and consent, status, and "life chance," among others.[37]

Sociologists of consumption have found Pierre Bourdieu's writings on the symbolic structure of resources to be especially fruitful for mining the relationship between class and consumerism, and I draw on his typology of capital throughout this book.[38] Bourdieu explicates the "three fundamental guises" under which capital may appear: *economic,* which translates directly into financial wealth; *cultural,* which corresponds to educational qualifications and intellect; and *social,* which can exist as a title of nobility but often reflects relational networks—all of which are more or less convertible to others.[39] Bourdieu eschews an economically deterministic model of class identity in favor of a more dynamic system that foregrounds education, experience, and social distinction, among others. A person's manner of dress is thus an expression of her *cultural capital;* it is rendered visible in the red-lacquered soles of Christian Louboutin footwear, the interlocking "C"s fashioned onto the enclosure of a Chanel clutch, the signature roundel that distinguishes a BMW, and the sleek band and oversized interface of the Apple Watch.[40]

Aspirational consumerism is thus understood as emulation of those with a higher level of *cultural capital;* the visible and social nature of material goods—both attributes that were highlighted by Veblen—remain central to this practice. Yet, while Veblen seems to condense conspicuousness and aspiration in drawing attention to the class-based performances animating consumer behavior, we would be remiss to read these terms as interchangeable. While ostentatious displays by the *nouveau riche* discernably communicate something about whom the individual *is,* aspirational consumerism is a projection of *who the individual may become.* The timeline for class mobility is therefore stretched out into an imagined future.

Ostensibly, appeals to aspirationalism are especially pertinent in the current, post-recession era, as many continue to seek out full-time, stable employment. In this so-called "age of austerity"—a phrase not without its critics—consumption is more likely to be focused on the future self, one living an improved life flush with shiny, new products. It is thus not incidental that when the publisher and chief revenue officer of women's fashion monthly *Harper's Bazaar* announced an e-commerce initiative called ShopBazaar in 2012, she reasoned, "We read to dream and aspire, but also to acquire." A designer I interviewed, Siobhan, made a similarly poignant remark when discussing self-presentation in the age of social media: "It circles back around to that same fashion trope, which is all about aspiration. . . . It's about selling an idea to somebody, and appealing to who they think they are, and/or who they want to be, and outside of the reality of themselves."

Though the indelible specter of "Mr. Breadwinner/Mrs. Consumer" still looms large—most unmistakably in representations in popular culture of the steely businessman or the shopping mall–cavorting female—this stubborn binary has been challenged on a number of fronts. For one, feminist scholars and activists have helped to lay bare the role of women's unpaid domestic and reproductive labor in maintaining the circuit of capital.[41] The lineages of this reasoning can be traced to radical Marxist feminism in Italy and, in the United States, sociologies of the gendered division of labor. Beginning in the 1970s, Italian feminists critiqued their Marxist brethren for failing to recognize housework, childcare, elder care, and other domestic responsibilities as the very "work that produces and reproduces labor power."[42] One especially influential voice was scholar-activist Leopoldina Fortunati, who identified the socio-political implications of the unequal exploitation of men and women under capitalism:

> Unlike the male worker . . . [the housewife] is posited as non-value, she cannot obtain money for her work, she receives no wage in exchange . . . she cannot hold money. . . . [W]ithin the family the housewife and her husband . . . enter into relations . . . without equal rights, therefore *not equal* in the eyes of the law.[43]

In an attempt to render visible the "women's work" that sustains modern capitalism, members of the International Feminist Collective orchestrated the International Wages for Housework Campaign in 1972. Assembling behind the rallying cry, "If women were paid for all they do, there'd be a lot of wages due," activists demanded material compensation for women's domestic labor—the very same activities that are often concealed behind heteronormative ideals of femininity. While the political gains of the campaign were—and still *are*—disputed, this project helped to draw attention to the structural inequalities inherent in the gendered division of labor.[44] And many of those involved with the campaign continue to advocate for bringing gender to the fore of Italian Marxism.

With the broadening recognition of the role of immaterial labor in powering the post-industrial economy, theorizations of women's domestic and/or care work have been shoehorned into critical writings on affective labor, defined as the "labor that produces or manipulates affects."[45] Yet to Silvia Federici, a co-founder of the International Feminist Collective, "women's work" is made all the more obscure by the "demystifying" language of affect. Taking particular aim at the writings of her Marxist contemporaries Michael Hardt and Antonio Negri, Federici outlines what gets lost in their designation of "affective labor": "the feminist analysis of the function of the sexual division of labor, the function of gender hierarchies, [and] the analysis of the way capitalism has urged the wage to mobilize women's work in the reproduction of the labor force."[46] Accordingly, the period since the 1990s has been experiencing an "affective turn" across the disciplines; despite this intellectual momentum, there is a lingering reluctance to think through "women's work" and affect studies.[47] A notable exception is Kylie Jarrett, whose notion of the "digital housewife" establishes parallels between unpaid domestic and reproductive (female) labor and consumer contributions to digital media industries.[48] Following Jarrett, I agree that "the uncanny, ghostly presence of women's labor can provide a framework to reinvigorate analysis of specific qualities of the laboring involved in the digital economy."[49]

Marxist feminism is not the only tradition to call attention to the profoundly gendered nature of certain forms of (under-valued) labor. With intellectual roots in American sociology, Arlie Hochschild explored the feminized nature of service work in her now-canonical 1983 monograph, *The Managed Heart: Commercialization of Human Feeling*. A key theme in the book is what she terms "emotional labor," which she defines as labor that "requires one to induce or suppress feeling in order to sustain the outward countenance that produces the proper state of mind in others."[50] Service professionals—she was looking at flight attendants and bill collectors, among other professions—are thus encouraged to *manage* their feelings according to organizational structures and scripts. Although Hochschild located the rise of emotional labor in the political-economic movement from a goods-based to a service economy, she also explores the various ways in which considerations of gender structure this system. Indeed, she seems to presage later discussions of the "feminization of the workforce" by noting the economy's demand for "skills in personal relations, the womanly art of status enhancement and the emotional work that it requires [which have] been made more public, more systematized, and more standardized."[51] One of my interviewees acknowledged the hidden costs of this labor quite explicitly: "There's a certain emotional labor that goes into being a female YouTuber. You just have to deal with people being shitty." I return to the topic of emotional labor later in the book; yet the remark from this vlogger suggests how gendered overtones structure such virtual interactions.

The traditionally gendered producer/consumer binary has been further eroded by the influx of women into the global workforce, predominantly in the aftermath of feminism's second wave. According to the U.S. Labor Statistics and Census Bureau, the number of female workers mushroomed from 30.3 million in 1970 to 72.7 million in the early 2000s. Though these raw statistics are staggering, they obscure less auspicious trends in the contemporary labor pool: the actual *percentage* of women entering the workforce has remained relatively stagnant since the 1980s, and many career sectors remain sharply divided by sex. For instance, the top-ranked positions for women in 1970 were secretaries, bookkeepers, and elementary school teachers; in the first decade of the 2000s, the leading occupations for female professionals were remarkably similar: administrative assistants, cashiers, and elementary and middle school teachers.[52] Further, the oft-cited wage gap statistic that *women earn $0.77 for every dollar earned by men* reveals the persistence of gender-based discrimination, with women of color faring significantly worse.[53]

These indicators have, perhaps unsurprisingly, emerged as catalysts for larger conversations about the presence and status of women in the workforce, including debates about the sex-based division of labor, the social demands of parenting and other domestic responsibilities, and labor policy reforms. In recent years, a handful of prominent female writers and executives have helped to steer the media conversation. In 2012, public policy scholar Anne-Marie Slaughter published a cover story in the *Atlantic* on "Why Women Still Can't Have It All"; notably, the online version was the most viewed article to date. In the op-ed, Slaughter poignantly detailed her decision to abandon her post as a high-ranking public official in order to spend more time with her family, including two teenage sons. A self-identified feminist and "high-profile career woman," Slaughter confessed that she never imagined she would face a choice between her career and her family; however, working for the government meant a demanding schedule over which she had little control. With the new position, then, Slaughter came to realize that "having it all was not possible in many types of jobs . . . at least not for long." Slaughter plainly denounced the workplace structures that force so many women to confront this decision, including inflexible work schedules and employers' expectations of the ever-present, connected employee.

Slaughter's piece has been held up as a rejoinder to Sheryl Sandberg, who in 2012 was gearing up for the launch of *Lean In: Women, Work, and the Will to Lead,* a book based on her wildly popular TED talk several years prior. Sandberg, the Harvard-educated COO of Facebook, prodded career-minded females to *lean in* as they endeavor to close what she calls the "global ambition gap" for women. Although Sandberg aligned herself with the objectives of feminism, she placed the onus on women for "lower[ing] our own expectations of what we can achieve."[54] Consequently, some public voices—including Slaughter—have critiqued Sandberg's dismissal of systematic barriers and structural conditions that stunt women's career progress. And, true to form, the mainstream media pitted these women against each other in a fierce debate.

A strong undercurrent of this so-called debate is the impact of new employment schedules—including the much-idealized flexible model. To be sure, widespread internet usage has figured prominently in modern arrangements that enable employees to work remotely and/or set their own schedules. It should be understood, though, that such changes are *also* symptomatic of the ideologies and processes of post-Fordism, a term that describes the progressive movement of organizations toward flexible specialization and decentralized production. Of course, post-Fordism amounts to much more than an altered system of production and is concomitant with a series of socioeconomic and technological shifts, including the rapid development of an information- or knowledge-based economy. Within this information economy, notions of flexibility assume a political valance. Indeed, for working mothers beset by the burden of balancing personal and professional demands, telecommuting and "smart homes" were introduced with a wave of euphoria. Just as mid-century technologies like the dishwasher and laundry machine were discursively positioned as "labor-saving devices" for the female homemaker, modern innovations have been celebrated for their ability to emancipate women from patriarchal work structures.[55] In a 2016 article published by Bitch Media, freelance writer Sarah Grey contended that women are increasingly being "squeeze[d] out of the workplace" by a constellation of corporate cost-cutting measures, including the "lack of paid maternity leave, inadequate time off, little flexibility, and unequal pay that doesn't always cover the cost of childcare."[56] For Grey, freelancing and contracting enable her to exert necessary control over her schedule as she juggles work with childcare responsibilities and a chronic illness.

Importantly, though, studies of flexi-work reveal that these tools have done little to unsettle structural gender inequalities—an issue Grey alluded to in the conclusion of her piece.[57] Internet scholar Melissa Gregg explores how "presence bleed"—the blurring together of the work and home spheres—disproportionally impacts female workers.[58] The women in her study had to "fight for time to perform paid work pursuits" because of the reverberations of the so-called "second shift" of domestic care.[59] Those I interviewed, similarly, noted how this always-on, multi-tasking mentality had impacted their personal lives: partners pleading with them to come to bed in the wee hours of the morning or turning the computer back on after putting the kids to bed. Heather recalled a family vacation from her days as a full-time mommy blogger: "My kids were swimming in the pool, and I'm upstairs in a hotel room on the Wi-Fi trying to get something published."

Though women's inroads into the employment economy are a marker of political progress, such laboring activities were historically steeped in appeals to feminine consumerism—particularly in the media and culture industries.[60] Whether as content creators, researchers, or sales professionals, women played a crucial role in the journalism, advertising, and beauty industries, shaping the direction of these businesses in the late nineteenth and early twentieth centuries.[61] Thus, while the post-Victorian beauty industry deployed enterprising women as a revolutionary, trust-building sales force, women's magazine executives relied upon female editorial voices to relate to the unique experiences of middle-class women. However, with women's magazines as texts *of* (i.e., produced by) and *for* (i.e., consumed by) women, the presentation of female staffers grew primarily out of a business logic—rather than a political one.[62] The owners of early women's magazines were guided by the assumption that female consumers would be inspired to follow the advice of female experts; thus, (male) executives invited female editors and columnists to join their staff.

Similar reasoning infiltrated the early advertising industry, as young women were hired and tasked with producing copy and visual appeals that could best address the (perceived) needs of the proverbial *Mrs. Consumer.* Consumer culture historian Jennifer Scanlon's study of female professionals in the J. Walter Thompson agency during the 1920s and 1930s seems to nuance the business-versus-politics understanding of the workforce composition; she argues that "these women often approached their work with a missionary spirit about the consumer culture, a spirit many of them carried over from the progressive politics of their college educations, suffrage activities or social work experiences."[63] Of course, this framing does not belie the fact that these female workers were part of an industry sustained by appeals to an overwhelmingly female audience. Who best to develop effective ad appeals for food, cleaning products, clothing, and cosmetics aimed at middle-class women *than other women?* Yet because of the disparity between these two groups—upper-class, former suffragists who sought independence in the professional domain and, by contrast, traditional, middle-class stay-at-homers—the former "remained invisible to the world of women's magazines and advertising for decades to come."[64] As should be apparent by now, "invisible labor" is a recurrent theme in thinking through the productive contributions of women across eras, contexts, and industries.

It was, rather unsurprisingly, the second-wave feminist movement that brought concerns about the unequal status of female media workers to public consciousness. Prime targets of the feminist movement were women's magazines—with their staid representations of domestic femininity emerging from a predominantly male editorship. During one widely publicized 1970 protest, more than a hundred women staged a sit-in at the office of then–*Ladies' Home Journal* editor-in-chief John Mack Carter; at the time, senior editor Lenore Hershey was one of the *only* female staffers. As feminist scholar Bonnie Dow summarized, "For eleven hours, protestors demanded an all-female editorial staff, childcare for employees and an end to advertisements on makeup and appliances. . . . They targeted every characteristic that defined women's magazines at the time."[65] The sit-in prompted various changes: Carter let the activists edit a portion of the magazine later that year, and by 1973, Hershey had stepped into the role of editor-in-chief.[66] The succeeding years saw massive workforce changes unfurl, largely spurred by the women's liberation movement. During a 1993 interview, two decades after the *Ladies' Home Journal* sit-in, *Glamour* magazine's then-editor-in-chief Ruth Whitney provided a snapshot of the composition of the women's magazine industry: "The staff at *Glamour* is almost entirely female. The editorial staff numbers more than sixty and another forty that comprise the business area." She enthused, "At Condé Nast itself, working conditions and attitudes have changed."[67]

Despite Whitney's optimism, executive teams of (almost exclusively white) men tend to dominate the upper echelons of the magazine publishing business.[68] This disparity is indicative of a more widespread gender gap endemic to nearly all of the major media industries, with the role and status of women especially bleak at the highest levels of contemporary media organizations. In 2015, on the heels of the Women's Media Center's release of its annual report on the "Status of Women in the U.S. Media," *Time* magazine highlighted some particularly "sad truths" about gender-based inequities: the percentage of women in sports journalism was an abysmally low 10 percent; male journalists had an overwhelming margin in the area of hard news; and the large majority (83 percent) of Hollywood executives were male.[69] Moreover, these gender imbalances have important intersectionalities with race and ethnicity; women of color fared worse than white women across all categories examined in the 2015 report.[70]

The statistics are grim in other geographic contexts, too. The publication of the first "Global Report on the Status of Women in the News Media," which drew upon a study of 500 companies in 59 nations, highlighted some of the stark disparities across nation-states. Overall, though, the 2013 survey revealed that men held 73 percent of top management jobs and nearly two-thirds of reporting jobs. Fortunately, the pattern was less dire among news-gathering, editing, and writing positions.[71] In making a case for the need to take the macrolevel relationship between media and gender—including policy, financial, and ownership structures—seriously, feminist media scholar Carolyn Byerly contends that the overwhelming control of media industries by men gives them the power to determine which messages and images to circulate to broader publics.[72]

While the national and global surveys listed above detail the prevalence of vertical segregation—the glass ceiling metaphor—David Hesmondhalgh and Sarah Baker produce compelling insight about horizontal, or occupational, segregation within the television, magazine, and music industries. Among the implications they identify: the tendency of jobs performed by a large majority of women to pay less; sex-based divisions which challenge ideals of autonomy and freedom; segregated cultures that make it more challenging for workers to "match their talents to their occupations"; and gender clusters which tend to perpetuate stereotypes.[73] Such findings tend to reaffirm studies of other creative professionals published over the last decade: while men dominate more prestigious creative roles as well as technical and craft fields, women are concentrated in marketing, communications, and service roles.[74]

The high ratio of women working in public relations—estimates range from 73 to 85 percent—has led to its designation of a "pink ghetto."[75] In 2014, *New York Magazine* writer Ann Friedman questioned why the field "remains synonymous with the worst female stereotypes":

> While there are many men in PR—including 80 percent of upper management—it's women, often young women, who are likely to be doing the grunt work of sending emails and writing tweets and cold-calling contacts. The very work that journalists, and the rest of us, are likely to see as fluffy.[76]

A year later, then–*Medium* editor Alana Hope Levinson invoked the "pink ghetto" aphorism in a poignant self-reflection on the marginal standing of social media workers within contemporary news organizations. Social media, she learned, is disparaged as a "girly job"—despite its central role in steering the twenty-first-century news business. Levinson notes the striking similarities between digital media work and PR, explaining that "they both, at their essence, involve promotion; and they're both—if done well—invisible."[77] This invisibility manifests itself in various ways—in the lack of female bylines, the shifting regimes of credit to male superiors, and the tendency of women to absorb the organizational "flack."[78]

There is, of course, another "pink ghetto" in the creative industries—the sprawling culture of unpaid internships. College students eager to pad their resumes and schmooze with prospective employers are prodded to "pay their dues" or "work for exposure" through these oft-uncompensated positions. And the market for unpaid interns is markedly gendered. In his exposé of exploitative conditions of the internship system, Ross Perlin pinpoints both gender- and class-based internship injustices, with the former attributed to "the fields women gravitate toward and possibly also [to the likelihood that] female students have been more accepting of unpaid, unjust situations."[79] Researchers at the University of Victoria and the Canadian Intern Association produced empirical research confirming the gender disparity in unpaid internships—or that "the unpaid intern economy rides on the backs of young women."[80]

Many of the creative aspirants I interviewed held internships prior to—or concomitant with—their social media productions. Reflecting on the general character of internships in the glamour industries, college student Nishita offered, "It's really hard to find a good paid internship when it comes to the fashion or creative industry. Mine wasn't paid. I just did it for the experience and just to learn more about everything." Lauren, another young woman seemingly indoctrinated in the "work for exposure" narrative, explained that though her internship was unpaid, she received "exposure to the industry and . . . to put [the position] on your resume, and it's a really good experience to improve your writing." Kelly, too, was optimistic in recalling her former stint as an intern at *Teen Vogue*. Though the unpaid position required her to commute back and forth between Philadelphia and New York (nearly one hundred miles) at least three times a week, she concluded that she "would not take back that experience for the world." The experiences of these creative aspirants corroborate research by Michelle Rodino-Colocino and Stephanie Berberick, who conducted a series of focus groups with former PR interns; their sample, perhaps not surprisingly, was 85 percent female. They learned that interns seem to render their "bitch work" more tolerable through individualized narratives of "hope, love, and luck."[81]

Disparaging terms like "fluffy," "bitch work," and "the pink ghetto" testify to the fact that inequalities in the creative sectors are more than just "numbers" issues. Rather, they are bound up with historical and social constructions of gender that have done little to unsettle assumptions that have rendered women a *particular kind of creative laborer.*

In stark contrast to their high concentrations in the promotional industries, women's roles and status in the tech sector are marginal, at best. The number of female tech workers employed by the industry juggernauts—Apple, Google, Facebook, and Microsoft—is astonishingly low; Apple is the only one to climb above the 20 percent mark, and the figures are especially bleak for women of color.[82] More alarming still, a study by the American Association of University Women found that the gender gap in computing is actually widening. In 2013, women held only 26 percent of computing positions, a marked decline from 35 percent in 1990.[83] Silicon Valley—with its über-hip lot of start-ups and innovation industries—is a notoriously inhospitable work climate for women. Discourses of (masculine-coded) entrepreneurship are firmly entrenched in tech culture, which, as internet scholar Alice Marwick argues, is doubly problematic for women: "Entrepreneurialism is a loaded concept that incorporates male-normative notions of behavior and success, and because entrepreneurs are so high status, this means that women have been systematically excluded from the highest levels of the technology scene."[84]

Some of the women I interviewed, particularly those who had more experience in start-up culture, shared their own experiences with subtle and not-so-subtle sexism in the tech fields. Siobhan, an aspiring fashion entrepreneur, spoke at length about the ways in which gender biases shape the experiences of women in business, particularly:

> I think that as a [female] entrepreneur, a lot of the resources . . . are limited because you are going to be in female-centric businesses, which tend to not have the capital interest that other ones do. I just think about in terms of some of the VCs [venture capital firms], and I can only think of really one that specializes in fashion. When you think about a start-up company, and they're going to get investment, it's usually a guy, it's usually a tech company. And even if it's not a tech company, the people that are giving the money are men.

Meanwhile, Ana R., a longtime computer programmer, left her career because of a pervasive sense of feeling "pushed out." During our interview, she challenged the common assumption that the lack of women in technology is a "pipeline problem." She explained, "If there's not enough women in technology, it's because women don't want to go into technology because there's so much bias."

In recent years, mainstream media have cast a much-needed spotlight on this issue, exposing forms of gender discrimination across the new media and technology industries. For instance, the *New York Times* reported that female computer engineers and programmers were abandoning lucrative posts because of an alpha-male culture where they are frequently dismissed, harassed, and even threatened.[85] An especially high-profile case concerns former Reddit CEO Ellen Pao, whom the *Washington Post* dubbed "one of the most recognizable faces in the debate over discrimination in Silicon Valley."[86] After she filed a gender harassment suit against her former employer, venture capitalist firm Kleiner Perkins, a jury ruled against Pao, who declined to appeal. Her self-reflection on the experience appeared in *Lenny*, a feminist magazine spearheaded by actress Lena Dunham:

> I saw inconsistencies in what people said and what they actually did. I saw many firms talking meritocracy but ignoring great opportunities that women brought in or giving men credit for them. I saw the bar for promotion move as soon as a woman crossed it. I saw inconsistencies in how aggressiveness and strong opinions were rewarded across genders. I heard stories about harassment and off-color jokes and sexist/ageist/racist conversations. Women founders were pushed out or into lesser roles as a condition for investment, while similarly inexperienced male founders were given the benefit of the doubt and supported.[87]

Although Pao went on to champion a series of anti-harassment measures at Reddit, she soon became the victim of a targeted attack by internet trolls. In late 2015, Pao publicly announced her decision to step down from the executive post.

The gaming industry is another creative field where misogyny and sexual harassment run rampant. Indeed, feminist game scholars Shira Chess and Adrienne Shaw note that while the number of women *consuming* games is relatively equal to that of men, women are a minority when it comes to the *production* of games. Institutional sexism is so pervasive that even those connected to the industry—game reviewers or critics like Anita Sarkeesian—have been subjected to rape and death threats. Chess and Shaw describe how they, too, became the target of online trolls as part of the #Gamergate scandal.[88] Unfortunately, even initiatives which are specifically designed to promote women in technology are mired by deeply ingrained stereotypes and lingering devaluations of gendered labor. For instance, Alison Harvey and Stephanie Fisher's study of the Difference Engine Initiative— a Canadian incubator designed to support female video game developers—revealed that despite the seemingly admirable mission of the initiative, unequal power relations were maintained through immaterial labor.[89]

Such findings are a testament to the substantial amount of invisible labor structured into an economy where workers are compelled to promote themselves and deploy their affective skills. And while the narrative that sustains this logic is the problematic assumption that women are uniquely positioned to engage in such modes of affective labor, it is a contemporary truism that all cultural workers face increasing demands to manage their self-presentations. The features of what Lisa Adkins called the "cultural feminization of economic life"—including flexibility, mobility, an emphasis on image/aesthetics, and various subjective performances—make clear how understandings of gender and labor must go beyond the sheer number of women participating in

At the same time, some of the grassroots, feminist sites that were launched in the early days of the web underwent a transformation as part of the progressive commercialization of the internet.[100] The years bracketing the new millennium saw the incorporation of several popular female-only sites; for instance, women.com merged with Hearst magazines, and later the site was combined with iVillage—another independently created site, which was purchased by NBCUniversal in 2006 before shuttering in 2015.[101] As Herring astutely observed of this trend, the web's shift

> from social action to individual fulfillment is consistent with a larger trend on the Internet whereby communitarian discourses and discourses about participatory democracy are receding in importance as commercialism comes increasingly to the fore.[102]

Herring's comment about commercialism "[coming] to the fore" seems nostalgically outdated now, in an era where the web's non-commercial roots are largely forgotten, buried beneath a veritable heap of sponsored messages, native content, and cookie-tracked conversations. And, perhaps not surprisingly, the construction of women as especially communicative digital consumers has found a welcome home in the social media economy. One particular way that historical and industrial constructions of gender get reified in the digital realm is through reports on the "social" nature of women's online interactions.[103]

As internet conversations have migrated from chat-rooms and message boards to Facebook, Twitter, and YouTube, the valorization of female internet users has only intensified. In fact, some have even suggested the second decade of the millennium marks a new phase: "the feminization of the internet."[104] This assumption is in part linked to the profound growth of social networks where women tend to cluster: female users have a slight majority over men across Facebook, Tumblr, and Instagram. The gender gap is especially pronounced on Pinterest, a site regarded for its arsenal of expressly feminine content, with neatly organized images of wedding ideas, home decor, recipes, and children's projects.[105] To this end, *Washington Post* columnist Petula Dvorak called the site "digital crack for women."[106]

The internet has also given rise to markedly gendered—and unabashedly commercial—genres of content production: fashion blogging, beauty vlogging, mommy blogging, and DIY design, among others. In the popular imagination, these activities are widely

2. *Maeve Stier, an aspiring model and the blogger behind Chic Now, showcases some styles for "between seasons." Photo Credit: Blogger.*

touted as platforms for self-expression and individualism—resonant ideals in discourses of post-feminism. By re-routing *consumption* as a mode of cultural *production,* these activities promise to disrupt traditional gendered hierarchies and financially empower (mostly) female participants.[107]

The gendered history of the producer/consumer binary is a multifarious one, structured through evolving norms about women's social positioning within various spheres, most especially the public and private domains. Fortunately, these rudimentary—and overwhelmingly patriarchal—norms have been challenged on a number of fronts, and once-airtight boundaries are being slowly effaced. Yet the specter of traditional, gender-based divisions—such as *Mr. Breadwinner* and *Mrs. Consumer*—lingers on. Thus, while female workers have made substantial gains in the labor force since the women's liberation movement, occupational inequalities and social hierarchies persist—though they are much too often brushed aside with narratives about innate "gender differences" or, alternatively, "pipeline problems."

The media and creative industries—including the particular career sectors of fashion, entertainment, and new media—offer a prism through which to examine various constructions and ambivalences surrounding gendered labor. Indeed, despite the glamorization of these career fields in the popular imagination, contemporary culture industries continue to be mired by systematic patterns of horizontal and vertical segregation. In the case of the former, whereby women cluster in the so-called "pink ghetto" of promotional or below-the-line jobs, feminized forms of emotional labor are rendered obscure by social constructions of women as intrinsically social communicators.[108] This argument does not deny the fact that men, too, are increasingly expected to engage in emotional or immaterial labor as part of the widespread feminization of the workforce in a service-based econo-my.[109] However, these progressive shifts have done little to overturn the antagonism in the discursive separation between "men's work" and "women's work." Specifically, patterned gender discrepancies mean that women shoulder most of the risk/low visibility/emotional labor—as they remain far removed from the executive suites.

With social media usage skyrocketing, seemingly feminized ac-tivities, like child-rearing, decorating, knitting, and fashion styling/modeling, are imbued with opportunities for female empowerment and financial independence.[110] Reflecting how digitally mediated modes of self-expression assume a progressive bent, Sarah Banet-Weiser and Inna Arzumanova argue that, for fashion haulers, "crafting one's personal identity in front of a web-cam . . . is not posi-tioned as narcissistic, but rather empowering, precisely because these activities nurture the promise of an entrepreneurial future."[111] Etsy-preneurs, mom-preneurs, and blogger-preneurs seem to represent the vanguard of female business success in the early twenty-first century. The fashion bloggers, designers, YouTubers, and Instagrammers I interviewed, too, see their activities as paths to potentially lucrative and fulfilling careers—despite the fact that they are centrally posi-tioned within the consumer sphere. But these laboring activities, like forms of status-enhancing consumption that preceded them, must be understood as fundamentally *aspirational*. Social media producers approach their activities as investments in a future self—*one who will (hopefully) get paid to do what she loves.*

3

(Not) Just for the Fun of It: The Labor of Social Media Production

Now I'm really trying to think of how I'm going to make this [blog], a brand [and] make money off of it . . . so that it's not just something I do after 9 to 5, but *it becomes my 9 to 5.*

—*Crystal, fashion blogger*

"Instagrammer" is now a six-figure job—at least according to a pithy headline that appeared in the news feeds of *Social Media Week* subscribers in early 2015. The article that followed was upbeat, and perhaps hyperbolic, as digital contest strategist Tanya Korobka assured readers they could "ditch [their] boring location-based nine-to-six job and enjoy personal freedom and creativity as a 'professional instagrammer.' "[1] Korobka profiled three insta-careerists (all women) who effectively transitioned from "using the app for fun" to "earning six-figure salaries and being flown around the world to take photos." To be fair, this siren song of social media entrepreneurship was no less than a project in organizational self-sustenance; *Social Media Week* charges attendees a few hundred dollars for a pass to one of its week-long seminars, convened in hip urban locales around the globe: New York, London, Milan, and São Paulo, among others. Yet in chronicling the digitally enabled evolution from *hobby* to *pro,* the article underscored the extent to which social media activities seemingly blur the boundaries between labor and leisure.

Indeed, with the rapid ascent of interactive technologies, social theorists have drawn attention to the economic and social productivity—that is, the *labor*—of online consumer-audiences.[2] Portmanteaus such as pro-sumption, produsage, pro-am, and playbour capture the nuanced ways in which production and consumption, work and play, and amateurism and professionalism bleed into one another in digital contexts.[3] Fashion blogging, beauty vlogging, and other activities chronicled in this book are positioned within such murky conceptual spaces: participants produce cultural products and/or content of economic value, at the same time that they articulate their practices as enjoyable and eminently expressive. The underlying tension here gives structure to what has come to be known as the "digital labor debate." Essentially, the debate pivots on the question of whether uncompensated online activities—for instance, commenting on a TV network's newsfeed, reviewing a restaurant on Yelp!, or participating in a user-generated ad contest—represent digitally enabled forms of creative expression or, alternatively, free labor exploited for profit by the greedy hands of capitalism.[4]

Some of the most vociferous critics of the internet's system of capturing and harnessing "digital labor"—Christian Fuchs and Trebor Scholz, for example—draw upon Marxist thought to highlight the exploited nature of the "work" performed by unwitting consumer-participants.[5] However, while I concur that a decisive economic logic underpins the digital labor system, the kinds of production taking place across social media platforms provide participants with forms of meaning-making and expression that must not be dismissed. Many social media creators derive pleasure from their digitally mediated "passion projects," but they *also* believe that they will benefit professionally from such value-generating activities.

I first recognized the need to take seriously digital participants' professional aspirations around 2008, after conducting a series of in-depth interviews with entrants in a user-generated advertising contest sponsored by Dove.[6] Marketing executives for the personal care company, likely eager to mimic the staggering success of the Doritos "Crash the Super Bowl" contest, encouraged women to submit thirty-second commercials featuring Dove Supreme Cream Oil Body Wash; the winning ad was chosen and premiered during the 80th annual Academy Awards. In stark contrast to the perspective that these contest participants were cultural dupes, unaware that their unpaid labor was being extracted for brand-building value, I found that most were keenly aware of their role in helping the Dove brand sustain its luster. More important to them, however, were the personal and professional benefits of the contest. Indeed, a number of the video creators participated in the promotion expressly to further their professional ambitions: they emphasized the potential to build their portfolios, add footage to their demo reels, and/or garner constructive criticism and feedback.[7] These content creators thus exhibited few symptoms of perverse indifference.

Let me be clear: I am not suggesting marketing initiatives such as these are unproblematic; to the contrary, I was—and *am*—quite critical of commercial messages delivered under the guise of creative autonomy or with a breathless promise of female empowerment. Yet I also think that the *career-oriented ambitions* of the content creators propelling our social media economy deserve further critical attention. And, fittingly, in the years since I completed the Dove study, there's been an uptick in research that identifies future career opportunities as a salient motivator for producing uncompensated digital content.[8] Kathleen Kuehn and Thomas F. Corrigan's notion of forward-directed, "hope labor" offers an especially productive framework for thinking about the role of (temporally deferred) career opportunities in configuring the activities of the digital economy.[9] Inevitably, it is the *hope* of securing a full-time career that propels certain forms of participation in the online economy.

Given a social history that has rendered women's work undervalued or—worse—invisible, it is discernibly clear that investments of labor do not get rewarded evenly across social categories. What is more, in the context of a feminized consumer culture, labor and leisure blur together; we must therefore open our eyes to what cultural theorist Angela McRobbie disparaged as the "gender blindness" to which many labor scholars fall victim. In my earlier research, I have critiqued digital labor scholars for succumbing to a similar shortsightedness; there is a tendency to overlook the importance of gender relations and subjectivities.[10] But forms of value-generating, gendered self-expression are rife in the social media world through blogs, vlogs, Instagram, and more. Though these activities are superficially framed as amusement and sociality, I contend that many young women don't produce and promote content *just for the fun of it.* Rather, they approach social media creation with *strategy, purpose,* and *aspirations of career success.* This chapter, therefore, exposes the deep cracks in narratives of social media leisure and amateurism. In so doing, I explore some of the most salient conditions and features of aspirational labor: narratives of creative expression, relationship-building in online and offline contexts, and modes of individualized self-expression that both reveal and conceal normative feminine consumer behavior.

The genre of personal style blogging, which I closely examine in this book, has been widely celebrated for transferring power from the elites to the "masses." According to the popular lure, fashion blogging had humble beginnings: the genre began its ascent in the early and

3. *Bryanboy, considered one of the pioneers of personal style blogging, poses for a shot at New York Fashion Week in February 2013. Photo Credit: Brent Luvaas.*

mid-2000s as (mostly) teens began keeping online diaries of their personal styles as well as commentary on fashion house runway shows. By 2008, the mushrooming popularity of blogs like Susie Bubble, The Budget Fashionista, Style Rookie, Fashion Toast, and Bryanboy (see Figure 3) attracted the attention of publicists and fashion designers, who extended certain bloggers invitations to Fashion Week shows.

From the beginning, fashion blogs were presented in opposition to traditional sources of fashion news and commentary (e.g., women's magazines).[11] Members of the fashion elite deployed the language of "amateur" as something of a defensive containment or, at least, an indication of bloggers' scrappy roots. In contrast to the well-established voices of the "old media" world (experienced *professionals*), early bloggers were seen as dilettantes. A particularly scathing comment about fashion-bloggers-as-amateurs came from Franca Sozzani, the late editor-in-chief of *Vogue Italia*, in 2011:

> These aren't people who have been working in fashion too long to end up criticizing everything, the shows, and they don't have a background in fashion so they are not conditioned by their knowledge or interests. There [*sic*] comments are naif and enthusiastic. They don't hold a real importance in the business. Of course not.[12]

Later, in a 2013 *New York Times Magazine* article denouncing the "The Circus of Fashion" at New York Fashion Week, longtime style critic Suzy Menkes critiqued the peacocking behaviors of fashion aspirants as well as the surfeit of attention paid by street-style photographers snapping away with their long lenses. Fashion, Menkes concluded, has "become mob rule—or, at least, a survival of the most popular in a melee of crowdsourcing."[13] Designations like *unprofessional, un-*

sites—or began to take them more "seriously"—when economic circumstances drove them to seek out new sources of income. Erika, who traced her interest in sartorial matters back to childhood, described her initial venture into personal style blogging as a "hobby." She immediately added that she was "in between jobs" at the time, had been a fan of blogs, and thought, "Why not start my own?" Meanwhile, jewelry designer Deirdre acknowledged how difficult it was for her to secure a creative career while living in Charleston—far outside the geographic clusters of U.S. "creative cities" like New York, Los Angeles, or the Silicon Valley region.[20] "I ended up [using social media] as a hobby and just something to do on the side because I knew I was going to have to go back to doing websites, which I hated [though it provided an income]." In contrast to the accidental entrepreneurs described earlier, Erika and Deirdre approached blogging with unambiguously professional ambitions; yet they also seemed to valorize the "hobby to pro" narrative—regardless of the extent to which it adequately characterized their own experiences.

Other interviewees were more candid about the situational factors that led them to devote additional time and energy to their social media projects. Alice explained how she began to take her blog more seriously after graduating. As she recalled, "[I reasoned that] since I don't have a job now, why don't I focus on my blog? And I started to [do] research about how do you have a blog? What do you have to do to get a following?" Hélène, likewise, explained that she became more "serious" about her blogging project five years in, at a time when she was having trouble securing full-time employment. Classifying this as a "pivotal moment" in her life, she recalled, "I was like, 'Okay, well, what do I do now?' And [I thought], 'I [studied] fashion [for] a reason [so] I should really do something with it.'" While Hélène *was* able to successfully grow her blog readership, she eventually landed a full-time position at a New York–based social media start-up. As a result, Hélène admitted, her blog had taken a backseat:

> [It's] not that my blog hasn't been successful, because I've had so many amazing opportunities come out of it. But when it sort of like came to [the question of]—"Okay, do I continue with this full time or do I start taking on consulting work and like writing jobs on the side to sort of like make ends meet?"— I started concentrating less and less . . . on the blog.

The blog thus effectively served as a career standby, which she largely moved on from once she was gainfully employed.

For Crystal, a recent layoff became (re)framed as an opportunity to actualize her dream of being a full-time fashion/lifestyle blogger. When the news broke that her company was downsizing, Crystal was initially disillusioned; however, as she recalled, a discussion with her partner made her realize that "this probably couldn't have come at a better time" for her. Crystal explained:

> [That's what] sort of set the wheels in motion for me really taking it seriously. I've done it, sort of, you know, "oh this is cool, I'll just make a little blog" and didn't really think about monetizing the blog, or gaining followers, or speaking to an audience, it was more just for myself. Now I'm really trying to think of how I'm going to make this [blog] a brand, a [real thing], monetizing it, making money off of it so that it's not just something I do after 9 to 5, but *it becomes my 9 to 5.*

Caitlin, too, articulated her shopping and lifestyle blog as a potential conduit to a more stable—and creatively fulfilling—career. As she shared:

want to see] a sample of your work." Marissa aspired to work in fashion photography, inspired both by the artistic license and opportunities for travel; however, she later told me, "in the end, my dream dream *dream* job is to be a fashion editor at a magazine or publication, and maybe even something like Anna Wintour, editor-in-chief of *Vogue,* so we'll see."

These three narratives—creativity as accidental entrepreneurship, managing uncertainty in the post-recession economy, and "breaking in" to the creative industries—offer something of a typology of aspirational labor narratives, although this typology is admittedly a partial one. Maeve, for instance, seemed to conflate these in explaining the motivations to begin her fashion and lifestyle blog: "I think it's a wonderful thing when you have found something that you love to do, and you're able to make it a part of your income. . . . But as of right now it's just something fun and creative." Yet she quickly added, "I'm hoping that the blog could eventually help with [my main occupation as a model] as well." Maeve's exposition highlights how origin narratives were structured around the creativity-economy axis. The relationship between art (creativity) and commerce (economy) has long been fraught with contradiction; the very ambiguity of the term "creative industries" attests to the continued slippage of capitalism into cultural spaces.[23] For denizens of the digital economy, this slippage represents a space of opportunity: social media producers see creativity as a route to entrepreneurial success. Conversely, many of the same bloggers view entrepreneurship as the key to a life of creativity. In line with the wider culture's promise, their origin stories position labor and love as productive partners.

Not only did careerist discourses structure digital media producers' origin narratives, but the language and logic of work guided the totality of their social media projects—regardless of whether or not they were compensated for their efforts. Such vigilance in the management of their creative content challenges the notion that social media production is merely a leisurely pursuit; more often, it involves robust professionalism. Sharing her perspective on the conditions and opportunities for a full-time fashion blogging career, Hélène offered:

> It has a lot to do with luck, but it also has a lot to do with hard work. . . . The [bloggers] that really do make it, either they know the right people or they were just at the right place at the right time, or they get picked up and they explode. It's . . . these very random things combined with, obviously, hard work.

Here, Hélène acknowledges the role of chance circumstance ("luck" and "right place at the right time") in catapulting producers above the flood of other aspirants. Yet she also dispels assumptions about leisure-time passions through her repeated references to "hard work." Similarly Julianne, a PR professional and fashion-blogging hopeful, reflected on the level of commitment required to build a social media following in an evermore saturated market for content:

> Blogging is very time-consuming . . . nine times out of ten, it seems that the mark of a successful blogger is that they just keep at it. You'll find many times that people start blogs and then they're unable to just juggle a life and work, and writing the blog. . . . I mean, it kind of ebbs and flows with me; there are times where I'm up until two o'clock in the morning blogging, making sure everything looks perfect, and that all my posts are scheduled in a timely fashion, and then, there are times where it's nine to five.

Julianne thus highlights the self-discipline required of creative aspirants; she later reiterated, "If you really want to do it well, it's a lot of work." This perspective on the importance of one's self-will dovetails quite well with neoliberal ideologies emphasizing reliance on the self, above all else.

Further, Julianne's comment about "keep[ing] at it" signals a common refrain among my interview participants: both fledgling digital media producers and well-established blogger-brands emphasized the time, energy, and discipline necessary to build and sustain a social media persona. Among their laboring activities were managing workflow, staging visual content, and circulating material across the vast social media landscape—activities that invoke the production routines and business logics driving mainstream media industries.

Similar to the structures and practices that journalists and reporters have instituted to control the flow of information in the face of uncertainty, social media producers thought carefully about the scheduling of their material.[24] And, overwhelmingly, they emphasized the importance of "being consistent" by posting content at regular intervals and building up a rich queue of material. Amber provided a sense of what the management of workflow looks like: posting daily, Monday through Friday, as well as at least once on the weekend. She continued, "Being consistent, I think, is a big part of it [and] promoting all of my posts on my various social media channels as much as I can; it's time-consuming, but it really does make a difference." Other social media producers organized their production schedules in ways similar to the editorial calendars found in monthly magazines. Hélène, for instance, noted how she had "plan[ned] out the sort of editorial calendar and what I was going to post for the week and the month." Alice, meanwhile, believed that adhering to a regular time-table lent a sense of predictability to her site. She framed this as a benefit to her readers, likening her weekly roster to a TV listing, "so people know exactly [what] they are seeing and what day." In explaining her strategy, Alice acknowledged how the daily mandates shared a close affinity to her self-brand:

> Like Monday I call it . . . the "French Diary," so I'm telling my experience as a French person in America. And then Tuesday "Tricks, Tips and Tricks"; Wednesday is "Product of the Week." . . . So people know what they're going to see when they come on my blog.

Danielle also reflected on her weekly schedule, although she framed this management of her time as a strategy that would help her better cope with blogging alongside her full-time career. Being "over[ly] ambitious" with her posting schedule had taken its toll, she recalled:

> I would do five outfit posts a week, and I would do two music posts a week. And I ended up getting incredibly overwhelmed by that . . . and it became more [important to] do a couple posts a week and have them be good quality than do seven posts a week and have them be sub-par.

Danielle's comment reveals how producers struggle to strike a balance between their ability to produce (quality) content and the expected demands of their followers. Likewise, when I asked Emily about the labor involved in maintaining her site, she offered the following accounting of her time: "This week, I've done a lot more because I'm traveling all next week for work, so I probably won't really be able to

of their personalities. Rachel L. remarked that the constellation of various social media platforms "go together to create my internet personality." She explained, "On Facebook and Twitter, I'm more honest and funny and more of myself than I am on Instagram because there's more room for in between mistakes and things. . . . [With] the other ones—Facebook and Twitter, there seems to be a little more room for personality."

Heather, similarly, recalled that with the ascension of new social media platforms, she felt compelled to project different aspects of her persona to *imagined audiences.*

> So there is a vast majority of the Twitter followers who only know me as someone who Tweets quite a bit about my children or the absurdities of my children, and you know, links to a few interesting things. . . . I mouth off quite a bit on Twitter. And Facebook is much more warm and cozy and they know who my children are, they know the faces, they know my dogs. They want the meatier part of my story.

Assumptions about the "imagined audience" of social networking sites invoke the notion of "context collapse," which, as danah boyd writes, occurs when "the lack of spatial, social, and temporal boundaries makes it difficult to maintain distinct social contexts."[32] Put simply, our socially mediated self is often broadcast to once-distinct social groups—friends, family members, colleagues, and more—simultaneously and singularly.

To circumvent the challenges of impression-management exacerbated by collapsed contexts, producers used discrete platforms (Facebook, Twitter, Instagram, Tumblr) as built-in filters to either conceal or reveal particular aspects of their personae (e.g., the "funny" me, the "warm and cozy" me). Accounts of self-presentations fine-tuned for individual platforms suggest how self-branding is guided by *platform-specific imaginings* of the audience.[33] The recursive development and monitoring of these performances of the self can thus be read as a response to the seeming inevitability of context collapse. Of course, the compulsion to deftly manage platform-specific presentations of the self amplifies the obligation to partake in incessant self-branding.

In an era of ubiquitous connective media, commercial institutions "engage" consumers through digital initiatives that require employees to provide paid—and, at times, *un*paid—emotional labor.[34] But these directives are not just the province of corporate brand-building missions; increasingly, they animate the activities of aspiring media and creative workers. Internet scholar Nancy Baym, for instance, found that budding musicians found it imperative to interact with fans in socially mediated contexts. To Baym, these communicative, self-promotional practices are constitutive of a unique mode of value-generating productivity that she terms "relational labor."[35] Although Baym dismisses the notion that relational labor practices vary by gender, my own research has revealed how social and industrial constructions of (digital) audiences reify assumptions about gendered sociality. As I argued in my analysis of the women's magazine industry, corporate discourses valorize gendered social sharing, compelling cultural producers to interact with female consumers in various digital spaces.[36]

Those I interviewed—from the neophyte personal style bloggers to the social media mavens with follower counts in the tens of thousands—similarly reflected on the imperative to engage with fellow bloggers, brands, and audiences. Fashion and lifestyle blogger Jessie said, "What helps businesses grow are relationships," adding, "All of my work has come from relationships now that I think about it." She then detailed a series of social niceties—both online activities and off—that have helped her augment her personal brand. My interviews revealed that relational labor was not a single activity but, rather, an organizing concept that included a wide range of affective practices.

In describing their interactive activities, some digital producers conveyed an overtone of urgency. Erika, a fashion blogger who successfully transitioned from hobby to career, explained her obligation to "keep on top of comments" and "try to respond right away." She confessed how she would initially get between 80 to 150 comments per post, and that it became "crazy" trying to manage this feedback loop. Alissa, meanwhile, articulated reader responsiveness as "part of [her] job."

> If someone leaves a comment under that post on Facebook, I need to reply to it. Or if they send me a message on Facebook, I need to reply to it. . . . Because sometimes people feel like, "Oh, you think you're too good," or whatever the case. For me, I want my readers to know that I'm accessible to you. Like, this is part of my job. I chose to be a blogger, so what you think and what you want to see is important, so I have to make sure I'm responding on social media just as much as I'm posting on social media.

Alissa's sense of obligation to readers ("*need* to reply") was framed as a demonstration of her relatable *accessibility,* a theme to which I return in the next chapter.

For full-time bloggers, especially those who are contractually bound to "deliver audiences to advertisers" (to use conventional media speak), such responsiveness is not surprising: when followers, likes, and shares are the bread and butter of a digital market, a decline in these metrics could mean a direct financial hit. Yet aspirants, too, believed that the provision of instant feedback was critical to their "success." Maeve, for instance, explained how she felt that it was really important to "reply" to feedback on her blog, reasoning, "Ultimately your audience is your success [so] if they are happy with what you're doing, then you're going to get a larger audience, they're going to tell your friends, their friends about it, and you're going to be more successful." Notably, the discursive shift from interacting with "readers" to creating content for "audiences" is a significant one that is bound up with the ascension of advertising/marketing opportunities for seemingly "ordinary" individuals.[37]

Like the persistent mandate to self-promote, social media producers acknowledged that relation-building activities were time-consuming. Caitlin, for instance, expressed frustration about the fact that these promotional activities can become a full-time job themselves: "Maybe, if I was doing this all day long, [or] if I had a million dollars and didn't have to work or didn't have a social life then, yes, I would spend all day [interacting] and probably build it up. . . . I mean you literally have to be on top of this, like, day and night." Meanwhile, Danielle remarked on the labor-intensive nature of one particular platform, Lookbook. "It's incredibly time-consuming, [so] in order for people to find you, you have to be commenting on lots of things, like you have to be very active with it." She framed her overall experience with the blogging community as a positive one, lauding the "online support network" of fellow bloggers who enjoy mutually sustaining relationships through tweeting, Facebook, Instagram. "The more I've gotten involved with doing the social media aspect, it's definitely grown significantly in views and readers and followers and support." Such narratives bring the self-promotional aspect of active commenting into stark relief (i.e., references to social sharing and "success").

Certainly, followers, friends, tweets, and comments are the currency powering the social media marketplace, and many of these interactions were shaped by an undercurrent of instrumentality. Professionalization resources routinely urge fashion bloggers to "give back to the blogging world" and "support" other members of the community by actively commenting on others' blog posts. For instance, *Fashion 2.0: Blogging Your Way to the Front Row* author Yuli Ziv encouraged digital content creators to "build your relationships with other bloggers based on the principles of partnership, as if you worked together for one big corporation called the Blogosphere."[38] Though commenting was superficially framed as an act of goodwill, the structure of exchanges was incentivized with offers of friendship, collaborative knowledge, or the potential for economic gain. For instance, in an article on the "Joys of Blogging," Independent Fashion Bloggers (IFB) member Lauren identified "community" as the "undisputed king of blogging reasons." After describing how novice bloggers are often "shock[ed]" by the feedback and friendships provided by the community, she added, "It is a delightful world even following commercialisation, all based on reciprocal behaviour, click through [clicking on a given link to land on a new page], and link love [posting a link to another blog one admires]!"

Expressions of reciprocity are considered increasingly salient in the online economy, bound up as they are with mutually beneficial systems of social relations.[39] Thomas Rankin, co-founder of the Instagram and Snapchat marketing platform Dash Hudson, explained how this mentality of "partnership" played out in practice. He detailed a unique system "that the really young Instagrammers are using to build their accounts: they work in a very collaborative way to build their followings and help get each other 'likes.' "

Perhaps unsurprisingly, not all forms of interactivity were equally valued among bloggers and vloggers.[40] Instead, social media producers were encouraged to provide feedback according to the narrowly prescribed norms of positivity and sincerity. Adherence to these norms is guided by blogger politics and more formally sanctioned codes (both formal policies and technical features) that govern behavior among various social media communities. As blogger/author Yuli Ziv noted in the earlier-mentioned manual, *Blogging Your Way to the Front Row,* "Positive relationships only help all of us grow in power and profitability, and there's more than enough wealth and prosperity to go around." One of the women I interviewed helped to illuminate what such *positivity* might look like in practice.

> I'll thank [fellow bloggers] for a compliment just to acknowledge them and make them know that . . . I am thinking of them and that, you know, I appreciate their compliments, or, I'll go onto their profile and maybe "like" some of their posts that are really cute, or that I [feel are great]. All the bloggers who are a part of [the blogging network], they're also great and each one is so supportive of one another so we're always, like, rooting each other on.

Megan, similarly, explained, "The internet is a really scary, mean place when it comes to the comment section, [so] my comment section is like, a fluffy cloud of positivity."

Negative comments, accordingly, were vociferously discouraged; members of the IFB network, for instance, disparaged the purveyors of these comments as "trolls," "vandals," or "haters." One site member urged bloggers to follow the age-old advice, "If you have nothing nice to say, don't say anything at all." Tying this into notions of individual taste distinction, she continued:

> No one expects you to like or agree with everything you read in the blogosphere. We all have different tastes and styles; it is completely normal to dislike someone else's outfit or post. That doesn't mean you have to be hurtful. Constructive criticism and differing opinions are welcome, but there is a nice way to say something and a rude way to say something. If you can't figure out how to say it nicely, don't say anything at all.

The blogger's reference to "constructive criticism" suggests there is room for systems of critique in the blogosphere; however, widely voiced contempt for negative commenting seemed to dispel this myth. Instead, bloggers were encouraged to provide positive feedback that would ensure that the blogworld continued to be what another IFB member described as "a positive, self-esteem-building place."

Although norms about positive comments were linked to notions of community support and the democratization of taste, the significance of positivity to self-branding practices should not be cast aside. Indeed, this emphasis on favorable comments has been documented in other studies of digital evaluation and reputation management systems.[41] While bloggers' emphasis on positive feedback can be read as psychological or ideological, it may also be understood as a calculated effort to build affective relations—an enactment of the neoliberal project of self-branding.

Collectively, these online forms of relational labor—responding to blog and Instagram comments, exchanging emails, engaging in reciprocal tagging, and retweeting—are validated by the economies of interactive media. Social media metrics are the *de rigueur currency:* the number of comments/likes/retweets a post receives is used to benchmark blogger achievement and status. As a member of the IFB noted on the site, "Comments are like currency. . . . It makes us feel like people are actually paying attention to what we put out there."[42] This underscores the emergent political economies of blogging, wherein bloggers hoping to achieve even a modicum of success from advertising partnerships must have a baseline level of followers or commenters. Affiliate marketers typically provide specific guidelines on the number of readers/comments a blogger needs to monetize her site.

A personal style blogger interested in joining an affiliate network, for example, needs to surpass a follower threshold; ten thousand was a figure thrown around at conferences and in blogger manuals. Advertisers looking for "partners" to produce "sponsored content" also require applicants to submit social media metrics. This translates into a system of value hierarchies that privileges those that seem best able to deploy their affective relations. For instance, a call for social media influencers to develop a sponsored post for a designer shoe launch (the name was withheld in the call) required the following:

1. Blog URL
2. Current Monthly Blog Traffic
3. Instagram URL
4. Current # of Instagram Followers
5. Facebook URL
6. Current # of Facebook fans & friends
7. Twitter URL
8. Current # of Twitter followers
9. Your current rate for sponsored posts.[43]

The reach of a producer's content, for instance, either allows or precludes her from being admitted to any number of the ad networks that are billed as *invitation only;* after being vetted, these metrics dictate her compensation rate. But these crude statistics—like other indexes of power—are often self-fulfilling. José van Dijck, a social media historian, describes the tendency of connective media to exacerbate hierarchies through the *popularity principle:* "The more contacts you have and make, the more valuable you become, because more people think you are popular and hence want to connect with you."[44] *Having and making these contacts* is exacting and time-consuming, and creative aspirants are compelled to invest their energy and human capital in building their affective networks. From engaging with followers and reciprocating feedback to formal networking and informal schmoozing, relationship-building activities were articulated as *work.*

Such modes of networked communication—particularly when incentivized by marketing structures that emphasize metric quantification—commoditize affective relations as they reproduce the problematic assumption that women turn to digital media to "be social." My point in exploring the instrumental function of these interactions is not to empty their significance; bloggers frequently remarked on the inspiration, encouragement, advice, and even friendship afforded to them by their participation in formal and informal blogging circuits. Yet I also want to highlight how these various practices are configured for professional, brand-building aims. It is in this vein that I echo Nancy Baym's argument that scholars "do not have to understand *relationships* in labor as inherently either genuine or alienating, empowering or oppressive." Rather, she continues, "they are all of these and more, often at the same time." Of course, these relational practices take place off the screen, *in real life,* too.

An unshakable myth about careers in the cultural and innovation industries is that they are intensely social or, perhaps more euphemistically, *informal*. Ethnographies of creative work cultures—detailing the extravagant fêtes of the fashion world, the raucous laughter and clinking-glasses parties of the advertising and publishing industries, and the annual influx of the Silicon Alley crowd to the Black Rock desert for the Burning Man festival[45]—have done little to dispel this myth. Instead, they have helped to draw necessary attention to the always-on, self-interested nature of these *not-quite-leisurely* leisure activities. Cultural theorist Angela McRobbie has argued that communicative practices embedded in the subcultural club scene have infiltrated the culture industries through a " 'club culture sociality' with its attendant skills of networking and selling the self."[46] My interviewees also engaged in forms of what scholars refer to as "compulsory sociality": necessary networking where work and non-work time bleed into one another.[47] Yet these activities were of a decidedly different ilk—less hedonistic, more affable, more saturated with unabashedly commercial messages. In other words, they were more feminized.

The most explicitly careerist events are professionalization workshops and conferences such as BlogHer (organized by the SheKnows online brand), *Lucky* Fashion and Beauty Blog Conference (FABB), Bloggy Bootcamp (women-only conferences by the SITS girls), and IFB Con.—in fact, a whole industry has sprung up to cultivate wannabe social media professionals. Although these events were all brimming with entrepreneurial euphoria, I found that each had a unique tone and feel. Some of the events were spearheaded by characteristic tech enthusiasts, while others featured inspiring presenters from the unlikely domains of politics and the academy; some presiders mandated live-tweeting, while others shared "off the record" market forecasts; some emphasized finding a creative voice, while others offered practical insight on the trade.

The fee structure of professionalization events is also highly variable—from the $20 charity donation for a rather informal blogger panel discussion at a crowded Philadelphia eatery to the $850 one-day registration for a digital fashion event that convened in a posh hotel in New York's SoHo neighborhood. Tickets to *Lucky* FABB range from $250 to $600 and involve a vetting process: interested parties must explain why they want to attend, their goals, and, of course, the name of the blog. I saw one blogger post on her Instagram feed, "I wish! I'm not 'big' enough yet. . . . It's my dream to go someday." Several dreams may have been shattered that particular year—2015—when *Lucky* announced they were cancelling the conference just a few days before the event.

Presumably, only those with material access can afford to lay down hundreds of dollars on a conference—not including travel and lodging expenses. As Kat admitted:

> I think it would benefit me if I went to some of these blogger conferences, [but] it's one of these things when it's during the day, and I can't take off from my day job and pay money. . . . It really is kind of nuts . . . they're kind of expensive, some of these things and it's like *Ugh* [expresses frustration].

Registration information is no doubt provided to the conference sponsors (Proctor & Gamble, for instance, primary sponsor of *Lucky* FABB, or Maybelline, sponsor of "Fun, Fearless, Life"; see Figure 4).

Ostensibly, brands and designers orchestrate events for the sole purpose of generating buzz through participants' social media feeds. Fashion and beauty bloggers, in particular, receive regular invitations

4. Participants at Cosmopolitan's *first "Fun, Fearless, Life" event in New York get their makeup done by event sponsor Maybelline. Photo Credit: Author.*

to launch parties and product premieres, sponsored by fashion and retail brands. Fashion blogger Alice offered a description of how brand-sponsored events work:

> When [brands] have events around New York or Philadelphia they will . . . send me an invite telling me, "We have an event about our new launch, our new product, would you like to come?" And then we go to the presentation, they give us a premiere, a bit before it's released out so we can write about it, and try the product, and give our opinions about it.

Other bloggers were less enthusiastic about these PR-generated happenings; Alissa admitted, "I don't always go to those because it's just kind of . . . looking at the collection, and the brand hoping that you write about them." However, she found another type of event more compelling: those that bring people from all walks of life together in a shared space.

While conference programs list formal speakers and panels, networking is the *raison d'être* to attend such events. Conference presiders roused attendees to "Meet new people!" during breaks and networking receptions. At the end of each event I attended, I had amassed an overflowing stack of business cards, most of which included individuals' Facebook, Twitter, Instagram, and/or Pinterest accounts. Kat compared the contact-building nature of these events to her time in PR: "There's just so many events happening—product launches, and dinners, and that kind of thing. So each time I go to one of those, I feel like I pick up another, sort of, contact."

To this end, participants justified their participation in these events—from formal conferences to grassroots blogger collectives—as an investment in the (future) self-brand. Although Danielle did not attend many of these events, she shared an observation about the merits of relation-building practices: "A lot of bloggers have grown in readership through networking. . . . And I know bloggers personally that they were kind of small, and they started hanging out with a lot of the girls that were very successful, and then they blew up overnight." Other participants conceded that the events might not be immediately gratifying; yet, they rationalized their attendance as something that may *one day* prove beneficial. For instance, Alissa explained:

> [You're] meeting not only people that are within your own niche, but you're meeting people outside of it because you're building relationships. And those relationships that you're building could possibly take you to the next level of

whatever it is that you're trying to do with your blog. So for me, it's always important to go to as many events as I can because I'm meeting so many different people from all walks of the fashion industry. . . . You're meeting designers; you're meeting people who work on the business side of fashion; you're meeting people who do marketing. . . . At some point, you may need to ask these people for a favor. Or these people may like how you carry yourself or like what you do and want to work with you.

Alissa signals a cognitive validation endemic to creative work, namely what Gina Neff, Elizabeth Wissinger, and Sharon Zukin describe as workers driven "by the promise of one Big Job being right around the corner."[48] Another fashion blogger, Alice, offered a strikingly similar account; however, for her, the obligation to network meant *being on* in all social situations. She explained:

I have my business cards, I have everything on me. So when I'm talking to somebody and [they ask what I do,] I give them my card, and then [I] follow up with people: I send them an email saying, "Thank you, it was nice meeting you, [let me know] if you have any project in mind."

Alice gave the example of a chance encounter with a web producer for a local TV show affiliate whose responsibilities included shooting funny or unscripted footage for the website. He told Alice he wanted to interview her "and the next day he made it happen." In this case, Alice offers a one-off example (meeting a web producer) to justify compulsory networking; after all, she could be seated next to an individual who might give her a *big break*.

Amber, too, framed events through the prism of *potentially* beneficial. She offered the hypothetical example of an event led by a makeup artist who will cover something that "could wind up being an inspiration for a post." She added, "If you're just sent products, that's great, and you'll certainly have things to write about, but I do think that it . . . inspires a lot of post ideas when I go to these events." For her, the challenge is to balance her schedule of events and appointments to ensure that she has "enough time to really sit down and write my assignments." Jessie made a similar remark about the unmanageable schedule of events, noting, "I get a lot of requests from people to have coffee, and I love to meet with people, but it's gotten to the point where I'm like, if I don't say no at times, I'm going to have coffee dates around the clock."

While Amber and Jessie nodded to the time-intensive nature of socializing activities, Kristy's critique was of a different ilk: during her tenure as a fashion blogger, she confessed, she had grown weary of the performative, self-indulgent nature of networking events. Over time, she explained, "I wasn't enjoying the people I was around. I wasn't enjoying the events. The events were tedious . . . they were boring." She recollected her experience at a blogger award ceremony as "an alternate reality where everybody thought or acted like they were really vain." In fact, Kristy found the self-aggrandizing behavior of certain A-list bloggers so off-putting that she sat with the web team ("they were the only other people in the room who were kind of 'with me' in the sense that they thought it was kind of silly the way people were acting"). She added:

The focus on status and exclusivity became discouraging. Each time I would take a step back and view it objectively, I thought it was pretty silly. It reminded me of being in high school and wanting to sit at the popular table. There was such a lack of self-awareness because everyone was so distracted by utter frivolity.

An exception, for Kristy, was London Fashion Week; she enthused, "Snapping pictures of beautiful designs in this very great lighting and stuff—that was awesome, I loved that."

The biannual spectacle that is New York Fashion Week is perhaps the definitive brand-building event for fashion aspirants, as swarms of status-seeking style enthusiasts cavort outside the Lincoln Center Pavilion, many hoping to catch the discerning eye of a fashion photographer (see Figure 5). British fashion critic Suzy Menkes offered one

5. *Two young women pose for street-style photographers outside of New York City's Lincoln Center during Fashion Week in September 2014. Photo Credit: Author.*

Though personal style bloggers drew upon the language and aesthetics of consumerism, many invoked a patterned series of discourses to reframe forms of physical self-presentation and transformation as *work*. Thus, though the images they project and promote are powered by practices of gendered consumerism, these activities were notably absent from informants' self-reflections. When bloggers *did* reflect on shopping, it was either part of a life story that expressed a longtime passion for fashion or, alternatively, reference to an addiction that was somehow overcome through the blog project. Sarah G., for instance, explained how her blog covers "what I do on a daily basis, which nine times out of ten is going through my closet, or shopping or like, my battle with my wallet, which is ongoing [laugh]." Jennifer, similarly, conceded that she "loved shopping a lot."

Much more often, the act of shopping was concealed behind the language of "styling," a term deployed to describe the production of a highly individualized "look." Of course, "styling" presumes an active subject—one who can resist the allure of the marketplace and is above all a cultural *producer.* Styling involved a visible display of the self on a consistent basis, a compendium of products, and forms of transformation that ensured that one stayed within the margins of her brand niche. Styling thus represents "the labor of self-fashioning," and a performance of expertise.[53] Marissa explained how much more involved the process of fashion blogging was because of the upfront work required, including styling/outfit planning, hair and makeup, and more. Personal style blogging, she explained, "is a lot more intense because you have to think through the outfit . . . if I don't have a piece that I want, I have to go find it . . . , so shooting will take some time, editing takes some time." The process, she continued, can take up to a full day.

Much like models and celebrities of the late twentieth century, bloggers, vloggers, and Instagrammers are compelled to attend to the stringent physical requirements of those in the public eye. Yet these demands are amplified by contemporary standards of airbrushed, Instagram-worthy perfection as so many of us are incited to participate in the image work and body discipline that constitute what Wissinger calls "glamour labor."[54] Several of my interviewees discussed aesthetics of self-presentation that seemed wrought by traditional codes of idealized femininity. Kimberly spoke to me about this, and after our interview went public about her struggle. As she wrote on her blog (pennypincherfashion.com/2014/01/looking-in.html):

> When I started this blog, my main goal was to connect with other women & to help them look and feel their best. But, after hearing a comment someone made recently, I realized I needed to take a moment to address it. She said, "I used to read your blog all the time, but it just made me feel bad that I don't look that pulled-together every day." I'll be honest, my heart completely sank. I never want someone to visit this site and leave feeling worse about themselves. . . . But it wasn't until last week when we were leaving the house for a photo shoot (that I honestly didn't feel up for) when it all clicked for me & her comment suddenly made sense. At the time, I was feeling miserably sick, but going out to take pictures where I would put on my sunglasses, paint on a bright smile & pretend my way through it so I would have a post for the next day. It dawned on me that my readers aren't always seeing the real me because I'm not letting them see it.

Kristy, meanwhile, was especially frank about the internal tumult she experienced from being cast in the limelight. She confessed that being in the social media spotlight made her "overly concerned about my body."

To this end, strict body disciplining is an especially controversial form of aesthetic labor, and certain fashion bloggers are beginning to attract the same ire that models and celebrities have long drawn for perpetuating unrealistic standards of physical perfection.[55] Kristy also waged a wider critique on the incessant culture of consumerism, which she believed deracinated the blogosphere's indie roots.

> I had been so excited about the blogging movement because I thought it would genuinely be helpful for women, for people. In some ways it has helped, but mostly all I see [are] more young women exploiting themselves for the profit of corporations, for fame, for money. It's all about excess. Never repeating the same outfit. Buy more to make you happy.

Kristy's comment lays bare the recursive nature of (gendered) aspirational production; it feeds back into the consumer marketplace. Media scholar Elizabeth Nathanson made a compelling argument to this end in her analysis of blogging as a "new" mode of consumptive pleasure amidst post-recession anxieties: "While blogging promises to be a career replete with the pleasures of self-determination, entrepreneurial success is predicated on marketing personal style, which fundamentally also serves the interests of the fashion industry by producing future consumers."[56]

Before drawing conclusions about the aspirational labor system, I want to pause to anticipate a potential critique—namely, that this career-centric orientation fails to characterize *all* forms of social media production explored here. To be clear: although the majority of my interviewees indicated a close affinity between social media production and brand-building, career-focused labor, there were outliers. Pharmaceutical sales rep and part-time fashion/music blogger Danielle was among the exceptional cases. Danielle explained that she began posting about her tastes in fashion and indie music a few years ago and was rather astonished by the reach of her site. "I never really thought it was going to go anywhere," she recalled, offering an origin narrative not unlike that of the "accidental entrepreneurs." Yet Danielle was adamant that the blog was an end (a "fun hobby") in itself rather than a means to a distinctly professional end: "My passion in life is not to work at a magazine or have a really big blog." In fact, Danielle told me that she enjoyed aspects of her "day job," including its presumed stability:

> I really like my day job. . . . I don't want it to get to the point where people are flying [me] around and giving sponsorships, like I understand from a financial standpoint that it's great but . . . I like to know what's gonna happen, and my normal job is a very stable job, and it's a good job.

Although Danielle was drawn to the expressive potential of social media, the tradeoffs of a creative career didn't hold the same sway over her; after all, she was gainfully employed outside the fashion world.

In contrast to my other interviewees, Danielle's work-style seems animated by the cultural ethos of the so-called "slash generation." As I explained earlier in this book, "slashies" are said to be a cohort of millennial workers who hold multiple jobs for self-actualization purposes, rather than out of necessity. Media coverage, not surprisingly, has valorized the "slashie" work-style/lifestyle. As one member of the putative slashie generation told a reporter, "The thought of a 40-hour week and then you're into overtime seems like nonsense to me. I'm lucky because it doesn't feel like work, it's creative and it's enterprising."[57] Although a small minority of the individuals I interviewed might be classified as slashies—they had full-time gigs and were maintaining blogs "just for the fun of it"—most others emphasized the fact that what they were doing was indeed *work*. It is not incidental that when I followed up with Danielle roughly a year after our initial interview, she had abandoned her site to make time for a new career in biotech sales.

Working as a "creative" is a resonant ideal in contemporary culture, and the stock of artists, writers, designers, and photographers on the quest for gainful employment is brimming. To better position themselves for career sectors with characteristically high barriers to entry, job-seekers utilize various strategies—from slogging away at internships to cultivating professional networks to more conventional forms of résumé-building. The women profiled in this chapter make clear how younger generations are increasingly relying on social media to pursue the well-worn ideal of "dream careers." Websites, blogs, and carefully curated Instagram feeds are thus articulated as "résumé-builders," "networking tools," or—most auspiciously—direct conduits to employment. Though my sources' self-descriptions seemed to indicate different approaches to cultural work—motivated by creative impulses or economic demands—professional drives are central to the rhetoric of both. Such accounts provide a sharp rejoinder to constructions of digital content creation as either *leisure* or *exploited consumer labor*. Neither of these perspectives adequately captures the purposeful, directed, and future-oriented nature of these practices. Aspirational labor, as I have shown here, involves discourses and practices shot through with contradiction.

Indeed, under the shiny veneer of seemingly "fun" work, the very real disadvantages of the aspirant work-style emerged. Producers described the compulsion to work long hours (including late nights and weekends), invest in their own skills-building and training, participate in a litany of formal and informal networking events, and deploy affective skills to inflate their "metrics." These activities were often justified by fleeting promises of success; with enough hard work, aspirants are assured that they will rise up the ranks. The social media economy was thus framed as a meritocracy. Recall Julianne's detailed exposition of the kind of self-discipline required for a blogger to be "successful": one who "just keep[s] at it" and who can "juggle a life and work, and writing the blog." Certainly, this valorizes a particular kind of subjectivity—one that Anita Harris seemed to foreshadow more than a decade ago, whereby "success and failure are constructed as though they were depending on strategic effort and good personal choices." Yet, Harris clarifies, "these designations have much more to do with economic and cultural resources than personal competences."[58] Similarly, a blogger's lack of success stems from her personal failure to "juggle" conflicting demands: the structural barriers that make this juggling especially difficult for certain subjectivities go unacknowledged.[59] It encourages a type of laboring subject who is *always* on, but only *partially* paid.

As these individuals reflected on the demands of creating, distributing, and promoting content, it became patently clear that the routines and logics of social media aspirants bear many of the marks of traditional media work.[60] Creative and promotional labor, efforts to "know" audiences, and a preoccupation with metrics—these are all tasks intimately familiar to producers in traditional media industries. Additionally, bloggers' inflections on the tradeoff between individual self-expression and external social approval can be contextualized within a larger tension between creativity and constraint that has long been characteristic of work in the culture industries.[61] Yet there is an important distinction between legacy and ostensibly "new" media: denizens of the latter seek to harness and deploy the commercial value of "authenticity."

4

Branding the Authentic Self: The Commercial Appeal of "Being Real"

I think the most important thing right now is to be true to your sense of style, be very authentic and different from other bloggers.

—Julianne, style blogger

At first blush, the three young women featured on the February 2015 cover of *Lucky*—the unabashedly commercial "magazine about shopping"—appear as typical magazine cover models. Arms entwined and traipsing in stride, they exude poised self-assurance. Their bodies are long and lean, and each dons a high-hemmed dress: bauble-embellished lavender, pastel and black color-blocked, and poppy lace. However, these striking women are *not* merely cover models; rather, they are social media dynamos who by all accounts have earned *Lucky*'s designation as "fashion's digital superstars."[1] With readership soaring into the hundreds of thousands, Chiara Ferragni (The Blonde Salad), Zanita Whittington (Zanita), and Nicole Warne (Gary Pepper Girl) are ranked among the world's top fashion and lifestyle bloggers. Yet despite astonishing career success—Ferragni was expected to rake in $8 million the year the magazine was published—these blogger-*cum*-digital entrepreneurs are suspended in the popular imagination as people *just like us*. Indeed, in the magazine's opening pages, *Lucky*

Since then, however, individuals have begun to contest these appeals to inclusivity by questioning what the appellation "real" implies for female subjectivities. As a *Huffington Post* writer complained, "Saying 'real women' is a way of throwing the more peopled category of women a bone in an industry that obviously favors shapes that simply aren't in the cards for nearly everyone."[9] In this same vein, numerous feminist media scholars have critiqued the extent to which the designation "real" remains inscribed within a normative culture of beauty.[10] Campaigns steeped in authenticity appeals can thus be read as expressions of "commodity feminism," wherein advertisers co-opt the political aims of feminism to make their messages compatible with marketplace demands.[11] As Sarah Banet-Weiser argues, the form of individual empowerment presented in the Dove Campaign is "not one that emerges from collective struggle or civic participation." Instead, she continues, "the individual is a flexible commodity that can be packaged, made, and remade—a commodity that gains value through self-empowerment."[12]

The presupposition that realness is a conduit to empowerment has found a welcome home in the social media sphere. In particular, the outwardly democratizing nature of production and distribution technologies coincided with a heightened emphasis on "authentic" public self-expression.[13] Marketing exec Juliet Carnoy's article, "Why Millennial Women Crave Authenticity," touted the virtues of social media:

> Today, more than ever, women want to be their most authentic selves. Whether it's embracing our natural bodies, refuting the need to be "likable," or considering the possibility that maybe no one truly has it all—women are tired of being manipulated to fit a mold that is shaped by brands for them, and not by them. . . .

In their search for authenticity, millennial women have turned to online channels. The prevalence of the Internet and social media has allowed women to represent their own ideals of beauty. They post and share photos of the products they love and create the very authenticity they are not getting from brands. Women upload millions of photos every day that reflect [their] diverse personalities and individual styles.[14]

Carnoy's closing point—"what's better for women is better for your brand"—indicated that the irony of celebrating *commercial authenticity* was all but lost.

Within the realm of fashion blogging, the values of "realness" and "authenticity" were born with the genre in the early 2000s and continued to gain traction during the so-called "golden age of fashion blogging." Lapping up the overnight success stories of Susie Bubble, Tavi Gevison, and Bryanboy, mainstream media situated this new generation of fashion voices in opposition to more exclusionary and hierarchical genres of cultural production, most especially women's magazines.[15] For instance, *Daily Mail* reporter Karen Kay wrote in 2007: "the [fashion] industry that is all about staying one step ahead is struggling to keep up with the plethora of bloggers who are revealing trends before they're set, passing on gossip before it's happened and rapidly diminishing the power of the glossy magazines."[16] Several years later, a BBC article on the "ordinary people who stole the show" at London Fashion Week articulated bloggers as those more in touch with "everyday life." A quote from Bryan Grey Yambao (Bryanboy) was included, explaining how blogs have "made everything more approachable."[17] Former fashion blogger Kristy, who launched her blog around 2008, recalled the intoxicating indie spirit of these digital pioneers: "I felt that blogging could be a great way to kill that iron grip rule magazines and advertisements had over us."

The authenticity of the blogosphere is also ascribed to its outward promise of diversity: plus-size, ethnic, and differently abled fashion bloggers testify to assumptions about digital fashion's inclusivity. Media trend pieces tend to valorize the distinctive aesthetics of fashion and beauty bloggers. Nicolette Mason, a "plus size" blogger/designer who proselytizes "body positivity," has received a spate of coverage in the mainstream media. As she told a reporter in 2016, "It's a really exciting time in fashion right now and we have seen a big shift towards a more democratic view . . . [and] that's a wonderful thing."[18] She traced the rise of political advocacy to online platforms, enthusing, "Social media has given a platform for people of all kinds, not just people who are in power and privileged and controlling media in whatever regard they are." Christina, founder of LoveBrownSugar, a blog for "savvy, multicultural women," was cautiously optimistic about claims of diversity. "There has absolutely been way more diversity and inclusion with the growth of digital media, [but] I think there's still a long way to go where that's concerned."

To some scholars, the blogosphere's appeals to diversity are dubious, at best. Based on an analysis of the highest-ranked U.S. personal style bloggers, Emily Hund and I argued that a narrowly defined aesthetic structures the upper echelon of the blogosphere; that is, top bloggers are young and overwhelmingly Caucasian or Asian, and have physiques that are often indistinguishable from fashion models'.[19] Claims of ethnic/racial diversity have also been problematized despite the global nature of social media production.[20] For instance, drawing on an analysis of Susanna Lau (Susie Bubble), Minh-Ha T. Pham contends that Lau's success is perhaps less about subverting historical norms and more about a feminization and racialization of labor that "implicitly charges Asian girls and women with the responsibility of the global economy."[21] Despite such scholarly critiques, discourses of "authenticity" and "realness" remain central to constructions of the blogosphere and serve as a foil to mainstream fashion culture.

Such ideals sit uneasily with the self-branding activities that drive social media producers to market themselves with intent. This chapter explores this contradiction as I examine how aspirational laborers' (seemingly incongruous) principles of authenticity and profit-making get reconciled as public expressions of the personal self-brand. More specifically, I contend that vexed notions of "realness," "amateurism," and "uniqueness" enable bloggers to simultaneously align themselves *with* and *against* mainstream fashion culture.

Despite the patterned similarities between "traditional" media work and online creative production, interview participants called upon the ideal of "realness" to justify their position that social media producers occupy a cultural space wholly distinct from so-called "legacy media." College student Lauren S., a blogger and "head style guru" for the College Fashionista social media site, explained her preference for reading other fashion blogs: "With a blogger, you feel like you can relate more to them . . . magazines are more like, just fantasized . . . and the blogger is just more real-life." Similarly, Philadelphia-based style blogger Danielle told me, "I think what blogs do that magazines don't do [is they] just give you real people style and real people representation." Danielle went on to declare her affinity for *Lucky* magazine because "they do a lot of street-style photos of people."

As Danielle's reference to "street style" suggests, this aesthetic is often contrasted with high-fashion imagery (i.e., what one would *expect* to see in a fashion magazine or advertisement), although the distinction is predictably murky. Offering a historical context, anthropologist Brent Luvaas notes that street-style photography has been a fixture of mainstream fashion magazines since the late 1990s, offering "a brief detour from the [magazines'] fantasy worlds" by featuring people " 'just like you and me,' albeit with a somewhat savvier style sensibility."[22] Danielle thus views the incorporation of "real people" into *Lucky* as a mode of representation for those traditionally excluded from women's glossies. Later during our interview, Danielle commented on the diversity afforded to the public by virtue of personal style bloggers:

> There are a lot of people of all different shapes and sizes that . . . [blog], and that's kind of the nice thing about it is like, for people that have a certain size or shape, there is a blogger out there for you that does a really good job of dressing themselves and showing how you can have personal style by being different sizes and looking different.

Danielle's references to individuals of "different shapes and sizes" attests to the common construction of fashion blogs as *diverse* or *inclusive*, assumptions which I question later in this chapter.

Lauren and Danielle were not unique in calling attention to the varying degrees of "realness" circulating in mediated representations of fashion. Indeed, several other bloggers posited that magazines were unable to safeguard their position within the fashion industry because they weren't responsive to the economic realities of their readers. As college student and style blogger Marissa explained: "A blog's more of a fashion magazine for street style, so people are always trying to see what's cool, what they can physically buy and wear themselves." By contrast, Marissa continued, "when you look at a magazine, nobody can afford half the stuff that's in there, or look half [as good as people] in there."

Jen, similarly, offered that unlike high fashion magazines, "[the products that bloggers] mention are affordable; they're easy to relate to."

For these individuals, then, *realness* was tantamount to accessibility—geographically, aesthetically, and most often, financially. As such, they sought out visual and textual cues that resonated with their own subjective position within the sprawling consumer sector.

The designation of "authentic" or "ordinariness" as a marker of social position is a familiar trope in popular culture and is especially pronounced in the reality TV genre. Scholars like Laura Grindstaff, Beverley Skeggs, and Katherine Sender have shown how representations of "real people" in reality programs are imbued with ideologies of gender, race, class, and sexuality.[23] Talk shows ostensibly offer class demarcations through the notion of "ordinariness," used to signal real people lacking status as well as media savvy.[24] Post-feminist discourses get invoked in reality TV culture, too. In a critical analysis of the self-presentation strategies of Katie Price, a British model turned media personality, media scholar Stéphanie Genz explores how the "currency of 'realness' [gets] harnessed to neoliberal and post-feminist expressions of self-branding, entrepreneurship and feminine agency."[25] One specific way that "realness" is coded is through the production of "working class" ordinariness, which ostensibly enables Price to connect with her fans as she positions herself *against* mainstream celebrities. The level of reflexive awareness attributed to Price concerning the "currency of 'realness'" testifies to the larger cultural import of these themes across mediated spaces, particularly those enabled by social media platforms.[26]

The aspirational laborers I spoke to also drew upon themes of "realness" and class-based accessibility to describe the standards that steered their creative projects; discourses of relatability thus served to articulate one's social standing. Often, and in spite of their presumed aspirations of upward social mobility through entrepreneurial ventures, most shared the perspective that *other* content creators—especially the exalted few who reached star blogger/vlogger rank—

had demonstrated behavior that was "inauthentic." These claims were embedded in critiques of A-list social media producers' presumed class status: they were perceived to come from well-heeled families, have an army of workers supporting their digital projects, and have enough disposable income to travel the world for the exclusive purpose of garnering exotic photo backdrops. Offering advice to fellow members of the Independent Fashion Bloggers network, Vahni of Grit & Glamour confessed:

> I am neither a professional model nor a professional photographer; I have neither the gritty gloriousness of London, nor the grandeur of the River Seine for subterfuge or support. I have no photographer/boyfriend, no boxes of goodies arriving at my doorstep daily. I am not 26 and snapping my way through exams, parties, and fashion design school. It's just me and my camera. In the clean and plainly pretty southeastern U.S.[27]

Similarly, those I interviewed sought to distinguish themselves from this imagined archetype of the blogger/model/jetsetter when providing accounts of their own self-brand. When I asked budget-style blogger Kimberly to reflect on how her blog has evolved over the years, she responded:

> One thing that I will say that I'm proud of is that [my blog has] stayed true to its original mission, which is finding affordable fashion that looks nice, and beauty [products] as well that are very accessible. I read a lot of blogs, and I look at a lot of magazines, and I draw inspiration from them, but there's so many that just are not realistic for the everyday woman. . . . I'm not going to spend $3,000 on a handbag.

Although Kimberly condenses "blogs" and "magazines" into a single category when discussing the inspirational-yet-unrealistic images pervading fashion texts, other content creators directed their critique exclusively at the former. As Julianne explained:

> I think it's also important to be attainable, and to . . . blog about things that the everyday girl can wear and use. I mean, don't get me wrong, who doesn't love a Chanel handbag? But not every girl can afford a different Chanel handbag every single day, so I think it's really important to bear in mind that chances are the majority of your readers are going to need to read something that's a little more affordable.

Presumably, inflated costs such as these (e.g., "$3,000 on a handbag," "a different Chanel handbag every single day") were invoked to distinguish individual content creators from a nameless class of *others* who seemed out of touch with the "everyday girl" reader. Allusions to excessively priced goods, though, were not the only way that bloggers sought to render themselves as *relatable*. As Kat explained of her blog, "I think of it as a beauty/lifestyle blog for everyday women. . . . I purposefully try to focus on either products or styling that is actually accessible to the everyday woman." She added, "I don't have a personal trainer and a personal chef, and I don't live this lavish lifestyle." By inoculating herself against assumptions of class privilege, Kat was able to establish a connection to an imagined reader while simultaneously shoring up her own brand identity in an increasingly saturated marketplace.

The imperative to reconcile one's own social position with the popular imagination of the "everyday girl reader" was brought into stark relief by Danielle. As I explained in a previous chapter, Danielle was unique among social media producers in the sense that she already had what she considered a fulfilling full-time career as a pharmaceutical sales representative. She acknowledged that her income may put her out of step with her social media followers:

> I've been working since I got out of college for the same company, so I financially do well in my normal job, [and] a lot of what I purchase a lot of people can't, and I try to be very conscious of that. . . . I don't want it to seem like it's a fantasy land; I don't want it to be out of reach for people, and it's personally one of the things when I read other fashion blogs that kind of irks me a little bit. I'm like, "I know this is unachievable for so many people."
>
> I don't want it to seem like I'm not an approachable person, or that I live in this great place where I can afford all these super expensive things all the time and that's all I talk about. Like I still want it to be *approachable* and *relatable* . . . to a broader audience. (italics added for emphasis)

Danielle's explanation indexes the significance of lifestyle markers to social media producers' construction of "realness"; thus, she substitutes high-status indicators (e.g., "super expensive things") with lower-cost goods in order to present herself as more "relatable" to her presumably middle-class readers. Emily R., similarly, reflected on what she saw as an obligation to present herself in a particular class stratum. She acknowledged that she "really [tries] to be aware of" the cost of items showcased on her blog, adding, "I have nicer things, not very many, but I do have higher-end products, and so I try to balance out any outfit when I may be wearing—[for example] my Tory Burch bag but wear Old Navy clothes." For Emily, this deliberate melding of brands was a preemptive defense to thwart being "called out" by members of the blogging community. She explained to me how readers critique bloggers who seem to rise to stardom overnight and subsequently lose touch with their readers: "[The blog followers contend that] 'you used to be so relatable, and I used to be able to wear what you have, but now when I look at your products, I can't afford a nine hundred dollar sundress.'"

New York–based model/blogger Crystal also presented an account of "realness" that was configured by class markers as well as a sense of candor. Describing how she sought to create a brand that was "attainable but also aspirational," Crystal offered:

> I want it to be *real,* you know, like, I'll be cooking something, and I completely fuck it up; I don't want to [be like], "okay let's practice, let's try it again." I want to say, "hey, this is where I fucked up . . . let me show you how to fix it when you do this cause you're gonna fuck up too. Or when you have to go to a black tie event but you can't afford a $5,000 gown. (italics added for emphasis)

Crystal thus implied that other bloggers lacked "realness" given the extent to which they conceal moments of (imperfect) everyday life behind the shiny veneer of carefully curated feeds, Instagram filters, and endless reserves of capital (e.g., a $5,000 gown). It wasn't until later in our conversation that Crystal acknowledged how her ability to relate to audiences may also stem from her racial and sexual identity. Asked about her long-term aspirations, Crystal said that she longed to join "one of those multi-women talk shows" such as ABC's *The View* or Fox's *The Real.* She continued, "I'm African-American, I'm from the south, I'm gay, like, all these different things. In totality of who I am, [and I would] bring that to a larger audience." Even here, then, Crystal continues to define relatability and distinctiveness through the language of audience-building. Each of these examples thus shows how "realness" is coded as *relatability to an imagined audience;* by channeling this ideal into their social media projects, individuals seek to carve out a unique space for their personal brands in a densely populated blogosphere.

Despite many interviewees' convictions that "realness" could still be found in the social media sphere, a small fraction felt that "authenticity" had largely become deracinated in digital spaces, supplanted by shameless self-indulgence and crass commercialization. The most vehement criticism came from two *former* fashion bloggers; this is not particularly surprising given the importance of reputation to those still hoping to rise up the ranks of the blogosphere. Olivia attributed her decision to abandon her blog to a series of factors: intensifying demands on her time, a nagging sense of discomfort about the necessity to put herself out there, and a feeling that the genre of personal style blogging had lost its distinctive qualities. She invoked the much-lauded ideal of "authenticity" when discussing the latter:

> [On their blogs, I] see girls running around San Francisco at 11 am wearing tutus and glitter shoes, and it's ridiculous! . . . These girls are trying to live out their fantasies by creating these worlds and it just seems so fake . . . these people are creating these perceptions of themselves that they want people to see them. Obviously, my life is not all dressing up in designer clothes, and going out to eat for every meal and drinking wine every night, and going to Paris, that's what these girls are showing you and you think that [lifestyle is] attainable in a sense. I think that you're given a false illusion.

Olivia thus claimed that the carefully curated and deftly managed personae showcased in the fashion blogosphere failed to resonate with her own lived reality. Yet her decision to frame these interactions as "fake" and a "false illusion" underscores the importance of "relatability" in organizing socially mediated performances of the self. Later in our conversation, Olivia mentioned "authenticity" again, declaring, "It's kind of gone" because of the blogosphere's overt commercial ethos. She added, "That's why people trusted bloggers [in the early days of blogging]: because they didn't feel like they were being forced down their throats, like these brands. And now it's the same brands over and over and over, and . . . it's fake." She added that bloggers have become nearly indistinguishable from models—a comment which is especially noteworthy given its apparent tension with the "real women" trope discussed earlier.

Kristy, too, expressed frustration about an aura of superficiality that she felt was pervading the world of fashion and style blogging. In contrast to Olivia, Kristy spent time working as a professional blogger after winning a contest called "Dream Job" sponsored by a well-known accessories retailer. Recalling the time she spent interacting with her pro-blogger peers, Kristy shared that despite some "beautiful experiences" meeting other young women, she was struck by the legions of "pretentious . . . conceited social climbers." She continued, "That's not behavior I had expected of bloggers. I thought we were all supposed to be *the down-to-earth type*" (italics added for emphasis). Kristy expanded upon these themes in an email she sent to me, which highlighted the vexed nature of "realness."

I wanted to share something honest, a new way of interacting with fashion and product. Instead, I had unwittingly become another sneaky advertiser. And it was almost worse

Fashion Week. Alice, a recent college graduate whose blog focuses on luxury brands, mentioned that she had been to New York City a few times over the last year for branding events; several others regularly attended professional conferences such as those hosted by the Independent Fashion Bloggers coalition. From these discussions, it becomes apparent that participation in productive socialization or "compulsory sociality"—necessary networking where work and non-work time bleed into one another—present impediments to many aspirants.[28]

These forms of networking require sufficient reserves of time and money; conference registration fees alone run several hundred dollars or more. They are also typically held in cultural epicenters—New York, Los Angeles, London, and Miami—meaning that travel costs escalate quickly. Recall from the last chapter how one of my interviewees bemoaned the fact that these conferences are held during the workday and also have steep registration fees. As a street-style photographer explained to *Fashionista*, "Travel is my biggest expense. . . . I fly something like 100,000 miles a year and spend almost a third of the year in hotels . . . travel gets really expensive."[29]

In addition to the economic hierarchy that configures the social media sphere, there is a telling map of social relations. Such webs of connectivity are indicative of what Andreas Wittel described as a "network sociality," a system of social relations propelling the culture of creative/new media work, which is defined by its transience, digital nature, and blurred boundaries between work and play.[30] Much like in the world of traditional media, it's *who you know*. Some of the most successful bloggers in popular culture tapped into existing networks in the fashion, marketing, and/or media industries. Blair Edie (Atlantic-Pacific) is the accessories designer for Tory Burch; Kristina Bazan (Kayture) hails from the world of modeling; and long before Olivia Palermo launched her eponymous site, she appeared in an MTV reality spin-off, *The City*, and enjoyed a string of modeling gigs.

Some of the bloggers I interviewed had an "in," too. Kimberly, whose blog has enjoyed tremendous growth despite her concession that she hasn't been "super proactive" at promoting it, explained the repeated coverage she received in *Lucky* magazine:

> I was very fortunate to know the editor-in-chief . . . at the time. They had the *Lucky* Style Collective, where they chose a certain number of bloggers to be a part of it. And they would put ads on your site, and you get money from the ads. And then there's this whole community page that they have on Luckymag.com, and just from that I got a lot of exposure with the people internally at *Lucky*, and was in the magazine quite a few times.

Kimberly's social ties with "legacy media" may have helped attract readers—and advertising partners—to her blog, highlighting the importance of existing networks as a marker of social capital.

Other aspirants drew upon careers, professional training, and/or personal connections in the advertising, marketing, and fashion sectors. Julianne, for instance, was able to glean professional knowledge from her career as a public relations representative at an agency specializing in social media. As she told me, "One of my clients was a shopping district, and . . . we had many, many meetings about working with fashion bloggers and incorporating them into our social strategy, so that kind of started to pique my interest." Later in our conversation, Julianne explained how she tapped into her existing social contacts to develop a strategy for her blog: "I also worked with a girl at the agency . . . [who] helped me develop a lot of my best much." Lauren B., who had fashioned a career as one of the first professional Instagrammers, explained why she seeks to maintain her visibility in other areas. "I make lots of time for interviews and media and anyone that reaches out to me, but if it's just for a personal blog, keeping yourself in the public eye is really important."

Directives to self-commodify one's personal life generated a great deal of ambivalence among my interviewees. Some young people, such as full-time fashion blogger Rachel L., felt that this mode of public sharing was an accepted, and even gratifying, aspect of the profession. She described the "documentary-style" of social media production as follows:

> For me, I think like more so than a lot of people, since I've been blogging for so long and like a lot of my stuff is very much like people have been following my life since I was in high school . . . I show my relationships and people know my different boyfriends from photos, like people I have dated and my different friend groups . . . stuff where *I really document my personal life*. (italics added for emphasis)

Rachel went on to tell me that her followers knew about her father's battle with cancer as well as her own health issues, signaling a level of deep intimacy with her (perceived) readers. However, Rachel did acknowledge the limitations of maintaining an always-on persona—particularly when she experienced dissonance between her own self-concept and the social media brand she had created over the years.

> I think [my readers and followers] really see me as this cute little girl in college who puts Barbie stickers on everything and is the size of a doll. And I know what my style is

and what my fans like to see. . . . I guess every blogger [who] wants to be a brand . . . has a look that they emulate. But sometimes, in my I guess "real life" or whatever, I'm mostly wearing like black leather skinnies and a black tee and little white or black flat boots, and I don't look like that character all the time anymore. Sometimes I feel like . . . they're *not as me* anymore. And so it's hard sometimes because I'm like: well, my followers want like probably this cutesy stuff.

Rachel thus expressed a tension between sharing an "authentic" version of herself and one that fits with the brand persona she had created *for* and *through* her audience. Though she recognized the promotional value of her socially mediated self-brand, this caricature she had created no longer squared with her "real-life" self.

Rachel was not the only one who felt pressure to express herself according to a pre-defined script. Explaining how blogs are a "personal extension of yourself," Julia discussed the task of sharing intimate details of her personal life to mediated publics. "As I go on in life, I might be interested in different things, or need different things, you know, maybe I'll have a baby, I don't know if I'll blog about that; I don't know if that's on brand for me or if I'd want to keep it private." Julia thus expressed anxiety that a deeply personal experience—motherhood—might produce a rift with the social media persona ("*on brand*") she had created over the last half-decade or so.

In other instances, participants spoke more generally about the demand to broadcast their personal lives, dissolving a boundary between one's personal and professional lives in a way that assumed a traditionally feminine subjectivity. Style blogger Hélène, who had recently relocated from Canada to New York, was quite forthcoming about the personal stakes of a social media career, particularly the compulsion to always be "on." For Hélène, maintaining a division between personal and professional life is filled with tension; she added, "It's just a very fine line to walk." Kimberly, too, regularly confronted the countervailing expectations of public and private life. Her framing of the issue, however, was markedly different. Reasoning that an omission of "real life" is a disservice to readers, Kimberly said she planned to

> shar[e] things that are, you know, a little bit more—making me a little bit more vulnerable maybe, but I think people have responded really well to that. And just being real with readers and not just, "Oh, here's another pretty picture of me in a cute outfit." But, you know, it's really what's going on.

Of course, such raw realness has a decidedly promotional value given wider discourses of authenticity mapped out earlier.

And, fittingly, some individuals seemed to conflate visibility with the potential for success. Alissa noted how when she began blogging, she "didn't even do personal outfit photos." Instead, she explained, "My purpose really was to be a resource for plus-size women to be able to find the best stylish clothes that fit them and how to dress their shape. That's really what it was all about." However, she believed that making her physical self *recognizable* was crucial to her blog's flourishing:

> I noticed that the only plus-size bloggers that were getting recognition were the ones who were showing how they dressed on a daily basis or a weekly basis. And so I had to start doing that so I could gain more traffic . . . [and] so people, other brands and company and people could recognize me. . . . That's something I struggle with because not all the

time do I want to put up a personal outfit. I want to stick to being informative, but . . . in the plus-size community, it's almost as if you can't be a plus-size blogger without showing *you*. (italics added for emphasis)

The account LoveBrownSugar's Christina offered in narrating her blog's trajectory was strikingly similar to that of Alissa. Christina recalled, "It wasn't until a year after I started the blog that I actually started to post pictures of myself on there." She added, "The blog really started to take off once I started to show more of my personality and show people who the person behind the keys was . . . and [I came to show] more [of] my personal life."

Not everyone I spoke with was as responsive to the market logic of compulsory visibility. Maeve confessed that one of the reasons she waited so long to launch a blog was because she was "a little intimidated by the idea of putting myself on the internet." She acknowledged that the statement may seem peculiar for someone in her position—an aspiring model used to being in front of the camera; however, there was a level of personal disclosure that made her feel more vulnerable in the blogosphere. Also recall Olivia, who abandoned her blogging project because of the discomfort she felt from the self-disclosure obligation. As she shared, "I felt too self-conscious to do it; I feel like you have to really be out there and want to pursue it. [That's when I realized I] didn't want to . . . continue [blogging . . . and] didn't want to promote myself and take a bunch of pictures."

Undoubtedly, the scope of public visibility is shaped by gendered expectations about self-promotion: across cultural and professional contexts, women disproportionately experience discomfort by the directive to "put themselves out there."[40] "Self-promotion," psychologists Corinne Moss-Racusin and Laurie A. Rudman contend, "violates female prescriptions to be helpful, supportive, and other-oriented."[41] In a study of female musicians, creative industries scholar Christina Scharff found that many were hesitant to engage in brazen self-promotion due to factors implicated in social norms. They include the contradiction between self-promotion and norms about women's performances of femininity; the fact that participating in commerce threatens their artist status; and finally, the negative connotations associated with "selling yourself" as a woman.[42] These considerations brush against attention-seeking commands embedded within social media culture.

Other bloggers and content creators sought to circumvent the pervasive cult of visibility through professional decisions. As a beauty blogger, Amber didn't feel that she had to share images of herself to the same extent as her peers in fashion blogging. Her manager, however, felt differently:

> [My manager] was telling me . . . I really need to up my photo game, and really try to only post original photography on my blog; so I've been trying to do that. But I kind of I struggle with having photos of myself on my blog. . . . It's not really my scene, but it would probably, you know, be more popular if I did because people respond really well to that.

Megan, too, distinguished her blog, which provided a female perspective on men's fashion and lifestyle, from the hordes of personal style bloggers who share an unwieldy stream of photos of *themselves*. "I think that both men and women who've established these personal style blogs—where they take pictures of their outfits every day and link to them and talk about why they wore them, what they like about them—I think that [it's] an amazing gig." Yet, she continued, "I certainly would never have the capacity for it, neither my wardrobe nor just my inclination to *put myself out there in that way*." Both Amber and Megan felt that their social media brands were infused with their personalities; yet, neither felt comfortable with the image-driven element of self-presentation.

Although these young women conveyed apprehension about broadcasting themselves to anonymous masses, others were more concerned about how those in their existing networks would react to their digitally mediated self-expressions. Emily R. initially kept her blog from her friends and family, fearing that they might react adversely. Back then, the blog was not part of what she called her "*life* life." She later overhauled her blog to "put it all out there"; however, she blamed her relative lack of financial success on this delay:

> I kind of regret . . . keeping it a secret the first time, just because I feel like a lot of the people who have been able to turn this into more of a career started at the exact time I started my old blog. [So], if I hadn't been so timid and scared to share my interest in it with people then maybe things could have turned out a little differently.

Alana, too, struggled with the self-disclosure imperative. She told me that despite being "outgoing" while growing up, she was "super private" on social media and set up privacy protections such that she was "hard to find on Facebook, MySpace." She continued:

> I think just putting yourself out there and knowing your high school friends that you grew up with are looking at these photos and just worrying about what they're saying, it was

really hard for me to do, so back when I first started my blog, I didn't tell anybody, and I think that kind of hurt me. I could have had more followers or more readers, but I really just kept it on the down low, and I just used hashtags to get people to come to my Instagram, and then finally one day I was like, "You know, I really don't care [to hide myself]."

Much like Emily, then, Alana believed her blog could have been more impactful had she not experienced so much self-doubt about sharing her content with digitally networked publics.

As the comments of these content creators suggest, an individual's failure to maintain a certain level of visibility is considered an impediment to career success. But the much-vaunted imperative to "put oneself out there" is fraught with complexity as social media producers must carefully tow the line between visibility and vulnerability, particularly as female producers who publish content in highly public digital spaces. For Sophie, the public nature of her blog opened her up to scrutiny from her college peers. She recalled, "When I first started it, some of the feedback that I got was, you know, as expected, was kind of [critical]. You know, girls are confused or don't know what it is." Kristy found this mediated visibility particularly insidious as it exacted a high toll on her feelings of self-worth. As she confessed:

I've never been more overly concerned about my body than when I was a blogger, which is weird because when I started blogging, I was very much like, "Yeah, we need people of all body types out there." I'm so not about hating on models—I think models are gorgeous, but I just want to see a little bit more representation, a little more variety, right? Yes, this is what bloggers will do. Bloggers will make it so there's a lot of variety, and we'll all be represented, and stuff. [But instead, my experience blogging] very much turned me into [someone who thought], "I need to lose weight." I was so overly concerned.

Indeed, as bloggers are expected to reveal their "personal" selves—as intimate self-brands as well as embodied physicalities—they are increasingly scrutinized through consumer culture's prescriptions about idealized femininity.

Online hate speech directed toward women is not new but, rather, is considered an unfortunate hangover of the male-dominated culture of geekdom that defined the early web.[43] Misogynistic expressions run the gamut—from vitriolic "e-bile" to revenge porn to physical threats waged from behind a veil of anonymity.[44] In an article on "The Harsh Realities of Being a Woman on Social Media," *Femsplain* founder Amber Discko offered a blow-by-blow of being "someone who gets a lot of attention online," including "ugly private messages, emails, the threatening phone calls, and all the stress and energy that goes into protecting yourself." Reporting survey data that 76 percent of women under thirty have experienced some form of abuse or harassment online, Discko shared her desire to "exist as a woman on the internet without having to 'deal' with harassment every day."[45] In a similar vein, YouTube comedian Gaby explained how "discouraging" the YouTube community can be for female aspirants. "I'm sure it discourages women from wanting to do YouTube. I've had people write in and be like, 'I would love to do this, but I don't want to get these fucked up comments.'"

While social media creators of all stripes are susceptible to online criticism, fashion and beauty bloggers may be easy targets of internet trolls *because of* their collective culture of "putting themselves out there." Reflecting on her decision to move away from creating beauty videos, Rachel W. explained how female viewers can be especially harsh critics:

> The audience [for beauty vlogs] is usually very young women . . . and they might not have gotten to the point yet where they can actively realize what is going on internally when they set out to destroy another woman's self-esteem. They haven't reached that point yet that [they] realize, "Hey, this is not okay, and I'm being immature, and I'm internalizing a lot of hate for my own gender here, so maybe I should chill."

Rachel attributed such abuse to more pervasive forms of sexism and discrimination. "I know that obviously male creators [justify], 'Everybody's gonna get shit online,' but I think that people online just judge women so much more harshly because that's just kind of how like we're all brought up."

One particularly popular destination for blogger snark is Get Off My Internets, which launched in 2009 and was later dubbed the "Craziest Destination for Blogger Hate."[46] According to the site's "About Us" narrative, "With the rise of blogging-as-a-job bloggers have become a new kind of 'reality star' for the modern world. GOMI provides a space for blog readers to share opinions about these web celebrities in a (mostly) moderation free zone." The site is populated by punchy critiques of blogger practices as well as salacious revelations. Over the years, the site has taken aim at a number of online influencers whose sites are deemed excessively promotional or fake, including those accused of excessive photo-manipulation (e.g., Photoshop). Ostensibly, GOMI's explicit construction of bloggers as "web celebrities" serves to deflect critique of the site itself.[47] As the popular argument goes, these individuals open themselves up to sur-veillance by thrusting themselves into the public eye. While the logic of this argument is flawed on a number of grounds, it may be espe-cially pernicious to digital media personalities precisely because of the requisite personal/professional blurring. Some bloggers offered defen-sive containments along these very lines. Alana described the personal strain of her encounters with "internet bullies": "They like saying mean things and comments, and I just have to tell myself that 'I don't know them, they don't know me, and it is what it is.'" Although she rationalized that you shouldn't take these harsh opinions personally, she conceded: "It was really hard for me to put myself out there on the internet, but I can't turn back now." Meanwhile, to Rachel W., this justification diverted attention from the fact that online hate plays out in patently gendered ways.

> [On YouTube], you still see endless comments about [a] woman's appearance, even if the video has nothing to do with the [creator's looks]. . . . It's just taken like, "Oh, well you put yourself out there so you deserve all of this abuse." And it's like, well, we should kind of be analyzing why we're getting these kinds of reactions.

The very real dangers of mediated visibility did not go unnoticed in blogger discourses. Even a *Teen Vogue* feature on "How to Make It as a Fashion Blogger" acknowledged the potential for bloggers to experi-ence public criticism or confront cyber-bullying from individuals in their online and offline social networks.[48] Yet these practices were ra-tionalized as inevitable side effects of the social media ecology. In the *Teen Vogue* article, for example, Man Repeller author Leandra Medine offered, "Success in any field of work will induce judgmental comments. I ignore them—most of them are rude." Essentially, narratives such as Medine's defend public evaluations and judgment as an inescapable part of the (professional) job that should somehow remain outside the personal sphere.

Academic inquiries into the pervasive cult of "realness" in popular culture have proliferated over the last decade as scholars attempt to conceptually locate reality TV, docudramas, and user-generated content in the context of profound shifts in the economies, technologies, and markets of media production and consumption.[49] To cultural studies scholar Graeme Turner, the mounting visibility of "ordinary people" is indicative of a cultural movement that he terms the "demotic turn"—an inflection that the shift is not necessarily a *democratic* one.[50] Against this backdrop, it is perhaps not surprising that social media producers positioned their digital activities as expressions of "realness," "relatability," and/or "authenticity." Yet these values had various—and at times contradictory—meanings; they were invoked, for example, to signal an aesthetic that differed from elite fashion culture, a sense of individual self-expression, or a level of material or financial accessibility. These terms were relationally defined, constructed against an imagined *other*—most often bloggers, magazine personalities, or mainstream fashion culture *at large*.

As other scholars have argued of the productive slipperiness of the "authenticity" ideal, I contend such conceptual imprecision enables bloggers to deploy these terms in ways that resonate with their ever-shifting allegiances—to themselves, to their audiences, to their advertisers, and to members of the public who celebrate them for wresting power from fashion's old guard.[51] However, it is this same imprecision that veils the problematic hierarchies configuring the aspirational labor market, including inequalities of social and economic capital. Indeed, appeals to "realness" were often structured through a middle-class sensibility—regardless of the aspirational laborers' own social class standing. Those in privileged positions seemed to veil their existing reserves of social and economic capital by sifting through various constructions of "ordinariness" or "relatability" that aligned with elements of their social media personae. While it's perhaps expected that well-to-do families bankroll their aspiring social media mavens, this trend helps to expose the fissures and ruptures in the narrative of digitally enabled meritocracy. The investments of time, energy, and money exacted of aspirants leave the playing field highly uneven. Such findings challenge existing articulations of fashion bloggers as "ordinary consumers"—defined as "individuals lacking professional experience and not holding an institutional or family position."[52]

Similarly, the infectious rhetoric of "realness" is not opposed to but, rather, in the service of, producers' tactical efforts to shore up the image of their self-brand. As I argued in the last chapter, such forms of self-promotion require considerable work and self-discipline—including enactments of aesthetic and emotional labor. And, for aspirational laborers, self-branding also necessitates highly gendered forms of self-disclosure: sharing details of one's personal life or reflecting on commodities that adorn the (female) body. Such efforts to "put yourself out there" help to bolster what Crystal Abidin describes as "communicative intimacies" between the influencer and her followers. The latter, Abidin explains, are thus privy "to what appears to be genuine, raw, and usually inaccessible aspects of influencers' personal lives."[53]

What must also be acknowledged is the extent to which this mode of personal "visibility" opens young women up to public surveillance and scrutiny. While some bloggers experience informal content

communication. Hyping the value of bloggers to advertisers, blogger-entrepreneur Yuli Ziv explained:

> The custom content that bloggers create on behalf of the brand is something that you can't compare with [traditional media] advertising because it's very personal and very authentic . . . if you compare [the] average advertising budget that brands spend on TV or print, what they can get for the same budget working with bloggers is incomparable.[4]

Ziv's account offers a framework to understand the skyrocketing of so-called "influencer marketing," wherein digital media personalities receive payment to puff various goods among their social media followings. Influencer marketing has become so pervasive that a whole industry has sprung up to broker deals between brand marketers and digital content creators: YouTubers, Instagrammers, and Snapchatters.

While accounts like Ziv's construct the blogger/brand system as mutually beneficial, such unrelenting optimism masks a series of deep-set power imbalances that characterize the social media advertising landscape. In fact, a writer for the Independent Fashion Bloggers coalition shared the grim statistic that fewer than 15 percent of bloggers earn a salary from their sites.[5] To be sure, some of my interviewees have been able to monetize their social media content through sponsorships, affiliate links, and more traditional forms of public relations, and a handful earn enough to make a solid living from these initiatives. Others, meanwhile, try to curry favor with prospective brands by performing what I call "entrepreneurial brand devotion," wherein social media creators visibly align themselves with certain commercial brands as they pursue income and recognition.[6] Often, these expressions of devotion are undercompensated, leaving participants to shill brand merchandise in exchange for free products or the mere promise of exposure.

The picture that emerges is one where existing social hierarchies are exacerbated both inside and outside these branded worlds. I thus argue that social media economies are unfolding in ways that are highly uneven, favoring particular subjectivities of race, class, and body aesthetics.

More than two decades ago, shortly before the social media floodgates burst open, serial entrepreneur/author Seth Godin prophesized that *traditional advertising is dead*.[7] While Godin was by no means the first industry insider to prognosticate the demise of the mass advertising system, he tapped into an ethos of uncertainty about the future of the ad-supported media system amidst profound currents of technological and economic change. And while not all media workers were as swift to adopt the "advertising is dead" rhetoric, marketing and PR professionals began to experience something of an identity crisis as they faced pressures to adapt to the rapidly evolving digital world.[8] Indeed, with consumers ostensibly seeking respite from the torrent of brand-laden messages disparaged as "spam," professionals began to strategize new ways to integrate consumers into the ad processes— from idea incubation to production to distribution.[9] User-generated ad contests such as those spearheaded by Doritos (2006–2016) and Dove (2007–2008) capture the spirit of this *purportedly* new era of marketing. By wielding "real people" as participants in the creative process, digital media companies supplant the work of paid researchers, producers, and distributors in much the same way that reality TV met the changing economic constraints of the new television era.

Media scholar Michael Serazio explores the rise of various forms of guerrilla marketing—essentially "*advertising that tries not to seem like advertising"*—against the backdrop of widespread transformations in the media and advertising industries. Among them: technologies that "empower" individuals to evade commercial messages, the fragmentation of audience categories, digitally enabled means of hyper-targeting, and the sheer ubiquity of ad messages on digital and mobile devices. To cultivate brand awareness and lure evermore-wary customers, marketers have turned to more surreptitious marketing tactics, delivered through "channels that exude a more underground ethos (a valuable pose to strike when catering to millennials, who are routinely conceptualized as jaded, resistant consumer targets)."[10] Forms of brand evangelism, which enlist the audience to deliver ad messages through their networks, harken back to the oldest—and presumably most coveted—form of modern advertising: *word-of-mouth promotion.*[11]

Of particular significance to the current study are historical exemplars of word-of-mouth advertising that coincided with cultural assumptions about the communicative nature of women.[12] As early as the nineteenth century, advertisers and publishers sought to leverage the respectability of "regular women" for promotional purposes. For instance, women's magazine owners and editors routinely crafted relatable, female personae to establish a sense of kinship between readers and (often fictional) magazine personnel.[13] Brand retailers, too, believed that *everyday women* would lend a sense of trustworthiness to the traditionally masculine practice of hawking products. In the early twentieth century, the founder of the California Perfume Company (CPC)—which was rebranded in 1939 as the now-iconic Avon cosmetics—made the then-bold move to hire a female sales force. These "worthy and enterprising" women were seen as reputable and adept communicators—factors that distinguished them from traveling salesmen, whose reputations were often suspect.[14] Cultural historian

Kathy Peiss's exploration of the nascent American beauty industry addresses the role of women as investors, distributors, and promoters. By the 1920s, though, men rose up the ranks to lead these cosmetics firms as they sought to "create a mass market and sell beauty products to all women."[15] Such histories reveal how female admittance into these fields was not politically motivated but, instead, driven by the financial exploitation of commercial femininity.[16]

With the unabated growth of advertising post–World War II, many creators sought to use seemingly "real people" in their ads in an effort to imbue their pitches with credibility and authenticity. Indeed, Dove began using "real women testimonials" in their ads in the 1960s, an era which saw the emergence of authenticity appeals within and across the commercial media industries.[17] As Thomas Frank explains of the ad industry more broadly, pervasive fears of conformity and the "faceless cogs in the great machine" led advertisers of the postwar years to integrate counterculture themes of individuality and autonomy into their campaigns.[18] Word-of-mouth advertising, then, can be understood as an outgrowth of a consumer sphere that prizes expressions of "authenticity" and "credibility."

Such assumptions made their way to digital spaces through early women-only communities like iVillage and SheKnows—sites which were markedly different from the politically charged cybercommunities that flourished on the early internet. Marketers on the quest to colonize these online spaces saw the value of these digitally networked participants as brand ambassadors. As media scholar John Edward Campbell contends, female internet users were understood above all as "commodity audiences."[19] Using the case of the iVillage network, Campbell explains how brand executives sought to exploit the "labor of devotion," a concept rooted in the assumption that "men loyally consume their favorite brands whereas women actively promote their favorite brands to other women."[20] And indeed, the countless dollars invested in research on the "social" nature of female shoppers reifies problematic discourses about gender and consumerism.

This brief history provides a useful backstory to the word-of-mouth zeitgeist that pervades the social media ecosystem. The market for fashion tastemakers and other influencers is voracious, with brands spending an estimated $1 billion on sponsored posts on Instagram alone.[21] The incentive for brands to partner with bloggers was not lost on my blogger-participants, who reflected thoughtfully on how the changing economic landscape of the ad industry has compelled brands to seek out "new channels" to promote their messages. As Sophie offered:

> Bloggers have an undeniable force of power in the industry: they're driving sales, they're contributing to campaigns . . . people love to follow bloggers because you feel like . . . you're following their story and you feel like you know them, and there's this personal connection. . . . So I think that's really the reason why girls have been so drawn to the concept. You know, girls are personable, and they like to know each other, and when you feel like you know a blogger and you like her, you like her personality, her writing, her style, you want to wear what she's wearing and it really does translate into numbers [and] sales.

Here, Sophie recognizes that brands are eager to leverage the networked capital of social media producers, especially given the ongoing valorization of such "organic" modes of product recommendation.

According to the 2013 Technorati Digital Influence report, blogs are "the third-most influential digital resource when making overall purchases," behind only official brand and retail channels.[22] A 2016 study jointly conducted by Twitter and the analytics firm Annalect found that roughly 40 percent of respondents purchased an item online that was used by a social media influencer on Instagram, Twitter, Vine, or YouTube.[23] The financial incentive to bring bloggers and advertisers together as "partners" has spawned a flurry of firms dedicated to brokering these relationships—from affiliate networks to services that make blog content "shoppable" to talent agencies that specialize in digital media personalities.

The same Technorati survey reported that among bloggers earning revenue (again, which is overall a small percentage), 41 percent make money from affiliate marketing programs, services that enable bloggers to earn a commission from product recommendations, based upon a percentage of sales dollars they funnel to their brand partners. Similar to the traditional function of advertising agencies as space brokers, affiliate networks mediate relationships between corporate brands and content producers (bloggers); their revenue is based upon a fee or percentage of bloggers' earnings. Several of my informants were members of affiliate programs geared toward the fashion and beauty subset: Style Coalition, Glam, and rewardStyle, among others. Each affiliate has a different roster of brands with which they partner, and some are optimized for a single platform. Ahalogy, for instance, is a content network that operates exclusively on Pinterest, branding itself as a leader in "revolutionary technology and network[s] that propel rapid, efficient growth in impressions, follower count, and site conversions."[24] The service Like to Know It, meanwhile, is an Instagram-only service operated by rewardStyle; registered bloggers use the app to tag various products or brands. Then, when Instagram

users "like" a post featuring a Like to Know It partner, they receive an
email that includes a "breakdown of links for buying all items in the
photo."

Recent years have also witnessed the emergence of firms specializing in the recruitment and representation of social media "talent."
Agencies such as GrapeStory, Cycle, and Gleam Futures, among others, position themselves as authorities in managing digital media personalities from YouTube, Vine, Instagram, and Snapchat. The landing
pages of many company websites feature a kaleidoscope of attractive,
quirky, or seemingly affable social media "stars"—a visual parade of
standouts in the attention economy. Clients' headshots and avatars
appear in neatly arranged rows, with either metric benchmarks or
pithy descriptors of social media sway publicly available upon clicking
on their likenesses. The profile for Gleam Futures client Tanya Burr,
for instance, promotes the British beauty blogger/vlogger as an "It
Girl" who has "taken YouTube by storm with her make-up and style
tutorials." Along with her YouTube stats (subscribers and views),
Burr's follower tallies for Twitter, Instagram, and Facebook are prominently displayed.[25]

Rather predictably, agency press kits celebrate the potential for
digital cultural intermediaries to siphon consumer-audiences away
from the "old guard" of fashion through the (ever-elusive) ideals of
"authenticity" and "engagement."[26] Mainstream media coverage,
similarly, hails these services for—as the title of a rewardStyle profile
summarized—"disrupting the fashion and blogging worlds."[27] The
profile, published in *Texas Monthly* in 2014, flaunted rewardStyle's
rather impressive statistics: the network has more than 4,000 retail
partners, which have grossed more than $270 million in sales, with
top-performing content producers raking in more than $20,000 a
month.

Meanwhile, a profile of personal style blogger Danielle Bernstein (We Wore What) in *Harper's Bazaar* highlighted how lucrative Instagram partnerships can be for the sartorially inclined. Bernstein, who agreed to participate in the *Bazaar* article on the condition that she was the *only* blogger featured, emphasized the premium placed on social media metrics. She explained how her Instagram count was hovering slightly below a million followers; reaching the seven-figure mark, she told reporter Kayleen Schaefer, would be a "big milestone," allowing her to command "a good amount more" for sponsored posts.[28] Bernstein works with a talent agency, Next Models, which charges anywhere from $5,000 to $15,000 for a sponsored post; however, those with six million followers can reportedly earn between $20,000 and $100,000 for a brand deal on Instagram.

Importantly, though, the industrial rhetoric of meritocracy serves as a gloss for characteristic hierarchies that structure contemporary social media economies. For one, the monetization system is rigged in favor of high-profile bloggers; that is, the services only compensate bloggers when they reach a minimum commission threshold. At the end of the previously mentioned *Wall Street Journal* article, blogger Taylor Davies explained her difficulty achieving the $100 baseline required for reward-Style to issue a check. "You don't automatically start making money," she told the reporter. "If people aren't interested in what you are saying, there isn't going to be much of an impact."[29] Several of my interviewees had similar experiences. Kat explained how, though she has joined several affiliate programs and works with advertisers through them, she makes "pretty much nothing in revenue" because of her low blog numbers. Daneen, too, has seen her revenue dwindle in the past few years because of the oversaturated market—along with bloggers willing to work for free—a theme to which I return later in this chapter.

The upbeat discourse about the social media advertising industry also veils the high barriers to entry that structure participation in this system. Indeed, though these firms bill themselves as "free" to join, they place the onus upon creative aspirants to demonstrate their position as digital "influencers" with the potential to hold sway over social media consumer-audiences. And they demand visible—and verifiable—benchmarks of such "influence" in the currency *du jour*: Instagram followers, YouTube subscribers, blog readers, or Facebook likes. Before admittance to an "invitation-only" affiliate program like rewardStyle or Glam, prospective members must undergo a vetting process to ensure they will draw sufficient traffic to retail partners' products. RewardStyle allegedly rejects blogger-applicants for failing to meet the minimum level of followers and stipulates that bloggers have "at least four months of consistent content . . . about monetizable products." The service also recommends that prospective members include hyperlinks to "linkable content" to direct fans to retailers' sites.[30] When I asked Thomas Rankin, co-founder and CEO of Instagram commerce start-up Dash Hudson, about what counts as an "influencer," he offered the following benchmarks:

> Typically we look for people who have, at minimum . . . 50,000 followers and up. . . . And then, of course, we've worked with people who are going up into the million range and looking at some people who are up even in the top 20 of Instagram. So you kind of get into "super influencers" at that level.

Of course, Rankin acknowledged that raw statistics may occlude more telling measures of influence, such as engagement or conversion.

Another metric that offers an index of blogger clout is the ratio of *followers to following:* 10:1 is often considered ideal for super-influencers in the Twitterverse. At one of the blogger conferences I attended, neo-phyte content producers were instructed to rely on various tactics to visibly grow their reciprocal followers; then, on a weekly basis, they were directed to enact a ritual "unfollowing" to maintain their ratios. One fashion blogger similarly admitted that she systematically "unfollows" people to ensure a higher ratio. Suddenly sheepish, she added, "I can't believe I'm saying this, [it] must sound so stupid. My boyfriend works in music production, and it's the same thing with that too, where people unfollow people [to keep a certain ratio]."

This blogger also discussed the imperative for potential affiliate program members to have "real" (verifiable) followers: "If all [of] your followers are from other countries, [brands are] going to know that those aren't your 'real' followers, those are paid." She added, "You have to actually build [social media audiences], otherwise they're not really valuable." The notion of "real followers" is a testament to the seedy black market for metrics that has infiltrated the ad-supported digital media sphere. In recent years, investigative journalists from the *Guardian, New York Times,* and *New Republic* have provided behind-the-scenes glimpses into the furtive practices of click farms, compa-nies that sell Twitter followers and Facebook likes from fake accounts for individuals seeking a bump in their social media metrics. Though "onlining" (as one click farmer described the practice) is a booming global industry, many click farms are based in the developing world, and some have abysmal labor conditions. As the *Guardian* reported: "It is miserable work, sitting at screens in dingy rooms facing a blank wall, with windows covered by bars, and sometimes working through the night. For that, they could have to generate 1,000 likes or follow 1,000 people on Twitter to earn a single US dollar." Accounts like these reveal just how wide the gulf is between sweatshop workers and the high-profile clientele; among those accused of click fraud are businesses (e.g., Coca-Cola, Mercedes-Benz, Louis Vuitton), celebrities (e.g., Paris Hilton, Diddy), and political candidates (e.g., Mitt Romney).[31] In the fashion blogosphere, some rather prominent voices have been accused of buying social media followers to superficially inflate their popularity. In each of the cases, the bloggers have been "called out" for sudden spikes in their social media metrics.[32]

The earlier-mentioned remark about the social media audience as "valuable" underscores the type of industrial incentives that animate social media producers to devote their time and resources to building and maintaining online relationships. While I have already detailed some of the particular tactics aspirational laborers deploy to build social capital, bloggers also talked to me about the importance of monitoring indexes of popularity and engagement. Most of my interviewees used Google Analytics to track visitors to their blogs and, in Danielle's words, see "what posts do well and things like that." Yolanda said she often tracks her Twitter and Facebook readers to "see what they're reacting to [and to] keep a close finger to the pulse of what is generating the reaction." As she clarified, "My blog readers [are] the meat and potatoes of my business." Julianne, meanwhile, waxed poetic over Instagram; she called it the "perfect platform" because you can "gauge what your readers like the most by how many likes you have, or how many comments."

This metric mania, with its quantifiable benchmarks of success (and failure), can have profound psychological consequences for social media producers. Jessie explained to me how draining it can be to work doggedly to grow one's social media follower tallies: "You can drive yourself nuts paying attention to numbers, and I have." She later reflected on the implications of the digital zeitgeist more broadly: "It's good because everyone is kind of at the same level, and so we all have to work really, really hard to build up our own numbers." At the same time, she admitted, "you can't just focus on your craft anymore because focusing on your craft is not enough." Jenn, meanwhile, described how she recently rethought the direction of her blog in order to get away from what she saw as a problematic "obsession" with metrics. She recalled: "[I was] like, oh my gosh, I have to get this many Twitter followers and this many people on Facebook to like [my site]." While Jenn shared her negative experience with metric valuation, other bloggers experienced dissonance when readers' demands brushed up against their own ideas about quality content. As one interviewee confessed:

> One article that has gotten a ton of hits [and] mentions [is about] Khloe Kardashian, and she wore this sheer top on *X Factor.* The post was super short, it was like, "Oh my gosh she wore this top, is this trendy or trashy? Give me your thoughts." That post shouldn't really get a ton of hits because it wasn't, like, a ton of words [and] the content wasn't super valuable, but it did because it was a hot topic in search engines that day.

My interview with Brittany, a college student majoring in advertising, was especially telling about how the drive to be eminently quantifiable can significantly impact the creative process. A Pinterest user with a staggering three million plus followers, she told me that she didn't even realize how many she had until U.S.-based marketing firm Hello Society invited her to be a paid Pinterest tastemaker, a position she had held for nearly a year at the time of our interview. Brittany admitted that she pays much more attention to metrics now that they are tied to economic rewards. "I follow the numbers more closely to see if my numbers are going up or going down and trying to determine what times [of day] work best." She also disclosed how she has to think more carefully about what she pins—explaining that she didn't want to overdo certain topics or "use too much repetition because people will un-follow you." Brittany's account is another instance of what I described in an earlier chapter as imaginations of the audience; that is, her creative decisions are based upon social constructions of followers, rather than actual user characteristics.

Rachel L., too, reflected on the extent to which these considerations recursively shape her social media practices. In addressing whether she thought about how individuals might respond to her content, she admitted, "Definitely more so now that I live in New York and it's my job, I think about sometimes what the client wants as far as like clothing posts go. And then I think about like how my readers see me, or what they kind of want." Here, Rachel indicates the (imagined) audience's sensitivity to her digital persona.

Of course, the emphasis on quantifiable data is by no means exclusive to the fashion and beauty sectors but, rather, is central to professional evaluations in the attention economy. As Hélène explained:

> I feel like when people in my industry [of social media] hire, it's almost as if they look to see what your numbers are: Are you already popular? Is this going to make the position that you're gunning for? Is that going to make it even better because they're hiring someone that has this big following?

Her comment reveals how the datafication imperative bleeds into various realms of cultural and economic life as one's value gets translated into quantifiable data. Moreover, it reaffirms traditional industrial discourses about the importance of audience-building as a resonant ideal about aspirational laborers.

Advertisers' gravitation toward digital media producers with the most "traffic" is not the only indicator that the ideals of the marketplace have become an insinuating presence within the blogosphere; indeed, the logic of *self-branding* is ubiquitous.[33] Creative aspirants jockeying for the attention of prospective employers, advertisers, and/ or audiences are commanded to construct themselves as a distinctive commodity: the book jacket of Yuli Ziv's instruction manual thus prods aspirants to "brand yourself as a top blogger and sought-after influencer!" Anthropologist Brent Luvaas, whose book *Street Style: An Ethnography of Fashion Blogging* offers a telling glimpse into the global ecology of street-style photography, aptly described his project as a lesson in "Brand Culture 101":

> You learn what kinds of content attract readers. You learn what kinds of content leave them cold. You learn to use the word "content" as if it were a pithy summation of your online thoughts and images, as if everything were reducible to something that can be posted online.[34]

A further testament to this "Brand Culture 101" mentality is the wellspring of advice urging individuals to cultivate a brand niche or unique selling proposition (acronym USP). On the "careers" page of *Fashionista,* for example, was a five-point guide to developing "a strong personal brand" in fashion.[35] The guide was culled from the advice of bloggerpreneurs and digital talent agents and emphasized the axioms of consistency, authenticity, specificity, and the cultivation of a unique point of view. The Independent Fashion Bloggers website, meanwhile, encouraged those seeking clarity about their niche to develop a brand pyramid: "If we assume that our blog acts as an extension, or representation of our selves, then we can also look to this aspect of branding to establish a foundation from which to clarify our blog purpose and personality."[36] Here, then, we can see how the evocative rhetoric of branding circulates throughout the aspirational labor market.

Most of my interviewees had internalized the self-branding directive, describing their social media products through marketing discourses or using the language of personal branding rather unequivocally. Marissa, who had begun her forays into blogging with ambitions of marketing herself as a blogger/model, believed that standout bloggers were distinguished by their brand aptitude: "It's how they brand themselves, online especially, because, you know, you [have to]

7. Rachel Lynch shows off an outfit she styled for her blog I Hate Blonde. Photo Credit: Blogger.

have the look . . . and be able to style the clothes [in such a] way . . . that other people like as well." Here again, considerations of the audience ("that other people like") are paramount. As Rachel observed, "[Bloggers] are our own brand, and we kind of essentially have to sell our lifestyle" (see Figure 7).

Alice, meanwhile, drew upon discourses of personal branding to explain how she strove to manage her persona in various contexts. As she explained, "You are your brand, so you have to market yourself and be professional at any time because you don't know who's sitting next to you, and you have to be ready all the time." Alice's statement is rooted in a common narrative about working in creative fields—every conversation could be a potential career prospect, or at least an opportunity to cut one's teeth in the fashion world—so it becomes important to keep the job-seeking antennae on high alert. And, fittingly, Alice was one of a number of recent college graduates who learned about the importance of self-branding within the walls of the classroom. Jennifer, too, explained how her courses in advertising, promotion, and marketing included assignments to curate her digital brand. She recently launched a personal website for one of her courses and concluded, "You have to really promote yourself and whatever brand that you're starting, which is really [insightful] because it teaches you how to market yourself and to really know what [your personal brand] is about."

The market-driven logic infiltrating higher education provides an important backstory to these anecdotes, especially as curricula undergo what sociologist Stanley Aronowitz called a progressive "vocationalization."[37] Such discourses do ideological work accordingly. As social theorist Nikolas Rose presciently argued of new mandates in the educational sector, "The new citizen is required to engage in a ceaseless work of training and retraining, skilling and reskilling, enhancement of credentials and preparation for a life of ceaseless job seeking: life is to become a continuous economic capitalization of the self."[38] For bloggers, such "ceaseless" work is rendered all the more pertinent given social media's obligation to unflinchingly maintain the brand in both online and offline contexts.

Content creators' reflections on self-branding are a testament to the market logic that propels much activity in the online worlds of fashion and beauty. It is against this commercial backdrop that style pundits have bemoaned the seeming corruption of fashion blogging—from an arsenal of sartorially inspired musings created at whim to adeptly managed content compliant with advertising demands. *New York Times* writer Ruth La Ferla is among the most unabashed critics of the market-driven fashion blogosphere. In a rather contemptuous article timed to coincide with New York Fashion Week 2012, La Ferla detailed a shift from the internet's halcyon days, when blogging was "fashion's last stronghold of true indie spirit," to the contemporary moment, "infiltrated by tides of marketers, branding consultants and public relations gurus, all intent on persuading those women to step out in their wares."[39] A centerpiece of her article was the surreptitious practice of content marketing, wherein designers "seed" clothes and accessories to bloggers who flaunt these goods before the fleet of photographers covering the event. Tom Julian, a fashion branding professional interviewed for the article, designated bloggers as "billboards for the brands," adding, "People still think street style is a voice of purity. But I don't think purity exists any more." As evidence of "purity"'s ostensible deracination by financial self-interest, the article mentioned that style influencers can rake in as much as $10,000 for a single appearance in a designer's merchandise.

Predictably, La Ferla's exposition of the blogger-marketing system was a lightning rod for controversy. A spate of writings published in the wake of the article questioned such knotty issues as blogger transparency, fair compensation, and the evolution of street-style fashion. Importantly, though, the recognition of bloggers as *brand billboards* tapped into a zeitgeist where marketing partnerships are structured by the currency of social media visibility. Amateur cultural producers may publicly express loyalty for brands with which they hope to partner as part of a mutually sustaining system of *entrepreneurial brand devotion.*[40] The blogger/vlogger/Instagrammer labor market is awash with young people eager to freely endorse branded goods in hopes of currying favor with desirable retailers and designers. Socialization resources—the Independent Fashion Bloggers network and various blogger how-to manuals—targeting this class of aspirants encourage them to make the first move. For instance, an online fashion magazine offered the following advice to aspiring style bloggers hoping to grow their impact: "Brands will not always know you exist until you show them. Tag, tag and tag them! Mention them within your posts and thank them." Another article recommended that content producers "pay attention to your captions—they make a difference. . . . Mention brands, use appropriate hashtags and add humor or emotion whenever you can!"[41] These discourses often play to the tune of the internet's siren song: social media as a platform for *getting discovered.* And brands are tapping their feet to the music in cadence.

In recent years, a torrent of marketing campaigns has used social media to scout talent or crowdsource content—including blogs that focus on the fashion blogger community. For instance, among *Postano*'s "Best Instagram Campaigns of the Year" was a social media promotion coordinated by fashion retailer Madewell, which put style bloggers, magazine editors, and employees to the task of tagging their favorite denim pieces from the brand. Dubbed #flashtagram (a clever portmanteau of *flash* mob and In*stagram*), the daylong campaign generated close to 2,000 tagged posts and 8.5 million total impressions; *Postano* billed it a "simple, cost effective way to put denim on the front of mind of the Instagram fashion community."[42] Promotions such as this rely upon the immaterial labor of participants, who willingly promote the particular brand within their social networks. But in contrast to the seeding practices La Ferla described, this marketing initiative was "unpaid," amounting to free advertising for the company.

Other social media campaigns are explicitly hyped as platforms for *getting discovered*—from Forever 21's "Declare Your Style" campaign to Refinery 29's "Next Big Style Blogger" contest to TJ Maxx's "Maxxinista of the Month."[43] Typically, these campaigns offer aspiring bloggers the opportunity to get noticed, align themselves with a high-powered brand, and even score a gift-card to their favorite store. Marketing executives tout these initiatives as "inexpensive" marketing and "a fantastic way brands can get their audience involved and interested in the company."[44] To be sure, the promises of exposure are realized for only a select few, such as Miami style blogger Julianne. I first learned about Julianne's blog during a conference breakfast, where I was exchanging early-morning pleasantries with a social media brand manager for TJX, parent company of TJ Maxx and Marshall's. He explained how he had "discovered" Julianne while scanning the company's Instagram feed for potential blogger collaborators who had tagged their TJ Maxx brand. I later interviewed Julianne, who offered the following account:

> TJ Maxx was doing a big social media campaign where they select one blogger each month and then they fly them up to New York and give them a shopping spree and ask that they . . . style a photo-shoot, and I think it was, like, fifteen looks in total, and then they hire a photographer, make up team, the whole nine yards, and they do it all over the city.

Julianne spoke glowingly of the experience; her account of the New York styling trip reads like a fairytale for the aspirational labor market. Yet she also acknowledged the role of strategy in garnering the attention of a marketing audience. "I really tried to be mindful about, especially in the beginning, and especially [when] trying to capture the attention of a brand . . . to post at times that you think that they would be receptive to it." While Julianne had a winning combination of style, looks, and PR savvy that enabled her to score a trip, free clothes, and a boost in metrics, legions of others engage in these activities without compensation nor a realistic prospect of discovery, yet still posting a digital catalogue of tagged styles that companies can mobilize.

Many companies seem to reward brand devotees through the promise of "exposure" or by supplying them with gratis products in hopes they will share them with their following. Of course, couture designers and their publicists have long "gifted" products to A-list celebrities in exchange for potential brand mentions, while "swag bags" are a widely discussed perk of awards ceremonies and film festivals. It is perhaps not surprising, then, that the economic valuation of social media has coincided with marketers' concerted efforts to rely upon digital media influencers, including bloggers, vloggers, and Instagrammers. Often, there is an expectation—if not an outright contract— that in exchange for the bounty, individuals will favorably review these products on their social media sites. In certain countries—the United States, United Kingdom, and Ireland, among others—bloggers are required to publicly disclose any gifts or services they receive from advertisers; however, ensuring that both parties adhere to these regulations is no easy feat.[45]

Seeding practices occur at other paparazzi-laden affairs, too. In 2015, the *New York Times* reported how advertisers and publicists were wooing members of the "new celebrity crowd" at Sundance, the

American film festival once held up as a bastion of indie spirit. At the luxury lounges and gifting suites, reporter Sheila Marikar explained, high-profile bloggers and Instagrammers were furnished with clothes, shoes, tech accessories, and more. These social media "influencers" were expected to share photos and reviews of the Sundance swag with their followers "in an 'authentic' way." The article cast a spotlight on highly gendered discourses of emotional labor, particularly in the context of the promotional "love fest."[46] As internet personality Justine Ezarik gushed, "I love products, and I love sharing if I love something. Like, you can probably guarantee that it's going to be posted, especially if I love it." A testimonial by a social media influencer like Ezarik enables retailers to rise above the flood of ubiquitous marketing messages through a seemingly "organic" brand promotion. Sophie, who was also profiled in the Sundance story, explained to me how brands had flown her from her hometown of Los Angeles to New York for events. Professional blogger Erika Marie had a similar account:

> I notice more companies want to work with bloggers in the sense that [when] I started . . . they would send me clothes, but now sometimes people just want you to talk about their brand or their product and sometimes you can even go on a trip just to experience firsthand because they want you to *give a real opinion of the product.* (italics added for emphasis)

At first blush, the accounts of Sophie and Erika seem to paint a rather glamorous portrait of the fashion blogger lifestyle—one flush with brand-sponsored globetrotting and A-list mingling. Yet both Sophie and Erika had remarkable social media followings—meaning that marketers were willing to invest in their brands to reach engaged audiences. Bloggers with hefty followings are provisionally "gifted" clothes from various brands in implicit exchange for an editorial (e.g., reviews, photos, styling), an incentive system that brings to mind the "information subsidy" that the public relations industry has long provided to news journalism.[47] In contrast, marketer-driven efforts to woo the aspirational crowd were discernibly scaled-down. Instead of comped trips, those lacking the requisite digital sway are expected to pay their own way to events, an investment that they hope will "pay off" through social and economic capital. And instead of free swag, lower- and middle-tier bloggers are compelled to invest their own capital in the latest fashions and accessories.

With swag as a marker of status, those seeking to bolster their status have presumably tried to game the system. *Fashionista* reported on an uptick in bloggers falsely representing freely given goods— including an anecdote about a popular blogger who, after being denied a free gift from a popular handbag chain, purchased the bag moments before thanking the brand for the "gift" across social media sites. Brands, for their part, have little reason to dispel these myths: Robbie Sokolowsky, creative director at ICED Media, told *Fashionista*:

> Bloggers who have inadvertently mentioned my clients in a positive manner (whether they are hungry for attention or rather "desperate" as you put it) will be rewarded and noticed whether I have sent them product or not. If they ever claimed it was gifted when it wasn't, yet they displayed the product in a positive light, I would most likely overlook that comment and thank them for their support.[48]

Swag, as an index of prestige, is embedded within a social media economy that is rigged to favor those with existing access to capital; it is but one marker of the deeply lopsided nature of blogger-brand *a solid* and, you know, give us the publicity we want [for free]." (italics added for emphasis)

This notion of "doing us a solid" involves the provision of promotional work for a name-brand client—without material compensation. There are obvious parallels between bloggers expected to shill products without remuneration and the system of unpaid internships, where college students are often tasked with running errands and performing menial duties as the oft-breathless promise of "full-time employment" looms large. In both cases, modes of free labor are articulated as stepping-stones to the "glamour industries" and opportunities to build one's personal brand by paying court to the powers that be. Other members of the creative precariat, including freelancers and contract workers, are routinely prodded to provide unpaid or low-wage work—all in the name of "exposure."

In recent years, several high-profile media companies have come under fire for exploiting the free or cheap labor of freelance journalists. In 2015, Australian reporter Tracey Spicer used her Facebook page to publicly disparage media companies that fail to adequately compensate writers. Her critique was in response to a message from an affiliate of the *Guardian,* which invited her to write a thousand-word "sponsored column" on financial empowerment—for mere pennies per word. As she wrote on her Facebook page: "Does anybody else see the irony here? Who else is being asked to work for next to nothing in this brave new world of branded media? Exploitation—especially of women and young people—seems rife." Cultural industries researcher Nicole Cohen contends that the freelance work economy is a key site to examine employers' capitalist exploitation of contingent workers in the culture industries. In addition to cheap employment, Cohen argues that companies get workers who, "motivated by the

relentless search for work and increasing competition, strive to produce their best works, providing capital ample choice from a pool of
skilled workers bargaining down the costs of their labour power."[52]
Perhaps predictably, a number of online programs have cropped
up that draw on the format and style of fashion blogs but bill themselves as "internships." College Fashionista, for example, calls itself an
educational program for "like-minded individuals all hoping to pursue careers in the fashion industry." After a vetting process, members
("style gurus") produce regular content for the site, including for
brand partners. Style guru Lauren, who described the experience as an
"unpaid internship" that offered "experience" and "exposure," detailed
a collaboration between College Fashionista and a retail partner:

> American Eagle Outfitters gifted a pair of jeans [to us]
> and you just show how you style it—and [those types of pro-
> motions are] how College Fashionista does a lot of their ad-
> vertising. . . . They'll do other campaigns on their Facebook
> about a giveaway for a pair of jeans, [and] they'll get people to
> like their page through entering this campaign. If you want to
> win twenty pairs of jeans you just have to "like" us and, you
> know, you're entered.

The ability of initiatives like these—populated by fashion-minded
millennials—to draw advertisers is not incidental. Jason Wagenheim,
who at the time of our interview was publisher and chief revenue officer for *Teen Vogue,* explained the role of one such program, Instalist:
Teen Vogue's Instagram A-list, in servicing advertising clients:

> We had our editors choose ten really prolific, up-and-
> coming folks on Instagram that we would deputize, for lack of

web: "How are they a 'personal style' blogger? In essence . . . they're a person with a following that's paid to [constantly] advertise different things."

Social media producers aspiring to *earn a living from their passion projects* must therefore tow a delicate line between earning an income and profiting from hollow, profit-driven expressions. A post from the creator of interior design blog decor8 highlighted how bloggers may be "called out" if they are deemed inauthentic product endorsers. After a commenter accused Holly of "loosing [sic] your magic touch by selling, selling and more selling," her husband and partner (and professional journalist) offered to reply on her behalf:

> I expect to be paid for my hard work, everyone does. Yet somehow bloggers have no right to that. They are expected to publish content for free. They are expected to do it out of the goodness of their hearts. They are expected to be magical creatures apparently living off of rainbows and hugs. Dare I say this holds true mostly for female bloggers. The moment a female blogger tries to find forms of compensation for her hard work she is chastised by a good percentage of her gender. She's selling out.[53]

Importantly, he draws attention to the tendency to render feminized genres of work invisible. As social media production becomes a stable source of income—at least for high-status bloggers—they are forced to construct a mediated persona that gets paid in more than "rainbows and hugs."

As the preceding discussion suggests, one of the hot-button issues polarizing various factions within the fashion and social media industries is the nature of marketing compensation. On one hand, the uptick in advertiser/blogger "partnerships" is a testament to the growing valuation of bloggers within the consumer marketplace; with higher status comes the awareness that these content creators (provided they have robust readerships) deserve material compensation for their *value-generating labor*. On the other hand, these economically incentivized relationships threaten to upend the heady ideals of "authenticity" and "trust" on which the first-generation blogosphere was founded—as elusive as these ideals may be. When discussing sponsored advertising, affiliate networks, and content marketing, many of my informants invoked the well-worn narrative of brand passion to reconcile these two perspectives. Much like the fictitious Brady family, who would only offer a *sincere* product endorsement, interviewees professed brand affection to reaffirm the conviction that they weren't doing it *just for the money.*

Among neophyte bloggers and those who had yet to reap financial rewards, the prospect of earning an income from retail brands was alluring. When I asked Hillary about whether she would be willing to accept advertising on her blog, she responded with an unqualified "Yes," adding, "I think the idea of getting paid to do something you love is just the coolest thing ever." Similarly, Emily R.'s plans for growing her blog were framed through the narrative of commercial-brand recognition.

> I find myself being very proud of seeing people react positively to what I've created, and want to be a part of it, and want to partner with me. And I think just growing that, too, and trying to get bigger partnerships and sponsorships and giveaways, and that kind of stuff is something that I definitely want to do in the next year. . . . And I think that's also a good

There's a brand that we worked with that is—because of the article—refusing to pay the production company. . . . I didn't mention the brand by name or anything in the article, but they're saying that because I wrote that I take brand deals for money and not because I like the company necessarily, they feel it undermines the brand deal we did, which obviously we took for the money.

Acknowledging the unmistakable irony of the situation, she added, "So me speaking up on [the difficulties of earning a living wage] actually caused a loss of income. That's how precarious this whole situation is, apparently."

Other social media producers discussed the emotional burden of feigning brand passion. Longtime "mommy blogger" Heather, for instance, grew weary of brand partners that expected her to "use my children" in sponsored posts, showing them with the paid products. She recalled, "[The process] became such an emotional and intellectual drain that I would have panic attacks. I was like, 'How am I going to pull this off, because I am not going to just shit something out. That is not how I work. That is not the quality of my work. And my readers will see straight through it if this isn't real.'" Heather eventually abandoned her post as a mommy blogger, and the announcement that she was going into semi-retirement sent shockwaves through the social media community.

Several others abandoned—or, alternatively, redirected—their social media projects for similar reasons. Lifestyle blogger Jenn admitted that she became disheartened by what she described as an "input/output" relationship with beauty advertisers. She explained, "Companies would send you products, and you would have to push out the review, and it became very heartless after a while. . . . It felt like I was kind of selling my soul in a way." Jenn subsequently shifted the focus of her blog from beauty to lifestyle in order to get away from being seen as a product pusher. Kristy, too, grew frustrated with the extent to which corporate sponsors sought to exert control over her image. She explained how she was chosen to represent a particular brand when focus group respondents lauded her unique personal style:

> [The brand] chose me because I was authentic but then tried to—I don't think they were trying to make me less authentic, but I think they really wanted my authenticity to kind of coincide with their desires perfectly. . . . [But] it doesn't work like that. It's one thing if you hire someone and you say, "Okay, you're going to write our [company] blog." But then that person who writes this blog is separate from the blog. It's just their job, okay and they get to stay anonymous and behind the scenes, and then they'll turn out whatever bullshit you want written.

Kristy found that her own ideas about content creativity clashed with the company's call for cannily staged promotional material. "They wanted someone to live this lifestyle and blog about it and be . . . a personality, and they wanted to use this personality for their own brand sales. And to an extent, I was fine with it until they started asking for a different kind of content." For Kristy, then, the same company that valued her authenticity sought to—paradoxically—siphon away her own creative impulses.

Heather shared a similar account of a brand trying to exert too much control over the artistic process. As part of a sponsored promotion, Banana Republic sent a handful of bloggers—including Armstrong, with her assistant and his partner in tow—to Deer Valley, Utah:

They wanted—I think the exact words were "not traditional, not boring, fun, thinking outside of the box type of
things." And I'm like, "That's me, I can do that." And I showcased the clothes in a beautiful way, and it was hysterical [and
included a joking reference to "hairy vaginas"]. But Banana
Republic completely flipped out, and to the point that they
threatened to pull all of their advertising dollars from my ad
network, which was billions of dollars.

In the aftermath, the company wanted her to remove the post or else
edit it to remove what they deemed controversial content. She re-
fused, reasoning, "If I take down the post, I have to tell my audience
what happened, because there's no way a post can go missing like that,
[especially one] that popular and got that much attention." After days
of back-and-forth communication, she was allowed to keep the post
but had to "omit the line about hairy vaginas." Of the experience,
Heather concluded, "That's not what I signed up to do. I signed up to
write stories from my heart and that came to me organically, and I was
manufacturing content, and I did not feel good about it."

Alternatively, Rachel W. highlighted the gender politics underpinning the system of sponsored content/influencer marketing within
the YouTube community. Certain cosmetics brands, she explained,
approach her about making videos without paying much attention to
the content and tone of her videos. "Then they look at [the] content,
and they're like, "Oh, wait, I didn't realize you actually curse in your
videos, and you talk about mental health and other sketchy topics
that we don't want to really associate our squeaky clean brand with, so
we can't work with you." She explained how marketers' treatment of
male YouTube creators is significantly less restrictive, ostensibly influ-
enced by cultural codes of masculinity.

Then there are men on YouTube that have worked with the same brands doing the same kind of language in their videos, and it's fine [for brands because] women have a certain standard that we're supposed to be held up to where we need to be like basically the face of *Seventeen* magazine 24/7 on YouTube in order to be able to be taken seriously.

While Rachel's comment draws necessary attention to the gender constructions that get reified in marketer-sponsored digital spaces, the emergent social media economy also favors certain subjectivities.

Put simply, marketers' definition of "female influencers" is a narrow one—often inscribed within heteronormative prescriptions of beauty and femininity. Although Gaby was not a beauty vlogger, she found herself questioning the limited aesthetics that circulate in popular culture while doing research for a media think piece. There's a tendency of the culture to focus on "waifish white women [as] standard. So, how do you subvert that?" She echoed a comment made by a fellow YouTuber about the beauty vlogging community: "It's supposed to be this egalitarian platform, but there's still something a bit structural about the type of woman you have to be in order to be a beauty blogger . . . it is a look that is upper-middle-class white girl." Although Gaby conceded that certain marginalized populations are receiving newfound visibility in digital spaces, she was dubious about whether their activities were *paying off.* "Now there's all these Hijabi . . . fashion bloggers and beauty bloggers. It's coming around to more diversity, which is great. But I am curious if any of those Hijabi women would get the same kind of deals that [other, conventional bloggers would get from marketers]." Alissa, similarly, critiqued the tendency of marketers to ignore black fashion bloggers:

When's the last time you've seen like a black blogger do a major collaboration? . . . And black women, we're spending billions of dollars a year on fashion. We are big players in spending money. And that's high-end stuff as well as—whether it's low or high, we're spending our money just as much. And to not see black bloggers get those kind of collaborations or have the same level of traffic or . . . it's mindboggling to me.

Such social realities render the promise of meritocracy patently superficial; those hoping to be compensated for their work inevitably find themselves in a system of cultural participation that, as Sarah Banet-Weiser reminds us, "unfolds within preexisting gendered and racial scripts and their attendant grammars of exclusion."[55]

Already, the burgeoning influencer industry is drawing criticism for its lopsided nature—one that defies the egalitarian spirit that digital media companies endorse so vehemently. After noticing a staggering disparity in *Entrepreneur*'s list of "50 Online Marketing Influencers to Watch in 2016"—nearly three-quarters were male and 86 percent were white—social media consultant Nichole Elizabeth DeMeré penned an essay on "The Problem With Influencer Marketing."[56] Through such a narrowly defined version of "influence," DeMeré argued, "the loud and privileged are even more amplified, to the point where they saturate the conversation and drown out voices from marginalized groups." It's a system that amounts to "the influencer version of 'the rich get richer.'"[57]

For more than a century, media and marketing firms have sought to harness the presumed *credibility* and *authenticity* of ordinary citizen-consumers—whether by deploying affable women as an unconventional, albeit "respectable," sales force; by utilizing "real people" as trustworthy brand advocates; or by seeding products to the buzz-provoking opinion leaders of youth subcultures. Against the backdrop of a sprawling social media landscape, this commercial ventriloquism is showing no signs of wear. Judging by the volume of dollars funneled into native advertising and sponsored content, contemporary market-ers seem convinced that social media "influencers" wield considerable sway over twenty-first-century consumers. The emergence of social media talent agencies and affiliate networks is further testament to the lucrative market for YouTube, Instagram, and Snapchat "brand ambassadors."

Of course, brand representatives may also reach out to bloggers, vloggers, and Instagrammers directly, hoping to lure them with vaunted promises of "exposure" or "portfolio-building." Social media producers' expressions of *entrepreneurial brand devotion*—modes of highly visible promotional labor that present themselves as opportu-nities for self-enterprise—are undoubtedly a tremendous boon to today's corporations. After all, these are the same businesses that con-tinue to feel the aftershocks of the economic collapse, the same ones that remain bent on breaking through the commercially cluttered me-diascape, and the same ones that are oft commanded to have a vibrant social media presence. To marketers, these un-/under-compensated brand ambassadors serve as what scholar Kylie Jarrett recently identi-fied as the "digital housewife," whereby laborers "express themselves [and] their opinions and generate social solidarity with others in com-mercial digital media while, at the same time, adding economic value to those sites."[58]

This compensation-by-visibility rhetoric is understandably seductive to young aspirants raised on neoliberal tenets of individual-ism and personal responsibility, both of which encourage the mobili-zation of one's personal brand capital. Yet in visibly promoting these products through their networked communities, often under the guise of *authentic brand passion,* their laboring role is elevated to new heights—or, perhaps ironically, rendered invisible by the lack of compensation. Moreover, aspirational labors are often compelled to establish marketable personae—growing their metrics, cultivating skillsets, and unselfconsciously promoting their self-brand—all of which amount to immaterial labor in the service of consumer capitalism. Social and historical assumptions of gender have lingering effects within this system. In particular, marketers reify constructions of women as uniquely social brand advocates and encourage their highly visible enactments of loyalty.

Of course, some aspirational laborers *are* compensated for their efforts, and a rare few profit handsomely from advertising, affiliate marketing, and retail/design deals. These individuals face a challenge of a different sort as part of their deft negotiations with big-name partners: they must ensure that their promotional communication seems "organic," "authentic," and "on brand." Tasked with presenting themselves as trustworthy brand ambassadors (recall the Brady family's charge), these influencers routinely justify sponsor-provided goods with affective sentiments of "passion" and "love." The passion-payout solution helps to deflect critiques that bloggers are doing it "just for the money" or "selling out." As a rhetorical strategy, though, the passion-payout solution relies on an ongoing performance, which entails emotional labor.

It must be acknowledged that considerations of "selling out" presume a privileged subjectivity, as brands are unlikely to partner with just *anyone.* Just as notions of "real people" adhere to existing codes from mainstream media, the selection of "real" brand ambassadors is typically limited to those who reaffirm traditional ideals of beauty and femininity.[59] Hence, the "top bloggers" are overwhelmingly young, white or Asian, and thin, and conform to conventional standards of beauty. This reality skewers the blogosphere's claims to diversity as the selection of "influencers" gets filtered through the prism of commercial femininity.[60]

The further melding of *social media life* and *commercial life* was brought to the fore by an *Atlantic* article detailing the "creepy new ads" popping up in Instagram feeds; the ads mirror the platform's aesthetic, namely what reporter Kyle Chayka aptly called "user-generated lifestyle porn." But it was the blurred boundaries that left Chayka unsettled: "Your friends look more like brands, and brands look more like your friends, so it's increasingly hard to tell which is which."[61] To his first point, the tendency of aspiring creatives to continuously present themselves through the aesthetics, tone, and layout of commercial brands raises questions about the stakes of living *in* and *through* a pervasive brandscape. To lure partners, and thus make a living wage, creative aspirants are not just encouraged to engage in self-branding practices but also to develop a social media persona that dovetails well with existing marketing discourses. And while commercial partnerships are endemic to life in an era of advanced capitalism, the implications for individuals' articulations of identity and selfhood need to be more carefully considered.

The next chapter examines these issues by looking at those who have achieved the coveted status of *going pro:* full-time bloggers, vloggers, and digital entrepreneurs. In offering a rare glimpse behind the curtain, I dispel—or at least complicate—some of the pervasive myths about "making it" in the digital economy.

6

The "Instagram Filter": Dispelling the Myths of Entrepreneurial Glamour

[Blogging is like] the fastest hamster wheel possible. You don't ever get to get off of it. There is no rest. You are always on.

—*Heather, mommy blogger*

Over lunch at a British-style tearoom located on Philadelphia's über-posh Main Line, Jessie, an effervescent twenty-something, recounted the circumstances that led her to launch a fashion and lifestyle blog four years earlier. Jessie had pursued a communications degree at a nearby liberal arts college while building impressive media credentials: experience writing for a local newspaper, where she had been freelancing since the age of sixteen; on-air radio training; and bylines in the features section of a respected regional magazine. Unfortunately, she graduated in the wake of a global economic recession when many businesses—including storied media publishers—were issuing layoffs. Such a turbulent employment market left newly minted graduates like Jessie hard-pressed, vying for positions that amounted to, in her words, "working a lot for free." She recalled, "I got out of school, I left my internship at [the magazine] . . . I couldn't get a job. I was interviewing everywhere, and I couldn't even get back at my old internship because they were too full now."

Though she eventually landed a magazine internship, Jessie decided that her time and talent could be put to better use, so she rechanneled her creative energies into her then-nascent blog Trend Hungry. Conjuring up her early forays into the blogosphere, she noted that her first year "was just a lot of cutting my teeth." She added, "I made hardly any money off the blog at all, [and] I was pretty much full-time waitressing [to pay my bills]." But that was several years ago, and she had since generated enough income from her digitally created brand to *go pro*. It is perhaps not surprising, then, that the "about me" page on her blog includes the siren song of social media entrepreneurship: "Life is good when you do what you love!" Jessie was similarly upbeat in person; at one point she enthused, "I cannot differentiate work from life because I love what I do so much." Yet over the course of our lunchtime interview, she pulled back the curtain on some of the less glamorous elements of the pro-blogger work culture: her incessant schedule of planning, styling, writing, and networking was taxing, and she lacked long-term stability. In fact, Jessie considered herself more of a "full-time freelancer," given that Trend Hungry was only *one* of her revenue streams:

> I do it all. I do styling, I write for [my blog] . . . I write for the fashion spot on Philly.com, I do TV segments, QVC, I have a weekly syndicated radio segment, and I just started a vintage jewelry business. . . . Being an entrepreneur, nothing is the end-all, be-all; everything is like your launch pad to the next thing.

At the same time, Jessie felt that many creative aspirants lacked a realistic sense of the time and commitment demanded of professional content producers in the digital age. Career hopefuls, she explained, "idealize [the blogger] life: they think that it's going to be really glamorous. So they see other bloggers maybe working [for] brands or getting free things, and they only see . . . everything that's through an Instagram filter that looks so fabulous."

Jessie's mention of the "Instagram filter" is a reference to the culture of vigilant self-monitoring on social media, particularly as individuals internalize directives to *brand the self* with resolve: we un-tag unflattering photos, we build credibility through "friend" and "follower" counts, and we harness our online personae to pithy self-descriptors that function as digital sound bites. For fashion bloggers, beauty vloggers, and other denizens of the feminine digital media economy, these activities are amplified; however, the work of such personal branding endeavors gets concealed behind a torrent of images and textual referents that ostensibly mask the labor required to *earn a living doing what you love.* Fashion bloggers and Instagrammers personify effortless glamour. As Emily Hund and I argued in our analysis of top-ranking female fashion influencers, their carefully curated aesthetics seem to offer an updated version of the post-feminist ideal of "having it all": Instagram feeds show them cavorting through the vibrant cityscapes of New York and Los Angeles, clinking champagne glasses against Parisian sunsets, and basking on the beaches of Bali and Bora Bora. Even moments of seeming candor do not unsettle the well-crafted social media personae of the Insta-*glam*.[1] Their shots are often cannily staged to ensure a particular aesthetic—one that cloaks the staging itself.

When digital *professionals*—including bloggers, vloggers, and designers who have achieved financial success from their self-starter careers—described "going pro," their accounts sound dissimilar to the romanticized ideal of female entrepreneurship. Christina remarked, "People have seen the success of some of the most notable fashion bloggers, and they want that. And they think, 'All I have to do is start a blog, show cute outfits, or just write anything, and I'm going to attain what that blogger has attained.'" One of the reasons the blogger market is awash with creators is, according to Christina, "because people are looking to get that fame and success." Yet, she added, "they don't realize that if you're going to do this, you need to be consistent, you need to be different, and you're going to have to put in some work before you even attain anything close to what a major blogger or YouTuber has attained."

Vlogger Rachel W., similarly, held there is a telling disparity between the upper echelons of social media fame and the lower cadres of content producers. In contrast with the popular image, she said, "it's definitely not this easy route of career that everybody in the media makes it out to be just because they talk about the top ten people on YouTube." The reality, she told me, is that only a handful of creators have succeeded in achieving "this super, amazing wealth out of their online careers."

Meanwhile, fashion brand strategist Sissi suggested that the patterned concealment of labor is endemic to the fashion industry.

> Glamour is fashion's way; historically we never see the labor behind the results. Social media hasn't done much to change this. The instantaneous nature of social media has been widely criticized for misleading followers about the sheer hard work behind Instagram-perfect photos, and rightly so.

Drawing attention to the potential implications of this pervasive misrepresentation, she added, "Social media can perpetuate a culture of supposed instant success and leads to a culture of insecurity, especially amongst young women who compare themselves/their work unfavorably to polished people/products."

Indeed, although the work styles of these creative professionals tend to be valorized in popular representations of online entrepreneurship, interviewees disclosed the less appealing features of their professional lives: a frenetic work pace punctuated by moments of uncertainty; the pressure to remain ever-accessible to audiences and advertisers alike; and a nagging sense of unease as one's personal life becomes folded into a carefully curated digital persona. Much like work in "traditional" media and cultural industries, social media careers are often characterized by long hours, temporary work arrangements, and the mentality that "you're only as good as your last [TV script, magazine article, commercial]."[2] Of course, laborers experienced these characteristics unevenly; for example, the accounts of the few working mothers I interviewed differed substantially from those women in an earlier life stage. Moreover, "flexibility," "independence," and even "entrepreneurship" assumed different valuations within and across participant categories.

Such precarity has come to epitomize contemporary regimes of independent work, as long-term positions are gradually supplanted by temporary work and other casual arrangements. And with an evermore-bloated labor pool, the shift toward worker individualization is showing no signs of decelerating. In fact, according to recent projections, nearly forty-five percent of the U.S. workforce will be considered "independent" by 2020.[3] Across Europe, the iPro (independent professional) category—which represents a segment of contingent workers across the professional sectors of science, technology, and entertainment—has witnessed a similar post-recessionary uptick.[4]

The sustained growth of the contingent workforce has generated a spate of media treatments, though with clashing perspectives. In a 2015 *Huffington Post* article, Gene Zaino, president and CEO of MBO

Partners—the same organization that published the above-mentioned study of independent work in the United States—was effusive about the possibilities and perks of independent labor. As part of a pseudo-treatise on why the "Independent Work Boom [Is] Good for the U.S. Economy," Zaino made the case that many independents self-select into these professions as they pursue the well-worn entrepreneurial ideals of "controlling my own schedule," "more flexibility," "being my own boss," and "doing what I love."[5] Other media reports have addressed the much less desirable elements of work in the "gig economy," including the lack of long-term stability and the dearth of benefits. As Freelancers Union founder Sara Horowitz opined in the *Atlantic:*

> The basics—such as health insurance, protection from unpaid wages, a retirement plan, and unemployment insurance—are out of reach for one-third of working Americans. Independent workers are forced to seek them elsewhere, and if they can't find or afford them, then they go without.[6]

David Hesmondhalgh and Sarah Baker, creative labor scholars who conducted in-depth interviews with workers across the TV, journalism, and music industries, found that the instability of the freelance lifestyle can have a psychological impact as workers internalize intermittent employment through feelings of low self-worth.[7]

To a large extent, the tenets of this debate framed the way the full-time social media producers articulated their work styles: they lauded the flexibility and autonomy of their pieced-together careers while drawing attention to some of the less glossy features of the independent work-style. Indeed, the social media professionals detailed careers marked by a chaotic pace of work, periods of insecurity, and the demand to be ever-present to both audiences and advertisers. These individuals, I conclude, engage in *aspirational labor*, albeit of a different sort: they labor persistently—and at times, invisibly—to maintain their status in the midst of what Ulrich Beck described as a "political economy of insecurity," where neoliberal ideologies and practices shift organizational risks and responsibilities onto the individual.[8]

The online laborers I interviewed helped to dispel some of the myths about the social media world's "dream jobs"—including the extent to which these activities offer the means to make a living. Recall, for instance, Jessie's description of the "Instagram filter," which obscures—or, at least, refracts—certain realities of the fashion blogger profession. Those seduced by the infectious rhetoric of "going pro," she explained, may be astonished to learn how much work is involved in this profoundly romanticized career:

> [Some bloggers] start, and they're not consistent, and it doesn't come as easily; it's a lot of work and there's a lot of competition, and they don't realize that a lot of people who are full-time are really . . . full-time freelancers; it's not the blog that's making their sole income.

Jessie was not the only one of my informants to illuminate the curious tendency among fashion bloggers to depict oneself as a *full-time* content creator—regardless of actual career status or financial earnings. Julia, a style blogger who juggles an adjunct professorship and a string of writing gigs, sought to demystify what she described as the "clout of blogging." As she offered, "A lot of people put up more of a front [or] façade [that] they do it full time, but meanwhile . . . they work part-time otherwise, or . . . they do freelancing for another site." New

York City blogger Alissa, similarly, remarked that professional status is often a "façade for bloggers" who have yet to garner sufficient income from their projects. She continued, "You'll be surprised at how many bloggers do still have their full-time job [aside from blogging]." Although this mentality of "fake it 'til you make it" is symptomatic of the airbrushed perfection of socially mediated performances, accounts from my informants revealed the volatility of this career path.

Those who had been able to monetize their social media projects had devoted years to their undercompensated hobbyist pursuits before bearing significant financial return. For some, this uncertainty meant balancing digital content creation with a full-time career in a starkly different field. Amber, for instance, worked for years as a financial analyst while moonlighting as a beauty blogger. It took four years before she felt financially secure enough to leave her position. Alissa, similarly, spent six years as a full-time hedge fund manager before she transitioned to blogging full-time. And as Christina explained, it took "about four years for me to get to a point where I felt like I could make [blogging] my full-time job." She reasoned, "In order for my business to grow, I knew that I had to be doing it full time." Moreover, many of these full-timers continued to manage other professional responsibilities—be it writing gigs, design, or contract-based work. Cultural theorist Angela McRobbie seemed to foreshadow this fragmented system of work more than a decade ago, when she argued that creative laborers "have to find new ways of 'working' the new cultural economy, which increasingly means holding down three or even four projects at once."[9] Managing uncertainty and instability through multi-skilled proficiencies is even more crucial in an era of fierce professional competition, when on-demand work is just an app click away.

With a dynamic career that spanned writing, styling, designing, and hosting, Jessie exemplified the cross-platform capabilities of contemporary social media workers. She endorsed the idea that such a multi-faceted career could help to contain some of the uncertainties of the labor market:

> If you see really almost any successful entrepreneur, they don't take that one platform and let that be the end-all be-all. Because blogging can be a flash in the pan; things keep changing, so who knows how long blogs are going to be here. . . . So it's really about diversifying [beyond the actual blog].

While Jessie described herself as "a one man band," another fashion blogger, Alice, likened the maintenance of her fashion blog to "running a company." Of the independent work-style, she explained, "It's a lot of work doing everything. [Be]cause I used to do photograph[y] by myself, [I am also responsible for] going to the event, tweeting at the event, coming back home and blog[ging]. . . . I did the videos too, like, it's too much for one person."

Perhaps unsurprisingly, then, some of the professional content creators I interviewed admitted to feeling stretched too thin by competing demands on their time and attention. Amber, for instance, described how draining it is to maintain a frenetic professional schedule when "you're essentially a team of one." To sustain her queue of content, including frequent product recommendations, Amber felt obliged to attend beauty product launches; the number of events she gets invited to on a weekly basis can be upwards of twenty—a number which she noted has doubled in recent years. "So that's the hard thing that I try to balance, having enough time to actually do my work during the week, and have time to write for my own blog and . . . my other [freelance] assignments," she explained. The imperative to juggle various priorities was not dissimilar to what Alissa experienced as a long-time hobby blogger who had recently made the decision to shift to full-time, professional blogging. When I asked her to address how she thought blogging compared to a more traditional creative occupation, she offered:

> It's harder because everything falls on you. You are the person for everything. You have to generate income. You have to decide what's worth writing about. You have to be in the know, in the mix. Like, there's no bigger company assisting you. *It's literally all on you.* (italics added for emphasis)

Alissa's account—particularly the individualized notion of business responsibilities falling "all on you"—is an apt characterization of contemporary worker subjectivities against the backdrop of progressive shifts toward neoliberal politics and economics. That is, individuals must increasingly shoulder the burden of risks that were once borne by employment structures: pay, training, benefits, and more.[10] Yet her comment also illustrates how her day-to-day responsibilities are continuously guided by the multi-skill demands of the independent career.

With these demands in mind, other bloggers remarked on how aspects of this glamorized profession get concealed from the public, distorted through digitally filtered depictions of *making a living doing what one loves.* LoveBrownSugar.com founder Christina detailed the seemingly mundane "day-to-day" business responsibilities that she is tasked with managing. Of maintaining a social media brand, she explained, "It is definitely something that requires a lot more work than just posting blogs." In addition to scheduling photo shoots and orchestrating various events, she told me how she devotes "a lot of time talking to my accountant" and other administrative matters.

Indeed, like many other young women featured in this chapter, Christina believed that these elements of the blogger profession are camouflaged in popular representations:

> I think a lot of people, when they decide to work on their blog for full-time, they're like, "Oh, I'm just going to be taking pictures all day and sampling products and having lots of fun." But no, it's probably forty percent of that fun stuff and sixty percent of the phone calls and conversations with sponsors about making sure I'm getting paid the correct amount of money for the work I'm putting in.

YouTuber Rachel W., similarly, estimated that about 70 percent of her workweek is dedicated to answering emails. She enumerated several other decidedly unglamorous tasks, detailing hours spent editing videos, long sessions of recording and checking podcasts, and routine administrative matters. She concluded, "Answering all of the correspondence and the editing of the videos and the podcasts is what takes up the majority of my time during the week."

Heather, whom the *New York Times* hailed as "Queen of the Mommy Bloggers" in 2011, addressed this systematic concealment— or perhaps *filtering*—of labor in an April 2015 blog post, in which she announced her semi-retirement. In a candid assertion about the extent to which members of the pro-blogging community are looming toward a "dangerous level of exhaustion and dissatisfaction," Heather lamented the permutation of mommy blogging into

> a peculiar livelihood that involves grueling and inhuman publishing schedules, hours spent on the phone with networks

and brands trying to convince someone outside of the relationship with that virtual audience why something will or will not work, email threads about those phone calls lasting months on end. *It's a lot like a traditional desk job.* (italics added for emphasis)[11]

When Heather and I spoke a few months later, she helped to shatter the pervasive myths of "dreams jobs" and entrepreneurial glamour. Her quote from the epigraph suggests how disingenuous these career fables are:

> This [profession] is not sustainable. . . . Emotionally, this is not sustainable for you, because it is a hamster wheel that is on—it's the fastest hamster wheel possible. You don't ever get to get off of it. There is no rest. You are always on. Always getting new content, always, always, always updating every social platform.

Heather found the administrative work to be especially onerous, and she explained how she often became mired in emails and contract negotiations; her reference to "a traditional desk job" connotes a baseline level of grunt work. She described the profession as "a vast, vast, vast amount of work that at some point became untenable, unmanageable by myself." As such, she eventually hired an assistant to help manage email communication and enlisted the support of her then-husband to fulfill other administrative obligations.

And, indeed, many of the full-time producers I interviewed relied upon the support of assistants as well as the expertise and networked capital of agents, managers, publicists, and web designers to help run their self-brand with alacrity. Yet because of the high value of their personal brand, social media producers felt compelled to ensure that their support staff would not tarnish their image. Heather, for one, explained how difficult it would be to farm out content because her blog's success was deeply bound up in her own voice: "I can't really delegate my website to anyone, and no one wants to come to Dooce and read someone else." Other bloggers expressed similar concern about maintaining the consistency of their editorial voice. Reflecting on the challenge of overseeing various elements of her blog business, Alissa remarked, "Some bloggers, they can hire people to do that. But for me, for someone who is very close and personal with my readers, it's like I have to be 100 percent involved in everything." Similarly, Megan told me how she finds it especially "important for me to be really present in the tone of the site and the voice of the site." Even when she publishes the content of contributors, she engages in "line editing [of] every single . . . piece," in an effort to ensure it retains the "voice" and "tone" of her self-brand.

In other instances, blogger-brands seemed to veil the professional contributions of their agents, publicists, brand managers, and even interns. The latter compose a growing coterie of individuals employed "behind-the-screens," a term Nina Huntemann applies to those invisible workers who produce, manage, and promote digital content.[12] Similar to the *behind-the-scenes* laborers employed in the film and broadcast industries, those working behind the *screens* engage in waged service work that is unseen to audiences. And though these jobs are technologically mediated, they entail what is often seen as "women's work," including "'soft' skills of verbal and written communication, management of emotions, diplomacy, and empathy[,] [which] are valued and exploited."[13] Amber, for instance, noted that she has a manager responsible for negotiating fees for advertising and advertorials on her blog who recently advised her to "up my photo

game, and really try to only post original photography on my blog."
Amber also credited this individual with developing a new name for
her site. Sophie, similarly, noted that she had a web designer helping
her "build the site from the bottom up."

Another blogger I interviewed was rather furtive about her reliance
on an agent: "I didn't want to say it [at a public event] because I didn't
want to be like, 'Oh, I have an agent,' I just felt like that sounded weird
to say." Her reluctance to mention her professional support system at a
public venue stems from a sense of unease about the perceived status of
someone with a talent agent. Presumably, it is only somebody making
substantial earnings—or with enough existing capital to support a
"passion project"—who can afford to hire support staff.

The incorporation of brand support specialists is a testament to
the pervasive obligation to market the socially mediated self; my interviewees reflected on the substantial human capital required to steer
one's personal brand. To some, like fashion blogger Erika Marie, the
marketing-centric orientation of social media was understood as part
of the job. "Every time there's a new outfit post," she noted, "I probably spend a couple hours that day just doing the [public relations]
for it, and then I got to get back to work on figuring out what's going
to be on the next day and so forth." Alissa, meanwhile, understood
the creative and promotional aspects of her career discretely, explaining, "You have to manage your social media, and then you have to
manage the blog." She continued, "So it's like you have to honestly
kind of be on social media all the time if you want your numbers to
grow. You have to post all the time. I try to do it every hour on the
hour or every two hours."

Megan, founder and editorial director of the men's lifestyle
blog Style Girlfriend, provided a similar account of her professional

responsibilities, particularly the ever-increasing importance of "outreach with brands." She estimated that her time is "probably split 50/50 between just editorial . . . and then, new [business] and pitching and projects and all of that." Lauren, widely hailed in the media as "Australia's first professional Instagrammer," was somewhat unique in favoring the business aspects of social media work. In contrast to "a lot of Instagrammers that are just the creative [type]," she described herself as someone who enjoys the creative element of her profession "but [is] also very business-minded and I understand what it takes to get this work over the line."

Other social media producers expressed ambivalence about the command to be hyper-vigilant with their personal branding efforts. Jessie, for instance, offered a deft appraisal of the extent to which the culture of promotion had effaced the more creative aspects of her blogging project. As she explained, "[Even if] you're the best, if people don't know you're the best it doesn't really matter; you just have to be good enough . . . and well marketed." Relatedly, Siobhan, an independent designer who was living in New York at the time of our interview, felt that the profile-raising elements of her nascent business tended to eclipse the expressive functions—particularly in an era of ubiquitous connectivity. Though Siobhan admitted that she "would be happy just sitting in a room and [designing] things all day," she understood the injunction to cultivate her digital reputation. "Your designs can be 'more special and more unique' or whatever it is, but if you're not competing in that [online market], which [involves] getting followers, getting fans, tweeting constantly and maintaining that presence, . . . [then] you're going to get beat by somebody else." However, this philosophy of "aggressive" self-branding didn't come naturally to Siobhan. She noted how "some people really have a gift with those sorts of [promotional activities], and they enjoy it." But the dizzying pace of social media activity was also something of a burden; as she noted, "It's Tumbler. It's Pinterest. It's Twitter. It's Facebook. It's Instagram. You could be doing that constantly and updating new content every day. It's a lot of work to keep it interesting for people."

Later in our conversation, Siobhan offered a frank account of how she draws upon image management tactics to burnish her brand:

> I try to only put photos up if it's something I think will fit the idea that I want to convey. . . . I'm definitely guilty of only sharing things that I think are going to present the right idea, and maybe be a little aspirational. [So] I'm not going to share the picture of, you know, the weird leftovers I ate for breakfast today, but I'll post pictures of the eggs Benedict I had for brunch on Sunday. . . . Because that's the world that I want the girls who wear my clothes to think [about].

What emerges from Siobhan's reflection is a tension between her own sense of self and the idealized version she tries to project to the world to satisfy branding directives. Scholars of digital media often invoke sociologist Erving Goffman's dramaturgical metaphor of front-stage (how we perform when there is an audience) and backstage (without an audience present) selves to conceptualize the performative ethos of online communication.[14] In the mid-aughts, for instance, internet researchers explored how individuals on dating sites sought to reconcile the disparity between accurate and favorable self-presentation, in part through the articulation of a future, "ideal self."[15] More recently, digital media scholar Alice Marwick has explained how social media culture incites users to craft an "edited self": a "self-conscious persona that makes the world think they are entrepreneurial, knowledgeable, positive, and self-motivated."[16]

In gendered sites of social media production, this "edited self" tends to adhere to predefined cultural scripts of femininity. Instagram's filtered and neatly cropped depictions of female perfection are so pervasive that they have spawned a series of irreverent parodies, including the YouTube clip mocking the "Instagram husband" and the satirical Instagram account created for Socality Barbie. The latter showcased a bespectacled, hipster Barbie frolicking through pumpkin patches, holding a frothy latte, and expressing gratitude for her #soblessed life. Socality Barbie's originator, photographer Darby Cisneros, said that she created the parody "to poke fun at all the Instagram trends that I thought were ridiculous."[17]

Alana, too, traced the incessant culture of online performativity to the ubiquitous photo-sharing site:

> Instagram is kind of like this world . . . of "one-up-ness," [where] everyone is like, "Wow, I want to be like her." One of my writers calls it the "Kardashian effect," like that's how you become a big blogger is [by emulating the] Kardashians, who have this lifestyle . . . that they portray on Instagram, so that's what bloggers have to do. And my lifestyle wasn't like that at the time.

To present the sort of lifestyle Alana alludes to, bloggers must suture their personal and professional lives. The image-enhancing work of fashion and lifestyle bloggers is similar to the "glamour labor" that sociologist Elizabeth Wissinger explores in her extensive fieldwork with fashion models. In an age of digital technologies, Wissinger notes, models described their careers as "never ending" and saw their labor and leisure activities bleed into one another.[18] More broadly, she explains, "both physical and virtual upkeep [have risen] to prominence, as new mediations of the social via Twitter feeds and online life exponentially intensified the demand for 'being seen at the right places at the right times.' "[19]

In light of the incessant pace of work wrought by digitization, social media creators seemed to internalize the charge to *be on*—tethered to their laptops or mobile devices at all hours of the day. To be sure, this preoccupation with connectivity is not exclusive to the blogosphere; it's an expression of twenty-first-century work culture as mobile technologies fuel expectations about the "constant contactability" of employees.[20] Melissa Gregg's study of knowledge workers helped to shed light on the implications of these cultural expectations for modern-day professionals—those who scan emails before breakfast, take their laptops into the bedroom, and internalize the need to be "on call" even during their holidays.[21] Media scholar Lynn Spigel, meanwhile, has detailed a marked shift from "conspicuous consumption" to "conspicuous production," where working *all the time* symbolizes the employee's role in the social hierarchy.[22] According to Spigel, "It becomes a sign of status to seem perpetually occupied and 'in touch' with anonymous others"; such "performative communication," she adds, "allows people to demonstrate their labor value as social actors in a networked world."[23]

For independent professionals—especially those contingent workers whose success is hitched to brand-building activities—the directive to be continuously available takes on a new urgency in the social media age. Interviewees interpreted the directive to *always be on* in disparate ways. Lauren, whose career as an Instagram influencer/campaign manager in the tourism industry requires her to travel incessantly, admitted, "I work really hard. I don't have much of a work-life balance at the moment. It is something that I intend to work on next

steering these blogs, she rhetorically questioned, "Is that how you really live, or is this how you want to portray you live?" Siobhan and I discussed at length the extent to which visually oriented sites like Instagram mandate glamorized depictions of lifestyle:

> I'm looking at some of these [bloggers'] feeds, and I'm [thinking], "There must be an assistant." But how can you keep tweeting and Pinterest and this and that? . . . What's the tipping point? What's the maximum capacity that we can intellectually and physically manage? I don't know, but I feel like we're getting close.

This notion of hyper-productivity as a path to exhaustion brushes up against a key trope about individual work, namely that digitally enabled careers offer unparalleled freedom.

The rise of connective technologies in an increasingly global economy has paralleled the ascension of flexible work arrangements; "9 to 5" has thus become a metaphor for bureaucratic employment structures inherited from the Fordist era.[26] Flex-work, meanwhile, is lauded for its ability to emancipate employees from these constraints by affording them the opportunity to work *when* and *where* they want. For female workers, this narrative assumes a political valance through discussions of "work-life balance."[27] By undertaking employment assignments remotely, the argument goes, working mothers can better maintain their "domestic responsibilities." To be sure, management researchers have found a positive correlation between the ability to work remotely and mothers' likelihood to return to their positions after maternity leave.[28]

Other studies, meanwhile, have challenged the female-empowerment perspective by drawing attention to the extent to which "flexible work" may exacerbate gender inequalities. In an early study of "new media workers," Diane Perrons argued that their much-hyped work-style seems "more concerned with accommodating life to rather demanding and unquestioned working hours rather than one of reorganizing work to allow time for domestic and caring responsibilities."[29] More recently, a study of female online entrepreneurs challenged common myths about flexible work, particularly for those from already disadvantaged positions.[30] Moreover, the rhetoric of "working mothers" fails to challenge the problematic assumption that women are naturally suited for the role of caregiver.[31]

Though interviewees described the insinuating presence of their "always-on" careers, many still found a way to articulate their social media ventures as "flexible." For mothers of young children in particular, spatial flexibility (i.e., the ability to work remotely) seemed to offer them a heightened sense of *presence.* Heather, despite lamenting the frenetic pace of her career, admitted that blogging provides the distinct "privilege" of working from home:

> I want to work [rather than be a stay-at-home parent], and this enables me to spend a lot of time with my kids while also getting to have a job. And it is a bit of an idealized situation that way. I mean, I see my kids all the time. I have a super flexible—I mean, if my kid is sick, I don't get to work for two days and then I get to play catch-up, but I get to be here when my kid is sick. As hard as that is on my work, that is a total privilege.

Budget fashion blogger Kimberly drew upon the familiar trope of flexibility-as-empowerment in discussing the benefits of her self-starter career:

It's empowering as a woman to feel like I can do this, basically run my own business, and do bills, and do everything, and still I get to do something that I love and that I'm passionate about. How many people can really say that? And I have the flexibility of working from home, and I can take my kids to school, and go on the field trip with them, all of that.

Yet she acknowledged that emulating the blogger lifestyle was not a reality for most. "I wouldn't necessarily encourage [aspiring bloggers] to think, 'Oh, great, I'm going to start this site, and it's going to take off and I will have my own business . . . and it will pay the bills,' because I think it's a very small percentage that can say that and that become that."

Ana R., who worked as a coder for fifteen years before leaving the tech industry, blamed the male-dominated work culture for forcing working mothers to conceal their home life. She recalled, "It always feels like, if you're a mother, you kind of want to hide that fact and not tell them. . . . You never want to say, 'Oh, my kids are sick today,' and all that kind of stuff." Ana's story is a testament to the retreat of female tech workers from patriarchal work environments; a 2008 study found that up to half of the women working in STEM fields will eventually leave "because of hostile work environments."[32] Full-time freelance writer and editor Sarah Grey reflected on this shift in an essay aptly titled, "Between a Boss and a Hard Place." Grey explained how traditional workplace structures provide insufficient support for working women, especially "those who are pregnant, parenting, or dealing with disabilities or chronic illnesses." She suggested that despite the characteristic instability of freelance work, there are "intangible benefits" for many women:

Working outside a traditional office setting can mean freedom from a host of gendered restrictions: no pantyhose, no high heels, no extra-tight uniforms or dry-cleaning bills. For those who work alone, there's much less emotional labor—faking smiles, making small talk, soothing others' feelings—and more freedom to drop difficult or abusive clients.[33]

For Ana R., owning her own business—especially one centered on app development for children's learning—has enabled her to integrate her children into the creative process.

Meanwhile, Ana D., an online entrepreneur with expertise in the beauty sector, helped to nuance the much-venerated ideal of flexibility. She left a storied career in corporate marketing to launch her own business; among the reasons was that companies failed to "have any processes in place to allow flexibilities . . . in employee schedules." She explained:

> I have two young children . . . and I really wanted to spend more time with them in the day-to-day [and] be more present in their lives, [but] not necessarily be a stay-at-home mom. . . . I actually still want to work full time because I really enjoy working, and . . . I find great fulfillment in having my own career. But I just wanted the flexibility to be able to drop them off at school a couple of times a week, pick them up, you know, maybe go on a school field trip, or just, kind of, be more present.

At the same time, for Ana, having the ability to set her own schedule translated into a sense of laboring around-the-clock: she recounted slotting in moments of work after she put her children to sleep or during hectic weekends. "It's almost ironic," she explained, "that I find it harder to actually stop working because I now work from home, and it's harder to just turn off my computer and just say, 'Okay it's done.'" She continued, "For me, [that aspect] has been really challenging, just because—especially with technology—you're always on, and you think that you can be so much more productive, but . . . it actually takes away a lot from you being present." Ana highlights a key tension in the notion of "flexibility," namely that *spatial* flexibility—working remotely—may correlate with a decline in *temporal* flexibility.

In other cases, flexibility was a euphemism for instability—or what critical scholars call "precarity," defined as "intermittent employment and radical uncertainty about the future."[34] Several full-time producers acknowledged the challenge of "making a living" in an economy where—as Sissi put it—"you can get hired over a tweet or get fired over it too!" YouTube comedian Gaby Dunn has publicly critiqued the precarious nature of social media work; her former career as a journalist made her well-aware of the parallels to a "freelance lifestyle" where one is always in flux. In a *Fusion* piece that detailed the exacting career of a social media full-timer, she confessed: "I've never had more than a couple thousand dollars in my bank account at once. My Instagram account has 340,000 followers, but I've never made $340,000 in my life collectively."[35] She explained that YouTube's loose compensation structure is partially at fault and that content creators are afraid to speak up: newcomers, in particular, "try to not say anything that will piss off 'people in charge.'"

Rachel W., a YouTuber and podcaster, professed that hers was "not the most stable career choice," especially given that "so many things go into factoring how much money you make each month." Her income was piecemeal, with multiple revenue streams: YouTube's

AdSense program, she noted, is "not a good way to make a livable wage." Rachel was frustrated with understandings of digital content creators in the popular imagination: "[Many people think], 'Millennials: they don't have to actually work hard. They can just sit in front of a webcam, and they're millionaires.'" But this was a profound misconception based upon faulty reasoning. She explained:

> People just expect us to all be doing really well because we're going to all these events, or we're getting these views, or we're working with these brands. But then a lot of us are at the end of the month trying to figure out how we're going to be paying our bills, especially because most of us get paid once a month too. . . . [Suddenly bills are] due, and you just got paid, so it's kind of like, "How much money am I going to have left over [for] this month?"

Rachel justified her decision to pursue such a financially unstable career path with the hallowed ideal of "passion." She professed to take great satisfaction in making the videos and acknowledged the perks of being her "own boss." Laying bare this trade-off, she concluded, "At the end of the day, if I wanted to be paid for every hour of work that I did, I would not choose this job."

The characteristic features of independent work—creative freedom, flexibility, and self-directedness—are fetishized in contemporary discourses of entrepreneurialism. As the accounts in this chapter have made clear, though, the attributes of the enterprising subject are marred by work patterns that are less than idyllic. For instance, *independence* is a celebrated ideal for creative producers; it connotes a sense of artistic license unencumbered by structural constraints, including commercial pressures that seem to render self-expression hollow.

Yet for full-time bloggers and other social media creators, being "independent" meant adapting to a protean style of work with the deftness to manage multiple roles simultaneously. These multi-skilled workers were—in the words of one participant—akin to "a team of one." In broader narratives about the labor market, de-specialization is articulated as a way to inoculate workers against the uncertainties of the employment economy; cultivating one's skillset across various sectors—and even industries—thus functions as a form of risk management.[36] Recall, for instance, fashion blogger Jessie's explanation about "do[ing] it all" as a way to diversify in the context of a rapidly evolving—perhaps volatile—career economy. Importantly, the image of the fast-moving multi-skilled worker obscures the reality that many of these tasks are fundamentally administrative. As a result, participants lamented the extent to which the creative elements of their profession had been eclipsed by instrumental business dealings. Though some aspects of their careers remained exhilarating, others amounted to grunt work: making phone calls, responding to emails, and adhering to a frenetic schedule of meetings and events. Similar to the Etsy sellers and DIY crafts persons Tara Liss-Mariño studied, including those who felt that the amped-up production demands rendered their work factory-like, I found that some of the professionals I interviewed "cast their businesses in a new, less-rosy glow."[37]

Worker *flexibility* also emerged as a profoundly contested ideal—one that seemingly entailed both *more* and *less* control over one's schedule. Youth studies scholar Anita Harris seemed to presage the problematic nature of the term in the early 2000s, when she contended that "flexibility" is associated with a particular type of (female) laboring subjectivity, namely one who can easily change work locations unencumbered by family or other commitments; is untroubled by flux such as downsizing, irregular hours, or retraining; will negotiate individual rates of pay and conditions without union or award interventions; and will perform a variety of tasks not limited to a traditional job description and duties list.[38]

My interview participants experienced similar ambivalence about the implications of flexibility. While mothers of young children experienced a sense of "privilege," and even "empowerment," from the ability to fulfill their professional obligations from the home office, this ideal failed to live up to its promises in other ways. Achieving a work-life balance was elusive—if not beyond reach—as producers felt the demand to be ever-present to audiences and advertisers alike. In this vein, they internalized the mandate to be *always on the job.*[39]

And, overwhelmingly, the social media producers chronicled in this chapter conceded that their personal and professional lives were increasingly indistinct. While some online professionals lauded this blurring as a harmonization of otherwise conflicting spheres, others expressed concern about the self-commodification of their personal lives: vacations doubled as photo opps as friends and family members stepped into supporting roles. A few women admitted that these factors—combined with the artifice of social media—created a perfect storm for anxiety and exhaustion.

Of course, such critiques of worker individualism are less relevant to those who have enlisted the support of production and promotion personnel. Professionals with the financial means increasingly rely on the hidden laborers of the social media ecosystem: web designers, agents, and brand managers, among others. Much like the "below-the-line workers" who provide physical—and increasingly emotional—

scaffolding for the production of TV and film industries, such "behind-the-screens" professionals support the activities of fashion bloggers and other aspirational laborers. A subset of my interviewees was fortunate enough to hire assistants, agents, and publicists to help manage the overload; however, the incorporation of behind-the-screens workers sits uneasily with understandings of the *personal self-brand.*[40]

Some producers' reluctance to publicly acknowledge these systems of support indicates vague dissatisfaction about the perceived status of someone with a talent agent. Such discretion might also signal the felt need to preserve the aura of *individualism.* In this sense, "behind-the-brand" might be a better title for the emergent class of professionals responsible for the public personae of today's social media entrepreneurs—despite the fact that their work remains largely invisible. Such hyper-vigilance about one's online persona is perhaps expected in a moment when digital media platforms are widely understood as central instruments of self-branding. Part of this self-branding involves cloaking the less glamorous aspects of careers, through socially mediated, Valencia-filtered images of "work that *doesn't seem like work.*"[41] Together, this vibrant kaleidoscope of images and textual referents seems to attenuate the time, energy, and investments necessary to *earn a living doing what you love.*

7

Aspirational Labor's (In)Visibility

Near the close of 2015, the chronicles of two different social media personalities were cast into the public spotlight; together, they reveal the consistencies as well as the contradictions that structure the aspirational labor system. First, in October, Australian Instagrammer/ model Essena O'Neill announced to her 600,000+ followers that she was "quitting" social media. This abrupt act of defiance, she explained, was a rejoinder to the internet's ethos of crass, narcissistic self-indulgence. On her final blog post, which was circulated by media outlets on a global scale, O'Neill declared:

> I'm quitting Instagram, YouTube and Tumblr. Deleted over 2000 photos here today that served no real purpose other than self promotion. Without realising, I've spent [the] majority of my teenage life being addicted to social media, social approval, social status and my physical appearance. Social media, especially how I used it, isn't real.[1]

O'Neill edited the captions on the remaining images, adding punchy language that called attention to the artifice of digitally mediated self-presentation—particularly among girls and young women. One of the reworked posts appeared adjacent to a mid-range shot of the flaxen-haired teen as she reclines on a rocky beachscape. Her neon-hued bikini

216

highlights a sun-kissed complexion, and she averts her eyes from the camera—an enactment of what Erving Goffman described as the female subject's "licensed withdrawal" in advertising imagery.[2] Highlighting both the physical labor *and* the production labor required to achieve the seemingly perfect shot, O'Neill's new Instagram caption reads: "NOT REAL LIFE—took over 100 in similar poses trying to make my stomach look good. Would have hardly eaten that day. Would have yelled at my little sister to keep taking them until I was somewhat proud of this."[3]

Along with the parting blog, O'Neill released a seventeen-minute YouTube video in which she blasts the rampant culture of social media performativity. After critiquing the smoke and mirrors of Instagram, she concludes that " 'having it all' on social media means absolutely nothing to your real life."[4] Unsurprisingly, O'Neill's video manifesto prompted something of a media blitz; in fact, *Time* magazine later listed her among "The 30 Most Influential People on the Internet"— an ironic choice given that she was no longer *on the internet*.[5] While some praised her public statement as refreshingly candid or even "brave," others were much less sympathetic. O'Neill's former YouTube collaborators claimed that the video was merely a "hoax" orchestrated to garner a bump in followers.

In the wake of O'Neill's self-exposé, another backstage reveal of social media labor was published on pop culture site *Fusion,* titled "Get Rich or Die Vlogging: The Sad Economics of Internet Fame." Author Gaby Dunn, the twenty-something co-host of the YouTube comedy show *Just Between Us,* offered a behind-the-scenes glimpse into the internet's lopsided compensation structure.[6] Her article spotlighted the legions of vloggers who constitute YouTube's bloated "middle class." Unlike the rarefied community of internet A-listers, these content creators, Dunn claimed, are "barely scraping by."

Indeed, Dunn chronicled how YouTubers with tens of thousands of followers hold low-status service positions just to pay the bills; their fans, of course, are stunned to find their favorite internet "stars" waiting tables or serving lattes. Some feel forced into these gigs because their fans cry foul if they produce an abundance of sponsored content (recall the discourse of "selling out"). Dunn attributed this trend to the internet's narrowly defined codes of self-presentation, hitched to ideals of "authenticity" and "relatab[ility]":

> Elsewhere, the trend is to show off wealth; that would be a major faux pas on YouTube. Whereas we're used to a CEO being a millionaire, a popular YouTuber's "business is predicated on 'hey, I'm just like you.'" That means fans don't want to see that you're explicitly on the hustle. Whether they realize it or not, they dictate our every financial move.

This logic of performativity requires vloggers and other internet personalities to maintain a delicate balance between retaining an aura of realness and earning a respectable income for their time and talent. These middle-range stars are damned if they do: fans accuse them of being inauthentic product shills if they detect sponsored content. And, as the reaction to Dunn's piece showed, they are damned if they don't: another "mid-size" YouTuber, Jared Polin, suggested that undercompensated content creators like Dunn merely lack business savvy. As he retorted, "You have to run your channel as a business. You have to do well. There's nothing wrong with going for the sell."[7]

Though the accounts of social media labor furnished by O'Neill and Dunn touched on different genres and networking platforms—and though each took aim at a distinctive facet of digitally enabled self-expression—the intersecting points of their critique are telling. Together, the pair reveals the extent to which social media producers must reconcile the tensions between labor and leisure, between the internal self and external publics, between authenticity and self-promotion, and between creativity and commerce. And it is these same patterned contradictions that configure the system of aspirational labor that I have outlined in this book.

Thus, while blogging/vlogging/Instagramming is framed in the popular imagination as individualized self-expression, I showed how social media producers tend to approach these activities with the commitment and purpose of full-time, paid employment. Indeed, many of the young women I interviewed had devoted significant time and attention to their social media brands. In addition to scheduling and producing textual material, staging photos, and promoting content across the vast social media landscape, these aspirational laborers worked vigilantly to build and maintain "relationships" in both online and offline contexts. Moreover, their relational activities were largely structured through appeals to "relatability" and "authenticity," a spirit captured by the statement in Dunn's article, "hey, I'm just like you." But the unconditional embrace of these ideals is decidedly problematic: constructions of realness, in particular, are deeply implicated in gender and class relations. Much too often, the significance of these social subjectivities in structuring the digital economy goes unnoticed. In particular, the deployment of various markers of authenticity helps to obscure the reality that social and economic capital are often prerequisites to pursue production, networking, and professionalization opportunities. The reserves of time and money exacted from creative aspirants leave the playing field profoundly uneven.

Further, on the perennial quest to project themselves as "relatable," aspirational laborers are incited to *put themselves out there.*

Social media's imperative to blur the public and private domains is not without precedent; Lauren Berlant has explored the commodification of women's intimacy in such genres as "chick-lit" and self-help literature as part of her exploration of the progressive sentimentalization of American culture.[8] Relatedly, Eva Illouz contends that the internet is among contemporary spaces of the therapeutic narrative, which—like support groups and talk shows—"converts the private self into a public performance."[9] The more recent incarnation of compulsory visibility, one largely born of the attention economy, is propelled by the currency of likes, shares, and followers. Many of the women I interviewed seemed to experience this visibility mandate in patently gendered ways: by adorning and displaying the body, by participating in a confessional culture, and by sharing one's life and career through the prism of the "Instagram filter."

Some of my interviewees found the self-disclosure obligation draining, and the buzz surrounding Essena O'Neill's social media take-down indicates swelling public interest in this issue. More recently, in a media think piece spotlighting the extent to which we "curate, script and filter ourselves online," author Michelle Duff addressed the potential implications of the visibility—spurred by celebrity culture and social media—for young women. Duff's piece included a quote from sociologist and anti-pornography advocate Gail Dines, who contended, "Everyone wants to be celebrities, because in a media culture all that matters is to be visible. In our culture, women are reduced to either f**kable or invisible, and you can't ask an adolescent to choose invisibility."[10]

What deserves increased attention is the extent to which the visibility narrative is deployed to normalize backlash and public expressions of hate. While I am by no means aiming to fan a moral panic, I find discourses of inevitable online behavior (e.g., "haters gonna hate") problematic. Such reasoning exonerates this behavior and attenuates the potential consequences of public criticism; yet it provides little recourse to those experiencing vitriolic speech and misogyny.

Meanwhile, the assurance of *future visibility* drives aspirational labor economies and ideologies. Corporate rhetoric urging young people's entrepreneurial brand devotion prods aspirants to serve as brand ambassadors who work not for money, but for potential "exposure." By shrouding this labor in the promise of impending rewards, brands capitalize on the energies and networked social capital of these female content creators. Like Brent Luvaas, who calls attention to the oft-illusory nature of the terms "collaborations" and "partnerships," I argue that brand-blogger relations are inherently rigged—particularly when the blogosphere is awash with content creators willing to "work for free."

Critiques about unpaid work bring to mind the digital labor debate that I reviewed earlier, which is concerned with the "free labor" we provide while live tweeting during our favorite TV show or liking a retail brand on Instagram. At stake in this debate are questions of power, agency, and value, all of which are bound by the assumption that many of our digital activities are productive—without our knowledge of the way these quotidian details generate value for digital capitalism. But it seems many *do* realize it: just as my students are well aware that they are served branded ads after "liking" a company's Facebook page, aspirational laborers are mindful that they are providing "free advertising" by sharing a brand's message through social networks. Thus, what I have detailed in the preceding pages reaffirms a claim I made earlier: we should not view social media laborers as cultural dupes. Instead, we must call attention to the dubious reward structures for aspirational labor. It is the unevenness of the system that is nothing more than a blip on the radar.

Celeb-bloggers and digital influencers are upheld in the popular imagination as individuals *just like us;* yet, the handful of pros who "make it" really aren't *just like* the legions of creative aspirants who don't. In this respect, the aspirational labor system is less of a meritocracy and more of what sociologist Andrew Ross described as the "jackpot economy." Model workers, Ross argued, are obliged to be "self-directed, entrepreneurial, [and] accustomed to precarious, nonstandard employment"—all in the hopes of "producing career hits." Yet as with any jackpot, the "glittering prizes" are won by only "the lucky few."[11] Though there are exceptions—including some of the social media professionals profiled in this book—the aspirational labor system is marked by a yawning gap.

As I have shown, the features of aspirational labor draw on the same market logics of audience building and ad-revenue generation that have long configured work in "traditional" media industries. And the social media version mirrors many of the social inequalities and hierarchies that mar traditional sites of cultural production. To be sure, women have long held marginal standing in media and cultural organizations: while they are overrepresented in administrative, service, or "below-the-lines" positions, very few occupy creative industry C-suites.[12] In recent years, scholars have shown the extent to which modern, "democratic" technologies—including the very same ones which promise to "empower" women—are *exacerbating* gender inequalities.[13] Indeed, the tech fields, including various sites of informational and innovation work, have been marked by a sharp division of labor; the lack of women in tech start-ups is especially dreadful, and gender-based harassment is rife. Other signs of exclusion—including a profound lack of racial/ethnic diversity—also plague the tech world. For years, internet behemoths like Google and Facebook failed to disclose information about their workforce diversity. Then, in 2014, Facebook admitted the appalling statistic that African Americans made up less than 1.5 percent of its workforce. The following year, Yahoo made public the news that African Americans and Hispanic workers were equally marginal—2 and 4 percent, respectively.[14]

On one hand, careers fashioned on the internet offer something of a retreat from inhospitable—even aggressively misogynistic—work cultures, particularly for women hailing from the tech world. But much too often social media labor is upheld as a path to a "unicorn job." Using luck, hard work, and free social media, the argument goes, "anyone" can "get discovered" or make a living from their "passion projects." In response to this digital idealism, I contend that traditional inequalities often endure, and that barriers to entry remain staggeringly high. Among the conclusions of this study is that those most likely to rise above the social media din are the same social types that have long dominated the tech and creative economies, particularly those with sufficient reserves of economic and social capital. Those seeking to build independently owned digital enterprises are expected to, in the words of one of my informants, "bootstrap it [with] funds from family at the beginning." Other studies, too, have confirmed that existing class privilege is critical to the experiences of budding entrepreneurs. Summarizing findings from the National Bureau of Economic Research, business reporter Aimee Groth noted, "The most common shared trait among entrepreneurs is access to financial capital—family money, an inheritance, or a pedigree and connections that allow for access to financial stability . . . it's usually that access to money which allows them to take risks."[15] The gendered, raced, and classed nature of self-enterprise renders notions of digital meritocracy superficial, if not discernibly false.

Throughout the book, I have drawn attention to another way that social divisions get reified in social media contexts, namely through the perpetuation of traditional norms about gender and femininity. Although the laborers detailed throughout the book self-identify as content *producers,* their creative contributions were largely inscribed in feminized sites of commodity capitalism (e.g., fashion, beauty, domesticity). Critiques of this gendered labor structure get deflected through feminine-coded traits of love and passion. As Miya Tokumitsu has argued, the media and fashion fields are flush with mostly female employees "willing to work for social currency instead of actual wages, all in the name of love." While unpaid internships are the most obvious source of uncompensated, "passionate labor" (fueled by the manic rhetoric of "getting discovered"), personal assistants and social media publicists (i.e., behind-the-brand laborers) are other arteries of this system. For these individuals, exciting, rewarding careers function as what Lauren Berlin describes as "objects of desire," with promises stirred by "the pursuit of 'the good life.'"

Many other features of aspirational labor are also coded as traditionally feminine. The emphasis on community building encourages the calculated deployment of affective relations while perpetuating industrial constructions of female audiences as innately social. But, importantly, efforts to boost follower counts, respond to comments, and attend events require enactments of emotional or relational labor.[16] As I have documented, this labor is largely *invisible,* a reality which captures the legacy of "women's work" as undervalued and unpaid activities—despite its central role in maintaining the capitalist circuit of production.[17] Moreover, the concentrated efforts of advertisers and marketers to deploy female influencers as an "authentic" sales force with socially networked capital draw on a legacy of understanding women as trustworthy and devoted brand advocates.[18] Yet we must keep in mind that the genre of fashion and style blogs ultimately "serves the interests of the fashion industry by producing future consumers."[19]

Though it could be argued that *all* labor has an aspirational element, it is important to keep in mind aspirational labor's historically rooted gendered bent. In the book's second chapter, I explored the historical positioning of women as aspirational *consumers,* with shopping practices articulated as modes of fulfillment, leisure, and self-expression. Although this construction persists in various incarnations, gendered consumption has in recent years slid into the system of *aspirational labor* explored in this book. Its ascension can be traced to changes in the economy and labor market that have affected women disproportionately, even if the ideology of aspirational labor will spread as part of the "cultural feminization of work."[20] Female aspirational laborers are the vanguard of digitally enabled "model" workers, and the conditions and rewards of their work presage larger socio-economic shifts in the gig economy.

Accordingly, it seems worthwhile to reflect on what the motivations, efforts, and investments of aspirational laborers can teach us about more pervasive narratives in the digital cultural economy. The desire for gainful employment in the creative industries is by no means a twenty-first-century phenomenon: the ideal of artistic license is a profoundly romantic notion, sharply contrasted with the blue-collar world of manual labor as well as white-collar careers of insipid monotony. Recent years have witnessed a fetishization of the technology industries, too, a shift that owes much to the rampant discourses of informal, "fun" work environments of "no-collar work." The Googleplex, located in Mountain View, California, is the paragon of this über-hip work culture; in the popular imagination, ever-sprightly employees cavort on sprawling campuses replete with volleyball courts, a gym, a massage parlor, and a series of gourmet cafeterias.

This idealized leisure/labor hybrid is a persistent theme in mainstream media, too, with creative workplaces celebrated in films and TV series such as *Ugly Betty, Gossip Girl,* and *Sex and the City* (perhaps another example of industrial self-sustenance?). At the same time, the ethos of fun and informal working has been amplified by the contemporary euphoria over self-employment, or—to use its more splashy euphemism—"entrepreneurship." Independent work is valorized in the popular imagination as *work that doesn't seem like work* or the opportunity to *be your own boss.*

Such constructions clash—or, at least, are moderated by—academic inquiries into the media, culture, and technology industries. Over the last decade, a number of scholars representing the "creative industries" paradigm have argued that traditional power structures have been supplanted by a new model worker-subject tasked with, as Rosalind Gill put it, "*managing the self in conditions of radical uncertainty.*" This idealized neoliberal worker-subject is entrepreneurial, self-directed, flexible, and available to work incessantly. The particular incitement to *be creative*, as Angela McRobbie contends, functions as a *dispotif* that involves a "mix of pleasure and discipline [which] . . . undertake labour reform by stealth and without even drawing attention to the old ways of organized labour."[21] Indeed, the overwhelming quest for autonomy and individualism displaces concerns about stability and security—as well as the hard realities of independent work.[22] Meanwhile, Gina Neff has shown how discourses inherited from the high-tech world have glorified risk while positioning uncertainty as crucial to economic success.[23] Within this milieu of creativity and tech, aspirational labor emerges as a seeming antidote to new anxieties about the culture of creative work.

While critical discourses of precarity and instability offer a bleak reckoning of the contemporary labor market, individualist appeals to passion and entrepreneurialism temporally reroute employment concerns. That is, affective mantras like "Do What You Love" shift workers' focus from the present to the future, dangling the prospect of a career where labor and leisure coexist. In his widely invoked 2005 commencement speech at Stanford University, Apple's late co-founder Steve Jobs told newly minted grads:

> Your work is going to fill a large part of your life, and the only way to be truly satisfied is to do what you believe is great work. And the only way to do great work is to love what you do. If you haven't found it yet, keep looking. Don't settle. As with all matters of the heart, you'll know when you find it. And, like any great relationship, it just gets better and better as the years roll on. So keep looking until you find it. Don't settle.[24]

Though Jobs offered that advice more than a decade ago, its spirit lingers in how-to manuals, career websites, screen prints peddled by Etsy vendors, and even street art (see Figure 8).

Similarly, aspirational labor is both propelled and sustained by the promise of a better future—with a fulfilling career where pleasure, passion, and profit meld. *But does it pay off?* In a handful of cases, these aspirational activities *do* provide laborers with economic and social capital. The success stories of social media celebs gaining entrée into the fashion, photography, or publishing circuits reaffirm the rewards of aspirational labor: while some are making a living from their passion projects, others have been hired into a traditional creative industry. Yet these tales of achievement should not obscure the practical realities of aspirational work. Only a handful have been able to realize their dreams of "going pro," and those who have toil around the clock

8. Street art hyping the mantra of "Do What You Love" on Primrose Street in London in May 2015. Photo Credit: Manuel Sechi.

to maintain their self-starter careers. We might conclude that aspirational labor doesn't pay off—if the benchmark is merely financial compensation. But aspirational labor has succeeded in one important way; it has glamorized work just when it is becoming more labor-intensive, individualized, and precarious.

The creative aspirants face this inconsistency alongside gig workers in the "sharing economy" and the part-time flexitariat. Unstable, benefits-stripped work is re-branded by cyber-enthusiasts as "free agency." In this respect at least, Uber drivers and would-be Instagram influencers face the same paradox: the very conditions of their work (flexibility on the one hand, creativity on the other) supply the narrative raw material that—rendered as a magazine cover line or italicized Pinterest post—papers over a less glamorous reality. This is, ultimately, a political problem, brought on by feeble labor laws and a frayed social safety net, especially in the Anglo-American world. One response is to reform labor and policy in ways that reduce precarity, in the social democratic spirit that Angela McRobbie champions in her important new book on cultural work in a European context. In the United States, grassroots worker organizations, such as the Freelancers Union and less formal intern collectives, can push for changes like these and provide collective support (however limited) for new economy workers of all stripes.

Support for policy reforms and wide-scale organizing depends, ironically, on the very social media platforms that host aspirational laborers. That is precisely why frank, widely circulated exposés like Essena O'Neill's and Gaby Dunn's are so crucial. The likes-and-clicks visibility culture, the lifeblood of the aspirational labor economy, is also the place to expose its myths. This book has sought to amplify the voices and experiences of young female aspirants, as one small contribution to the myth-slaying project.

EPILOGUE
The Aspirational Labor of an Academic

As an academic, I cling tightly to my self-identity as a *"critical media scholar,"* in part to distinguish myself from those analysts who take an administrative approach to communication research.[1] However, I hope by now I have made clear that this book is not a *critique* of the individual content creators who constitute the swelling aspirational labor class. To the contrary, over the course of this project, I've developed tremendous respect for the women (and handful of men) who generously shared their insight and experiences with me. I interpret their enterprising activities as an attempt to contain the uncertainties of an employment market that rests upon quite shaky foundations—and not as expressions of false consciousness. But there is another—and admittedly more personal—reason that compels me to reiterate that the object of my critique is the structure and not its inhabitants: I'm something of an aspirational laborer, too. That is, I have found that the ideologies and social practices propelling the social media sphere bear a striking resemblance to contemporary academe.

With its staid, ivory tower façade, the academy might seem far removed from the creative industries, a cluster of professions marked by an aura of bohemian cool. But it's much less of a conceptual leap to understand the creation and dissemination of knowledge as a form of *cultural work*. And many of the same venerated ideals—autonomy, flexibility, the perennial quest to "do what one loves"—seem to animate workers in both arenas. Indeed, art historian/author Miya Tokumitsu's observation that academia is unique among professions that "fuse the personal identity of their workers so intimately with the work output" might well be said of the creative industries.

There are much less idealized features that are associated with creative—and increasingly academic—labor, including long hours, heightened instability, and an over-reliance on contingent employees: freelancers, unpaid interns, and spec workers in the former case, adjunct faculty in the latter. Against this backdrop, cultural theorist Rosalind Gill has urged fellow academics to "consider academic labour as a species of cultural work, beset by many of the same challenges and experiences that characterize work in the cultural and creative industries."[2]

For me, though, the analogous nature of these professions was a happenstance discovery, unveiled during an interview with one of my study participants. As the interviewee—a relative newcomer to the fashion blogging scene who had amassed a remarkable following—reflected on her profile-raising strategies, I found myself pondering whether I, too, should be utilizing some of these best practices for social media self-branding. After all, as a junior scholar, I am well-acquainted with the injunction to promote one's work. But something about this particular impulse—*to be advantageous about the timing of my Twitter posts*—made me uneasy. It was at that moment that I realized how similar the worlds of creative production and academic production really are—and thus how *aspirational* much of my *labor* was.

Let me be clear: I have no plans to become an internet entrepreneur—nor do I expect corporate brands to lavish attention on me in exchange for shilling product. But other points of overlap seem irrefutable, most notably the individualized nature of these career sectors. Academics, especially in the qualitative social sciences and humanities, are independent workers *par excellence:* though we are embedded within departments, schools, and/or colleges, our programs of scholarship are of our making.[3] There are constraints of course—disciplinary, ideological, and increasingly, market-based ones—but it's an individualized career for many of us. Discourses of branding seem particularly apt here: our research specialty is our niche, and the "academic elevator pitch" we've honed with vigilance is our slogan. This pitch shapes our introductory interactions at academic conferences, post-lecture receptions, and informal gatherings; such events, like creative industry meet ups and other forms of "compulsory sociality," are a peculiar hybrid of labor and leisure.[4] These activities are rationalized as an investment in the future self, but they may or may not "pay off." And they may not be paid *for* either, as diminishing budgets have forced some universities to suspend faculty travel funding.

Like the aspirational laborers chronicled in this book, academics are afforded some freedom to set our own schedules—though this obviously varies based on the institution and the organizational culture. Certain phases of the year—summer and winter breaks, for instance—allow for spatial flexibility (i.e., teleworking), too. I, for one, did much of my sabbatical writing from home, and many college campuses are eerily quiet during the summer. Yet there are trade-offs for these ostensible freedoms: much like online entrepreneurs, academics are compelled to remain ever-accessible—to students, faculty colleagues, collaborators, and more. Work hours bleed into all moments of the day, and deadlines come at a frenetic pace. As the joke goes, *"There's a lot of flexibility in the academy; you can work whatever 80 hours a week you want!"* There's more than a kernel of truth here; indeed, I found myself nodding with gusto as my interviewees detailed overflowing inboxes, vacation-induced angst, and laptops as steady bedside companions.

While some of these reactions are my own, they are also symptomatic of a saturated academic labor market with a glut of highly specialized workers. An upshot of this hyper-competitive system is that job-seekers and those fortunate enough to find full-time employment internalize the "publish or perish" mentality. Moreover, to bolster their tenure files, scholars must demonstrate their productivity in eminently quantifiable ways. "Evidence of scholarly impact" may include a scholar's citations, h-index, and journal acceptance rates—metrics not all that different from social media producers' benchmarks for "influence": blog reach, Twitter followers, and Instagram comments. Though such indexes have long helped to calibrate the career successes of academics, increasingly it is incumbent upon researchers to build these numbers "organically"—through their own social media activities. I feel compelled to keep my website updated, post my research on sites like Academia.edu, and above all, disseminate my publications with colleagues across a raft of social media platforms.

It is this last activity that leaves me the most strained. Like my interviewees who expressed anxiety about "putting themselves out there," I feel a sense of unease every time I share a professional accomplishment on Twitter or Facebook. But I'm surrounded by advice touting the importance of "brand[ing] oneself"[5] or, as the *Chronicle of Higher Education* framed it, "How to Curate Your Digital Identity as an Academic." And so, I find myself thinking strategically about my online persona. Concerns about "context collapse" are brought to the fore when colleagues, former professors, students, friends, and family members occupy the same socially mediated spaces.[6] I've chided those closest to me for uploading pictures that stray too far from my role as an academic, and I'm fully aware that my friends and family members have no interest in the calls for papers I routinely circulate.

These and other forms of personal branding are, of course, deeply entangled with social norms: studies have confirmed that men are more likely than women to boast their accomplishments, and that members of marginalized groups are less likely to engage in self-promotion.[7] These disparities have staggering cultural and economic implications for workers. In the academy, we see these effects with citation practices: there is a marked gender divide in self-citation rates (31 percent of men and just 21 percent of women cite their own work), with real consequences for how others perceive the researcher. According to sociologists studying gender and citation practices, "While self-promotion enhances competence assessments, it also reduces a woman's likability. These gendered perceptions of self-promotion likely influence perceptions of self-citation."[8]

Such socially encoded reactions take on an added layer of complexity for feminist scholars. Reflecting on her own work as a feminist activist, Alexandra Juhasz explains how she understood her blog as "public engagement in thinking out loud, honing a voice, self-naming, community-building, and stake-holding." Yet, a newer generation of feminist scholars understands this same social practice—academic blogging—as a form of personal "self-promotion" rather than collective politics.[9] I agree there is a gap: senior scholars never urged me to "promote my work," but I now find myself advising doctoral students to make sure they create and maintain websites, blog about their research, and even strategize about the titles of their article manuscripts: "short titles are better cited," I counsel.[10]

The institutional backdrop of this aspirational labor is the increasingly corporatized university system, which has embraced marketplace ideals in the face of dwindling public support. This shift in higher education assumes many guises: "cash cow" master's programs, incessant demands for accountability and metrics, the rise of celebrity professors, and what culture industries researcher Casey Brienza describes as a "neoliberal rhetoric . . . [that] recast[s] students as customers and tutors as service providers."[11]

Media scholar Jeff Pooley explores another manifestation of this market logic, namely the uptick in socially mediated academic publishing sites (Academia.edu and ResearchGate are two of the most popular) that represent a "parallel universe of academic microcelebrities" who engage in digital reputation-building practices. As such, Pooley contends, "the sociology of academic reputation—traditionally fixated on citations and mass-media visibility—should be updated to account for the 'demotic turn' in *scholarly* life."[12] His call rouses us to think carefully about the stakes of a system of knowledge production shaped by the mutual influence of corporatization and celebrification. It is in this vein that I close with a call for a second, parallel updating within digital media studies: academic research on cultural laborers that continues to put their experiences at the center—both *despite* and *because of* the persistence of market-based structures. We have more to learn from them than ever before—not just because of profound changes in social and economic life but also because they allow us to hold a mirror up to ourselves—as aspirants, as academics, and as creators of culture.

APPENDIX
Method and List of Interview Participants

Method

From fall 2013 through summer 2016, I conducted 55 in-depth interviews. The majority of my interviewees were female, and the average age was mid-twenties; roughly a quarter were still in college. The racial/ethnic composition of my sample roughly maps onto existing findings about the (lack of) diversity among professional bloggers (see Chapter 4). Although I did not specifically ask questions about participants' socio-economic statuses, class emerged as a sensitizing concept through discussions of technology access, education, and professionalization opportunities, among others. As such, I explore class through its intersectionality with gender, an acknowledgment of the "multidimensional," interacting subjectivities of those occupying marginalized positions.[1] Interviews were conducted in person (for participants in the region) or over the phone or Skype. Questions were developed to address participants' educational backgrounds and professional expertise; career interests, aspirations, and passions; online and offline interactions with other social media participants; processes and considerations of content creation, distribution, and promotion; self-presentation strategies; and reflections on monetization (advertising, sponsorships, affiliate links), among others.[2]

While I began to solicit interview participants by asking members of my own (traditional and digital) social networks to connect me with potential participants, I increasingly relied upon socially mediated networks such as LinkedIn, Instagram, and the blogs themselves to *scout* potential interviewees across categories. A snowball method of sampling was also used to grow my interview pool, and I was fortunate that participants graciously offered to connect me with others in their networks. A further word about recruitment seems necessary here given that I consider my participants foremost *cultural producers*. I certainly did not confront the same challenges related to access that are standard fare when trying to score interviews with corporate cultural producers (e.g., magazine editors, TV producers, advertising executives). Nor did I have to undergo a frustratingly rigorous vetting process by an organization's gatekeeping PR/media relations representative. Instead, my interviewees were incredibly generous with their time, combining careful insight with seemingly candid anecdotes and appraisals.

However, such expressions of sincerity do not belie the potential limitations of qualitative interviews. Let me be clear: I am not suggesting participants' accounts are inaccurate or dishonest in any way. Instead, I believe their self-descriptions are likely structured by what Katherine Sender described as the "pitch," whereby those inculcated in the advertising and marketing professions endeavor to portray themselves (or their organizations) in a favorable light; this orientation thus shapes the contours of the interview experience for both the researcher and the participant.[3] That some of my own interviewees exhibited self-conscious, pitch-like approaches was less a product of professional marketing or advertising training (though I do contend that these fields are over-represented among fashion bloggers) and more a symptom of their aspirational ranking. That is, as social actors seeking a career amidst an overinflated supply of potential laborers, these individuals may have framed their interactions with me in a particular way given the public nature of this project (i.e., a book). Put simply, the opportunity to be "interviewed for a book" could be read as another mode of "exposure" for career-hungry social media aspirants. Reflexivity entails an honest appraisal of the various, often intersecting, ways in which the researcher's subject position may impact the research process; underpinning this is the recognition that "knowledge cannot be separated from the knower."[4] As an interviewer, I often experienced uneasiness surrounding the implied narrative of book-interview-as-a-route-to-exposure, which perhaps stems from my own concern with being duplicitous when approaching potential interviewees. Moreover, it was difficult to elide the power dynamics implicated with my role as a *professor* interviewing numerous college *students* about their career aspirations and prospects. I occasionally found myself stepping into an advising capacity as I queried them about particular course assignments, curricular initiatives, and position requirements. I gleaned great insight from these discussions despite my admission that I could not "turn off" my role as an educator.

Nor could this orientation be "turned off" at the wide range of conferences I attended during the research process, including the Women Get Social "Bloggy Boot Camp"; the annual Digital Fashion Commerce summit; Philly Tech Week Fashion Blogger's event; and *Cosmopolitan's* "Fun, Fearless, Life" event. I also conducted participant-observation at less structured events, including fashion blogger–hosted promotions and New York Fashion Week. Although I was initially reticent to reveal my outsider status, I came to learn that my position was much less in the margins than I anticipated. Participants at NYFW, for instance, included professionals moonlighting as street-style photographers, and some blogger conference attendees were employed in wildly dissimilar fields. Moreover, many of these boundaries were seemingly erased as we shared Facebook "friend requests" and Twitter handles. While the degree of participant closeness has long posed a quandary for researchers—most especially anthropologists—the kinds of researcher-subject intimacy enabled (or perhaps incited) by digital technologies merit more careful consideration.

List of Interview Participants

Hunter Abrams
Crystal Anderson
Heather Armstrong
Danielle Audain
Daneen Baird
Lauren Bath
Olivia Brenman
Christina Brown
Tess Candell

Alice Chan
Sarah Chipps
Megan Collins
Jenn Coyle
Brittany Cozzens
Ian Michael Crumm
Erika Marie de Palol
Julia DiNardo
Ana Divinagracia
Gaby Dunn
Kristy Eléna
Sophie Elkus
Alana Garcia
Sarah Greene
Hélène Heath
Carly Heitlinger
Kat Henry
Julianne Higgins
Jessie Holeva
Sissi Johnson
Amber Katz
Yolanda Keil
Nishita Lulla
Chrisi Lydon
Rachel Lynch
Madeline McCallum
Jennifer Morgan
Siobhan Murphy
Tanya Pham
Marissa Pina
Hillary Puckett
Thomas Rankin
Ana Redmond

Kelly Reid
Emily Rhodes
Jennifer Sikic
Dom Smales
Kimberly Smith
Lauren Snyder
Maeve Stier
Caitlin Sweeney
Emily Ulrich
Jason Wagenheim
Rachel Whitehurst
Alissa Wilson
Deirdre Zahl

Notes

Chapter 1. Entrepreneurial Wishes and Career Dreams

1. Mattel, Barbie website.

2. Dwyer, "Briefcase in Hand."

3. Garber, "Barbie Leans In."

4. Roy, "New 'Entrepreneur Barbie.'"

5. Bentley University, "The Millennial Mind Goes to Work."

6. Tokumitsu, "In the Name of Love."

7. McRobbie, *Be Creative*, 3, 11.

8. Fantozzi, "Guess and Marc Jacobs."

9. D'Onfro, "Meet the Snapchat Stars."

10. Saul, "Instafamous."

11. Edward McQuarrie, Jessica Miller, and Barbara J. Phillips describe the growth of fashion bloggers through the lens of the megaphone effect, or "the fact that the web makes a mass audience potentially available to ordinary consumers." McQuarrie, Miller, and Phillips, "The Megaphone Effect," 136.

12. Veselinovic, "Bloggers Turning Social Savvy"; Farzan, "Meet the 22-Year-Old Blogger."

13. Gregg, "The Normalisation of Flexible Female Labor."

14. Fuchs, "Labor in Informational Capitalism"; Andrejevic, "Watching Television without Pity."

15. Terranova, "Free Labor," 33.

16. Burgess and Green, "The Entrepreneurial Vlogger," 90.

17. Herring, Kouper, Scheidt, and Wright, "Women and Children Last"; Shade, *Gender and Community in the Social Construction of the Internet*.

18. Garber, "The Digital (Gender) Divide."

19. Banet-Weiser and Arzumanova, "Creative Authorship," 164.

20. Ibid.

21. Jarrett, "The Relevance of 'Women's Work' "; Shade, *Gender and Community in the Social Construction of the Internet;* McRobbie, "Reflections on Feminism."

22. Neff, *Venture Labor;* Kuehn and Corrigan, "Hope Labor"; Neff et al., "Entrepreneurial Labor."

23. Kuehn and Corrigan, "Hope Labor," 21.

24. See, for example, Sennett, *The Culture of the New Capitalism;* Neff, *Venture Labor;* Ross, *No-Collar.*

25. Hearn, "Meat, Mask, Burden"; Marwick, *Status Update.*

26. Pooley, "Consuming Self."

27. Senft, *Camgirls,* 25; Marwick and boyd, "To See and Be Seen."

Chapter 2. The Aspirational Ethos

1. See Perlin, *Intern Nation;* Rodino-Colocino and Berberick, " 'You Kind of Have To' "; Corrigan, "Media and Cultural Industries Internships."

2. Haughney, "Condé Nast Faces Suit from Interns over Wages."

3. Buckley, "Sued over Pay, Condé Nast Ends Internship Program." *Glamour* intern Rosana Lai, quoted in the *New York Times,* spoke for future interns: "We're no longer going to have that foot in the door."

4. Baker, "Interns Go out of Vogue at Condé Nast."

5. As Brooke argues, "Even if a whistleblower's intentions are good, they can wind up stigmatized or perceived as a legal liability." Brooke, "Could Former Condé Nast Interns."

6. Conor, Gill, and Taylor, "Gender and Creative Labour," 10.

7. Infante, "Hipster Is Dead."

8. Ibid.

9. Bullas, "Blogging Statistics, Facts and Figures in 2012."

10. Grit & Glamour, "Fashion, Beauty & Lifestyle" Survey. October 29, 2013. http://www.gritandglamour.com/2013/10/29/fashion-beauty-lifestyle-blogger-survey-results/.

11. De Grazia, "Introduction," 3. Similarly, Sharon Zukin and Jennifer Smith Maguire argue that "since its emergence . . . consumption has been viewed as both amoral and gendered" ("Consumers and Consumption," 175).

12. De Grazia even critiques feminist scholarship for articulating the consumer sector as an "exploitative force to which women are more vulnerable than men

because of their subordinate social, economic, and cultural position." De Grazia, "Introduction," 7.

13. Zukin and Maguire, "Consumers and Consumption," 174. See also Slater, *Consumer Culture and Modernity.*

14. Zola, *The Ladies' Paradise.* Quoted in Segrave, *Shoplifting,* 23.

15. Marvin, *When Old Technologies;* McPherson, *Digital Youth.*

16. Segrave, *Shoplifting.*

17. Slater, *Consumer Culture and Modernity,* 57. See also Marchand, *Advertising the American Dream,* 66.

18. Veblen, *The Theory of the Leisure Class,* 72.

19. Ibid., 81.

20. Ibid., 83.

21. See Juliet Schor's "In Defense of Consumer Critique" for an outline of these debates, particularly between the Veblen school and Frankfurt school.

22. This includes book-length studies by William Leach, Ronald Marchand, Lizabeth Cohen, T. J. Jackson Lears, Gary Cross, and Joseph Turow.

23. Ewen, *Captains of Consciousness,* 25.

24. Marchand, *Advertising the American Dream,* 66.

25. Sandlin and Maudlin, "Consuming Pedagogies,"188.

26. Damon-Moore, *Magazines for the Millions,* 15.

27. Edward Bok is known as the first editor to "run editorial material through the advertisements traditionally segregated at the back of the magazine." Waller-Zuckerman, "Old Homes," 736.

28. Walker, *Shaping Our Mothers' Worlds,* 37.

29. Ibid., 64.

30. Not all scholars agree with this narrative about the exclusion of women from the public sphere. Mica Nava challenges certain assumptions of this feminist historiography about the invisibility of women on the street. She does, however, acknowledge the role of the department store in women's increasing freedom to travel through the city streets. Nava, "Modernity's Disavowal."

31. Rappaport, *Shopping for Pleasure,* 167.

32. Leach, *Land of Desire,* 137–38.

33. Ibid., 79. Similarly, Mica Nava explains that "modern" women were at the heart of these "taxonomies of signification . . . which conveyed symbolic meanings about their owners." Nava, "Modernity's Disavowal," 48.

34. American ads produced, between the 1920s and 1940s, ad copy and images focused on an idealized consumer, a "Mrs. Consumer" with "upper-class status and modern tastes." Marchand, *Advertising the American Dream*, 80.

35. Walker, *Shaping Our Mothers' Worlds*, 38. See also Marchand, *Advertising the American Dream*.

36. Sivulka, *Soap, Sex, and Cigarettes*.

37. See, for example, Wright, "Social Class."

38. For a useful discussion, see Featherstone, *Consumer Culture and Postmodernism*.

39. Bourdieu, *Distinction*, 47.

40. Contextualized with a vibrant global economy, aspirationalism has assumed a political valance. Focusing on post-colonial India, anthropologist William Mazzarella shows how appeals to aspirational consumerism draw upon a Western model that "equates the generality of consumer desire with the particular norms and forms of the nascent middle-class imaginary." Mazzarella, *Shoveling Smoke*, 101.

41. Federici, "Precarious Labor." See also Jarrett, "The Relevance of 'Women's Work.'"

42. Federici, "Precarious Labor."

43. Fortunati, *The Arcane of Reproduction*, 37–39.

44. Kathi Weeks, for instance, critiqued the campaign for "feminism's own idealization of waged work." Weeks, *The Problem with Work*, 12, 138–46.

45. Hardt and Negri, *Empire*, 108.

46. Federici, "Precarious Labor."

47. McRobbie, "Reflections on Feminism."

48. Jarrett, *Feminism, Labour and Digital Media*. For a discussion of the turn in affect studies, see Clough, *Affective Turn*, or Wissinger, "This Year's Model."

49. Jarrett, "'Women's Work,'" 26.

50. Hochschild, *The Managed Heart*, 7.

51. Ibid., 171.

52. Baig, "Women in the Workforce."

53. Covert, "The Gender Wage Gap Is a Chasm."

54. Sandberg and Scovell, *Lean In*, 8.

55. See Spigel, "Designing the Smart House."

56. Grey, "Between a Boss and a Hard Place."

57. Gill, "Cool, Creative and Egalitarian," 88.

58. Gregg, *Work's Intimacy*.

59. Gregg, *Work's Intimacy,* 54. The "second shift" comes from Hochschild and Machung, *The Second Shift.*

60. See Duffy, *Remake, Remodel;* Conor, Gill, and Taylor, "Gender and Creative Labour."

61. Duffy, *Remake, Remodel;* Scanlon, "Advertising Women"; Peiss, *Hope in a Jar.*

62. Duffy, *Remake, Remodel.*

63. Scanlon, "Advertising Women," 201.

64. Ibid., 121. See also Mayer's work on the early twentieth-century "telephone girl" phone operator. Mayer, "To Communicate Is Human."

65. Smith, "Scholar Speaks on Feminism."

66. Ibid.

67. Reed, "Be Somebody," 96.

68. In 2013, I consulted the executive team pages of leading magazine publishers in the United States—Condé Nast, Time, Hearst, and Meredith, which was later bought by Media General. The ratios of women to men were 2/7, 2/12, 1/14, and 0/5.

69. Alter, "8 Sad Truths about Women in Media."

70. Women's Media Center, "Status of Women," 7.

71. Byerly, *Global Report on the Status of Women in the News Media.*

72. Ibid., 107.

73. Hesmondhalgh and Baker, "Sex, Gender and Work Segregation," 25.

74. Ibid., 27–29. See also Duffy, *Remake, Remodel.*

75. See Friedman, "Why Do We Treat PR like a Pink Ghetto?"; Grose, "How Did I, a Woman, End Up in Women's Media?"; Pan, "Pink Collar."

76. Friedman, "Why Do We Treat PR like a Pink Ghetto?"

77. Levinson, "The Pink Ghetto of Social Media."

78. Ibid.

79. Perlin, *Intern Nation,* 27; See also Schwartz, "Opportunity Costs."

80. Schultz, "The Unpaid Intern Economy."

81. Rodino-Colocino and Berberick, "You Kind of Have To," 498.

82. Molla and Lightner, "Diversity in Tech." Apple (22%), Google (18%), Facebook (16%), and Microsoft (17%).

83. Peck, "The Stats on Women in Tech."

84. Marwick, *Status Update.*

85. Miller, "Technology's Man Problem."

86. Kaplan, "How Ellen Pao."

87. Pao, "Silicon Valley Sexism."

88. Chess and Shaw, "A Conspiracy of Fishes."

89. Harvey and Fisher, "Making a Name in Games," 375–76. Specifically, the authors note how many unpaid activities—"training in the range of software tools, largely solitary programming and design, self-promotion through social media, and entrance into numerous festivals and competitions in the hope of winning some recognition, awards, or legitimacy"—involved the immaterial or affective labor of those women who had the least amount of power.

90. Adkins, "Cultural Feminization," 669.

91. Negra and Tasker, "Introduction: Gender and Recessionary Culture," 7. See also Mayer, "To Communicate Is Human."

92. Nielsen Media Research, CommerceNet/Nielsen Media Research Survey. See also Morahan-Martin, "Gender Gap in Internet Use."

93. See Herring, "Gender and Power in Online Communication," for a discussion of these and other biases.

94. Turow, *Breaking Up America*, 60.

95. Jenkins, Ford, and Green, *Spreadable Media*, 29.

96. For a discussion, see Shade, *Gender and Community in the Social Construction of the Internet*.

97. Zobl, "About: The Global Grrrl Zine Network."

98. Gregg, "Feeling Ordinary"; Herring, Kouper, Scheidt, and Wright, "Women and Children Last"; Lopez, "The Radical Act of 'Mommy Blogging'"; Harris, *Future Girl*.

99. Herring, "Gender and Power in Online Communication."

100. Crain, "Financial Markets and Online Advertising."

101. In 2013, iVillage was folded into NBC's Today.com.

102. Herring, "Gender and Power in Online Communication." Similarly, Consalvo has argued that "women are an important demographic for marketers, and the Internet during this period has become more of a place for selling than for exploring or creating." Consalvo, "Selling the Internet to Women," 133. Feminist internet scholar Leslie Regan Shade, too, observed that "the internet is becoming domesticated." Shade, *Gender and Community in the Social Construction of the Internet*, 2.

103. Duffy, *Remake, Remodel*.

104. The article drew on data from the Pew Internet and American Life Project, which found that, among Web users ages twelve to seventeen, significantly more girls than boys blog (35 percent of girls as compared with 20 percent of boys) and create or work on their own Web pages (32 percent of girls as compared with 22 percent of

boys). See Rosenbloom, "Sorry Boys, This Is Our Domain"; Allen, "It's Arrived: The Feminisation of the Net"; Lee, "Why Women Rule the Internet."

105. According to the Pew report, "44% of online women use the site, compared with 16% of online men." Duggan and Brenner, "The Demographics of Social Media Users."

106. Dvorak, "Addicted to a Web Site."

107. Banet-Weiser and Arzumanova, "Creative Authorship."

108. See Mayer, *Below the Line.*

109. See Adkins, "Cultural Feminization"; Negra and Tasker, "Introduction: Gender and Recessionary Culture."

110. Banet-Weiser and Arzumanova, "Creative Authorship"; Luckman, "Etsy"; Nathanson, "Dressed for Economic Distress."

111. Banet-Weiser and Arzumanova, "Creative Authorship," 166.

Chapter 3. (Not) Just for the Fun of It

1. Korobka, "'Instagrammer' Is Now a Six-Figure Job."

2. See, for example, Andrejevic, "Watching Television without Pity"; Fuchs, "Labor in Informational Capitalism"; Kuehn, "'There's Got to Be a Review Democracy'"; van Dijck, *Culture of Connectivity.*

3. See Ritzer and Jungenson, "Production, Consumption, Prosumption"; Bruns, *Blogs, Wikipedia, Second Life, and Beyond.*

4. See, for example, Campbell, "It Takes an iVillage"; Duffy, "Empowerment through Endorsement?"; Kuehn and Corrigan, "Hope Labor."

5. Fuchs, "Labor in Informational Capitalism"; Scholz, *Digital Labor.*

6. Duffy, "Empowerment through Endorsement?"

7. Ibid.

8. See Postigo, "America Online Volunteers"; Brabham, "Myth of Amateur Crowds"; Murdock, "Political Economies."

9. Kuehn and Corrigan, "Hope Labor," 9. They define it as "un- or undercompensated work carried out in the present, often for experience or exposure, in the hope that future employment opportunities may follow."

10. Duffy, *Remake, Remodel*; Duffy, "The Romance of Work." See also Ouellette in Andrejevic et al., "Participations"; Jarrett, "'Women's Work.'"

11. See Duffy, *Remake, Remodel*; Marwick, *Status Update*; Luvaas, "Indonesian Fashion Blogs"; Rocamora, "Hypertextuality and Remediation in the Fashion Media."

12. Sozzani, "Editor's Blog."

13. Menkes, "Circus of Fashion."

14. Keen, *The Cult of the Amateur.*

15. Bobila, "Susie Bubble and Bryanboy Respond."

16. Ibid.

17. Rocamora, "Hypertextuality and Remediation in the Fashion Media."

18. Neff, *Venture Labor,* 57. Neff uses this typology to describe Silicon Alley web-publishers-turned-entrepreneurs whose careers "were not calculated or rational moves. Rather they were attempts at being creative." Neff, *Venture Labor,* 58.

19. Jackson, "After Recession"; Meece, "On to Plan B."

20. Pratt, "Creative Cities."

21. Neff, *Venture Labor.*

22. Wittel, "Toward a Network Sociality."

23. In the new economy, as Angela McRobbie and others make clear, "the new relation between art and economics marks a break with past anti-commercial notions of being creative." The business side, she explains, now has a central place in artistic identity. McRobbie, "Clubs to Companies," 520–21.

24. Tuchman, *Making News.*

25. Lewine, "Outside Voices: The Visual Web Is Changing Everything."

26. Gill, "Life Is a Pitch."

27. Duffy and Hund, " 'Having It All' on Social Media."

28. Hearn, "Meat, Mask, Burden," 198. See also Banet-Weiser, *Authentic.*

29. Pooley, "From Flappers to Facebook."

30. Ibid, 79.

31. Peters, *Brand You 50,* emphasis added.

32. boyd, *Taken Out of Context,* 49. See also Marwick and boyd, "I Tweet Honestly," 122; Vitak, "The Impact of Context Collapse and Privacy."

33. Van Dijck explains that users challenge the identity affordances of sites by deliberately presenting "multiple personas across platforms . . . [as] a powerful strategy for users to 'perform' their identity." Van Dijck, " 'You Have One Identity.' " See also Cirucci, *The Structured Self.*

34. Drawing on notions of the "professional cool," Melissa Gregg contends that today's cultural workers are "increasingly charged with spreading the organization's message in web-based forms" as part of the performance of affability. Gregg, *Work's Intimacy,* 131.

35. Baym, "Connect with Your Audience!" 16.

36. Duffy, *Remake, Remodel*.

37. McQuarrie, Miller, and Phillips, "The Megaphone Effect."

38. Ziv, *Fashion 2.0*.

39. Chia, "Welcome to Me-Mart"; Gaudeul and Peroni, "Reciprocal Attention."

40. Duffy, "Link Love and Comment Karma."

41. Kuehn, " 'There's Got to Be a Review Democracy,' " 8.

42. IFB, "The Comment Challenge."

43. Personal email communication.

44. Van Dijck, *Culture of Connectivity*, 13.

45. Wissinger, *This Year's Model*; Cronin, "Advertising"; Nixon and Crewe, "Pleasure at Work?"; Turner, "Mass Production of Celebrity 'Celetoids' "; Marwick, "Silicon Valley"; Neff, *Venture Labor*.

46. McRobbie, "Clubs to Companies," 521.

47. Gill and Pratt, "In the Social Factory?"; Gregg, "On Friday Night Drinks."

48. Neff et al., "Entrepreneurial Labor," 319.

49. Menkes, "The Circus."

50. Garcia, "Life: The Diary of a D-List Blogger at NYFW."

51. Banet-Weiser and Arzumanova, "Creative Authorship," 168.

52. Wissinger explains "the look" through notions of affect; in the case of models, "the look" has an"ineffable quality." Wissinger, *This Year's Model*, 10.

53. Nathanson, "Dressed for Economic Distress," 147–48.

54. Wissinger, *This Year's Model*, 3.

55. Addressing the potential implications of the rise of ultra-thin fashion bloggers, Harriet Williamson argued that young women may find these images especially distressing because the bloggers, in the words of an eating disorder sufferer she interviewed, "are more like real people, with social lives and drama and success stories." Williamson, "Are Ultra-Thin Fashion Bloggers."

56. Nathanson, "Dressed for Economic Distress," 145.

57. Nathanson, "Meet the Slashies."

58. Harris, *Future Girl*, 32.

59. Under this meritocratic framing, the failure to realize a return on one's investment can be explained away as an individual's lack of talent or hard work, or by simply not playing the hope labor game smartly enough or for long enough. Kuehn and Corrigan, "Hope Labor," 18.

60. Burgess and Green, "The Entrepreneurial Vlogger."

61. See, for example, du Gay, *Production of Culture;* Hesmondhalgh and Baker, *Creative Labour.* More recently, in an in-depth study of Etsy sellers and DIY bloggers, Tara Liss-Mariño noted a trade-off between success and pleasure. She thus concludes that "the more successful a maker becomes and the bigger her business grows, the farther away she moves from personally experiencing *jouissance.*" Liss-Mariño, "Sell (It) Yourself."

Chapter 4. Branding the Authentic Self

1. McCall, " 'Lucky.' "

2. Chen, "Editor's Letter: Who's That Girl?" 16.

3. Gottlieb and Maleri, "New Girls," 69–75.

4. Jacob, "Stop the Presses!"

5. Banet-Weiser, *Authentic.*

6. Frank, *Conquest of Cool;* Pooley, "The Consuming Self"; Duffy, "Manufacturing Authenticity."

7. Here I refer to Dove's highly controversial 2015 "Love Your Curls" campaign, which focuses on the discourse of "taming" curly hair. See, for example, Duffy, "Empowerment through Endorsement?"; Duffy, "The New 'Real Women' of Advertising"; Banet-Weiser, *Authentic.*

8. Sieghart, "Real Women, Real Beauty." Of course, there were some early critics of the campaign, especially when the news broke that even the "real women" ads were digitally retouched.

9. Hoffman, "Stop Calling Us 'Real Women.' "

10. See, for instance, Banet-Weiser, *Authentic;* Duffy, "Empowerment through Endorsement?"

11. Goldman, Heath, and Smith, "Commodity Feminism."

12. Banet-Weiser, *Authentic,* 17. See also Duffy, "Empowerment through Endorsement?"; Murray, "Branding 'Real' Social Change."

13. See Marwick, *Status Update;* Duffy, "Amateur, Autonomous, Collaborative"; Banet-Weiser, *Authentic.*

14. Carnoy, "Why Millennial Women Crave."

15. Duffy, *Remake, Remodel;* Rocamora, "Hypertextuality and Remediation in the Fashion Media."

16. Kay, "The Fashion Blog Stars."

17. Murray, "Fashion Week."

18. Bryant, "Plus Size Designer Slams."

19. Duffy and Hund, " 'Having It All' on Social Media."

20. Pham, " 'Susie Bubble' "; Luvaas, "Indonesian Fashion Blogs."

21. Pham, " 'Susie Bubble,' " 261.

22. Luvaas, *Street Style.*

23. See Grindstaff, *The Money Shot;* Skeggs, "The Moral Economy of Person Production"; Sender, *The Makeover.* Skeggs's study of British reality "transformation" series also highlights the salience of participants' social positioning: working-class women are among the most frequently featured makeover subjects, and the transformation narrative is typically structured through class relations, such as when one group is depicted as uncouth. Meanwhile, Sender suggests that "ordinariness" is positioned somewhat differently in the context of U.S. makeover shows; class difference, she explains, "is less obviously polarized and is replaced by the fantasy of the American Dream."

24. Grindstaff, *The Money Shot,* 72–73.

25. Genz, "My Job Is Me," 3.

26. Ibid.

27. Grit & Glamour, "Photography for the Amateur."

28. Wissinger, "Modelling a Way of Life." Neff refers to "compulsory networking" (Neff, *Venture Labor*), and Gregg and Gill and Pratt refer to "compulsory sociality" (Gregg, "On Friday Night Drinks"; Gill and Pratt, "In the Social Factory?").

29. Sherman, "The Unexpected Costs."

30. Wittel, "Toward a Network Sociality."

31. Givhan, "The Golden Era of Fashion Blogging Is Over."

32. See Chittenden, "Digital Dressing Up"; Marwick, *Status Update;* Rocamora, "Hypertextuality and Remediation in the Fashion Media."

33. Nathanson, "Dressed for Economic Distress," 147, emphasis added.

34. Cho, *Blog, Inc.,* 147.

35. Illouz, *Cold Intimacies.* See also Pooley, "The Consuming Self."

36. Illouz, *Cold Intimacies,* 37.

37. Harris, *Future Girl;* Banet-Weiser, *Authentic;* Genz, "My Job Is Me."

38. Harris, *Future Girl,* 125.

39. Banet-Weiser, *Authentic;* Banet-Weiser and Arzumanova, "Creative Authorship."

40. See, for instance, Moss-Racusin and Rudman, "Disruptions in Women's Self-Promotion"; Scharff, "Blowing Your Own Trumpet."

41. Moss-Racusin and Rudman, "Disruptions in Women's Self-Promotion," 187.

42. Scharff, "Blowing Your Own Trumpet," 109.

43. Phillips, "This Is Why We Can't Have Nice Things."

44. Jane, "Your a Ugly, Whorish, Slut."

45. Discko, "The Harsh Realities of Being a Woman."

46. Lieber, "Inside the Internet's Craziest Destination for Blogger Hate."

47. Senft, *Camgirls;* Marwick, *Status Update.*

48. Lewis, "How to Make It as a Fashion Blogger."

49. Banet-Weiser, *Authentic;* Duffy, "Empowerment through Endorsement?"; Grindstaff, *The Money Shot;* Sender, *The Makeover;* Turner, "Mass Production of Celebrity 'Celetoids.'"

50. Turner uses the term "demotic turn" to suggest that the growing visibility of "ordinary people" in media should not be understood as fundamentally *democratic.* Turner, "Mass Production of Celebrity 'Celetoids,'" 155.

51. See ibid.; Grazian, *Blue Chicago;* Pooley, "The Consuming Self"; Marwick, *Status Update.*

52. McQuarrie, Miller, and Phillips, "The Megaphone Effect," 137.

53. Abidin, "Communicative Intimacies."

Chapter 5. "And Now, a Word from Our Sponsor"

1. I admittedly rewatched the episode while writing this book to confirm the details and was rather surprised at the emphasis on "real people."

2. Holmes, "How Style Bloggers Earn Sales Commissions One Click at a Time."

3. Strugatz, "The Blonde Salad at Harvard." According to reports, the students offered key insights as Ferragni sought to transition her brand to the luxury marketplace. The case study was later published as Keinan, Maslauskaite, Crener, and Dessain, "*The Blonde Salad.*"

4. Veselinovic, "Cash a la Mode."

5. Sabra, "The 6 Marketing Principles Every Fashion Blogger Needs in 2015."

6. I introduce this term in Duffy, "The Romance of Work."

7. Deuze, *Media Work,* 126.

8. Ibid., 130.

9. Duffy, *Remake, Remodel;* Turow, *Breaking Up America;* Serazio, *Your Ad Here;* Zwick, Bonsu, and Darmody, "Putting Consumers to Work."

10. Serazio, *Your Ad Here,* 3. See also Aronczyk and Powers, "Blowing Up the Brand"; Einstein, *Black Ops Advertising;* Serazio and Duffy, "Social Media Marketing."

11. Serazio, *Your Ad Here,* 93–100.

12. See also Duffy, *Remake Remodel.*

13. Braithwaite, *Women's Magazines,* 33. This seemingly made it possible for readers to feel a familiar connection with magazine editors whom they may never meet. An editorial excerpt from a 1919 edition of the British women's magazine *Peg's Paper* reveals just how conversational that tone had become: "It is going to be your weekly pal, girls. My name is Peg, and my one aim in life is to give you a really cheery paper like nothing you've ever read before. Not so very long ago I was a mill girl too. Because I've been a worker like you, I know what girls like, and I'm going to give you a paper to enjoy. Look on me as a friend and helper. I will try to advise you on any problem."

14. Manko, " 'Now You Are in Business for Yourself,' " 10.

15. Peiss, *Hope in a Jar,* 98.

16. Peiss, " 'Vital Industry' and 'Women's Ventures,' " 219.

17. Haymes, "Advertisers Model Campaigns."

18. Frank, *Conquest of Cool,* 11.

19. Campbell, "It Takes an iVillage," 494.

20. Ibid., 500.

21. Schaefer, "How Bloggers Make Money on Instagram." Although Technorati's 2013 report noted only 10 percent of brands' digital spending goes to social media, 65 percent of brands participate in influencer-based marketing. Technorati Media, *Technorati Media: 2013 Digital Influence Report,* 4, 11.

22. Technorati Media, *Technorati Media: 2013 Digital Influence Report,* 13.

23. Swant, "Twitter Says Users."

24. Ahalogy, Ahalogy website.

25. Gleam Futures, "Tanya Burr."

26. Marikar, "Turning 'Likes' into a Career."

27. Mari, "The Click Clique."

28. Schaefer, "How Bloggers Make Money on Instagram."

29. Holmes, "How Style Bloggers Earn Sales Commissions." Of course, the particular gauges of authority continue to evolve; according to the most recently available "digital influence report" published in 2013, measures of audience index, Twitter followers, Facebook friends, and blog views trumped one's number of LinkedIn connections and Klout score.

30. Wicker, "You Need to Know This about Your Favorite Fashion Blogger."

31. Clark, "The Bot Bubble"; Perlroth, "Researchers Call Out Twitter Celebrities."

32. Lieber, "The Dirty Business of Buying Instagram Followers."

33. Alice Marwick, who explores the rise of status-seeking in the context of Web 2.0 discourses and practices, contends that ethos of self-branding "would be impossible without the affordable means of information distribution that the internet provides, is intrinsically linked to the features of social media technologies that make self-promotion of a wide scale possible." Marwick, *Status Update*, 166.

34. Luvaas, *Street Style*, 221.

35. Phelan, "How to Brand Yourself in Fashion."

36. Noricks, "How a Personal Brand Pyramid Can Help Define Your Blog's Direction."

37. Aronowitz, "The Knowledge Factory."

38. Rose, *Governing the Soul*, 161.

39. La Ferla, "Who Am I Wearing?"

40. Duffy, "The Romance of Work."

41. VanderBeek, "Why Instagram Captions Matter."

42. Gibson, "The 14 Best Instagram Campaigns of 2014."

43. Lazauskas, "The Anatomy of a Killer Content Marketing Strategy."

44. Edelman Digital, "Friday Five: How Fashion (and Other) Brands Can Leverage Instagram."

45. Serazio and Duffy, "Social Media Marketing."

46. Marikar, "Sundance Courts a New Celebrity Crowd."

47. Gandy, "Information in Health."

48. Sherman, "Desperate Measures?"

49. Luvaas, *Street Style,* 223.

50. Pathak, "Confessions."

51. Jarrett, *Feminism, Labour, and Digital Media.*

52. Cohen, "Cultural Work as a Site of Struggle," 147.

53. Becker, "Can Full-Time Bloggers Live Off of Rainbows and Hugs?"

54. Email communication.

55. Banet-Weiser, *Authentic,* 89.

56. DeMeré, "The Problem with Influencer Marketing."

57. Ibid.

58. Jarrett, *Feminism, Labour, and Digital Media*, 4.

59. Murray and Ouellette, *Reality TV,* 8. See also Duffy, "Empowerment through Endorsement?"

60. Duffy and Hund, "'Having It All' on Social Media."

61. Chayka, "Instagram's Creepy New Ads."

Chapter 6. The "Instagram Filter"

1. Duffy and Hund, "'Having It All' on Social Media."

2. Blair, "'You're Only as Good as Your Last Job.'" See also Ross, *Nice Work If You Can Get It*; Neff, Wissinger, and Zukin, "Entrepreneurial Labor among Cultural Producers."

3. MBO Partners, *The State of Independence in America*, 3.

4. Leighton and Brown, *Future Working*.

5. Zaino, "The Independent Work Boom."

6. Horowitz, "The Freelance Surge Is the Industrial Revolution of Our Time."

7. Hesmondhalgh and Baker, *Creative Labour*. The authors cite interviews with freelance magazine producers who confessed to "chasing up things that you should be paid for" and approaching people for work meaning "you are constantly living sort of on the edge." See also Nicole Cohen's work on freelancers.

8. Beck, *Brave New World*.

9. McRobbie, "Clubs to Companies," 519.

10. Neff, *Venture Labor*; Ross, *Nice Work*; McRobbie, *Be Creative*.

11. Armstrong, "Looking Upward and Ahead."

12. Huntemann, "Introduction: Digital Labor behind the Screen."

13. Kerr and Kelleher, "The Recruitment of Passion and Community," 180.

14. Ellison, Heino, and Gibbs, "Managing Impressions Online."

15. Ibid., 425, 432.

16. Marwick, *Status Update*, 195.

17. Cisneros, "Instagram: Socality Barbie."

18. Wissinger, *This Year's Model*, 163.

19. Ibid.

20. Gregg, "The Normalisation of Flexible Female Labour," 290.

21. Ibid.

22. Spigel, "Designing the Smart House," 415.

23. Ibid., 416. See also McAllister et al., "Fetishizing Flo."

24. Gregg, *Work's Intimacy*.

25. See Halpern and Humphreys for a discussion of "aura" among digital filter apps.

26. Like Perrons, I agree that it's important to clarify that these "developments have not happened because of new technologies but rather because of the ways in which technological developments occur within a capitalist and increasingly global economy." Perrons, "The New Economy and the Work-Life Balance," 72.

27. See Gregg, "The Normalisation of Flexible Female Labour."

28. Cranfeld School of Management and Working Families, *Flexible Working and Performance.*

29. Perrons, "The New Economy and the Work-Life Balance," 69.

30. Thompson, Jones-Evans, and Kwong, "Women and Home-Based Entrepreneurship," 228.

31. As Gregg argues, "Few policy-makers, let alone feminists, currently seem interested in interrogating the *requirement* for women's flexible workplace arrangements *in particular,* instead taking it as given that women will retain the historically and culturally ascribed role of carer—if not by choice, then by default." "Normalisation of Flexible Female Labour," 286.

32. Lien, "Why Are Women Leaving."

33. Grey, "Between a Boss and a Hard Place."

34. Ross, *No-Collar,* 4.

35. Dunn, "The Sad Economics."

36. Neff, *Venture Labor.* See also Gill, "Life Is a Pitch."

37. Liss-Mariño, "Sell (It) Yourself," 206.

38. Harris, *Future Girl,* 39.

39. Conor, Gill, and Taylor, "Gender and Creative Labour," 5. See also McRobbie, "Clubs to Companies"; Deuze, *Media Work.*

40. Huntemann, "Introduction: Digital Labor behind the Screen," 158–59.

41. Duffy and Hund, "'Having It All' on Social Media."

Chapter 7. Aspirational Labor's (In)Visibility

1. McClusky, "Teen Instagram Star."

2. Goffman, *Gender Advertisements.*

3. O'Neill, Instagram post.

4. O'Neill, "Why I Really Am Quitting."

5. McCluskey, "The 30 Most Influential People."

6. Dunn, "Get Rich or Die Vlogging."

7. Gutelle, "Are the Economics of Internet Fame Really So Sad?"

8. Berlant, *The Female Complaint.*

9. Illouz, *Cold Intimacies.*

10. Duff, "The Gap between Us and Our Online Selves."

11. Ross, *Nice Work If You Can Get It,* 9–10.

12. Conor, Gill, and Taylor, "Gender and Creative Labour"; Hesmondhalgh and Baker, *Creative Labour.*

13. Nixon and Crewe, "Pleasure at Work?"; Mayer, *Below the Line.*

14. Cannon, "Yahoo Admits Workforce."

15. Weissman, "Entrepreneurship: The Ultimate White Privilege?" She cites research from the National Bureau of Economic Research, which found family money is a much better predictor of venture success than any inherent "entrepreneurship gene" for risk-taking.

16. Hochschild, *The Managed Heart*; Baym, "Connect with Your Audience!"

17. Duffy, "The Romance of Work"; Jarrett, " 'Women's Work.' "

18. Peiss, *Hope in a Jar*; Campbell, "It Takes an iVillage."

19. Nathanson, "Dressed for Economic Distress," 145.

20. Adkins, "Cultural Feminization."

21. McRobbie, *Be Creative*, 13.

22. Conor, Gill, and Taylor, "Gender and Creative Labour," 2.

23. Neff, *Venture Labor.*

24. Jobs, "Find What You Love."

Epilogue

1. Lazarsfeld, "Remarks on Administrative and Critical."

2. Gill, "Academics, Cultural Workers," 12–13. See also Banet-Weiser, "Rate Your Knowledge"; Brienza, "Degrees of (Self-)Exploitation."

3. This is perhaps overstated as debates about "academic freedom" have been thrust into the media spotlight of late.

4. Gill, "Academics, Cultural Workers."

5. *Inside Higher Ed* published "Branding Yourself Not as Painful as You Think."

6. Marwick and boyd, "I Tweet Honestly."

7. King, Correll, Jacquet, Bergstrom, and West, "Men Set Their Own Cites High."

8. Ibid.

9. Banet-Weiser and Juhasz, "Feminist Labor in Media Studies/Communication."

10. Letchford, Moat, and Preis, "Advantage of Short."

11. Banet-Weiser, "Rate Your Knowledge"; Brienza, "Degrees of (Self-)Exploitation."

12. Pooley, "Open Media Scholarship."

Appendix

1. Crenshaw, "Mapping the Margins."

2. These interviews were semi-structured, and I encouraged participants to move around to various topics of conversation and reflection rather than meticulously following the script. Interview sessions ranged from fewer than thirty minutes to several hours, and all participants granted me permission to tape-record our conversations to facilitate interview transcription. Participants had the option of using their real name or a pseudonym.

3. Sender, *Business, Not Politics.*

4. Steedman, "On the Relations between Seeing, Interpreting and Knowing."

Bibliography

Abidin, Crystal. "Communicative Intimacies: Influencers and Perceived Interconnectedness." *Ada: A Journal of Gender, New Media, and Technology* 8 (2015). http://adanewmedia.org/2015/11/issue8-abidin/.

Adkins, Lisa. "Cultural Feminization: 'Money, Sex and Power' for Women." *Signs* 26, no. 3 (2001): 669–95.

Ahalogy. Ahalogy website, n.d., accessed February 22, 2016. http://caleblummer-40sa.squarespace.com/publishers.

Allen, Katie. "It's Arrived: The Feminisation of the Net." *Guardian,* August 23, 2007, accessed February 21, 2016. http://www.theguardian.com/media/2007/aug/23/digitalmedia.radio.

Allen, Kim. " 'Blair's Children': Young Women as 'Aspirational Subjects' in the Psychic Landscape of Class." *Sociological Review* 62, no. 4 (2013): 760–79.

Alter, Charlotte. "8 Sad Truths about Women in Media." *Time,* June 5, 2015, accessed February 16, 2016. http://time.com/3908138/women-in-media-sad-truths-report.

Andrejevic, Mark. "Watching Television without Pity: The Productivity of Online Fans." *Television & New Media* 9, no. 1 (2008): 24–46.

Andrejevic, Mark, John Banks, John Edward, Edward Campbell, Nick Couldry, Adam Fish, Alison Hearn, and Laurie Ouellette. "Participations: Dialogues on the Participatory Promise of Contemporary Culture and Politics: Labor." *International Journal of Communication* 8 (2014): 1089–1106.

Armstrong, Heather B. "Looking Upward and Ahead." *Dooce,* April 23, 2015, accessed February 16, 2016. http://dooce.com/2015/04/23/looking-upward-and-ahead.

Aronczyk, Melissa, and Devon Powers, eds. *Blowing Up the Brand: Critical Perspectives on Promotional Culture,* in Popular Culture and Everyday Life series, Vol. 21. New York: Peter Lang, 2010.

Aronowitz, Stanley. *The Knowledge Factory: Dismantling the Corporate University and Creating True Higher Learning.* Boston: Beacon Press, 2000.

Arvidsson, Adam. "Brands: A Critical Perspective." *Journal of Consumer Culture* 5, no. 2 (2005): 235–58.

Baig, Mehroz. "Women in the Workforce: What Changes Have We Made?" *Huffington Post,* December 19, 2013, accessed February 16, 2016. http://www.huffingtonpost.com/mehroz-baig/women-in-the-workforce-wh_b_4462455.html.

Baker, Katie J. M. "Interns Go out of Vogue at Condé Nast." *Newsweek,* October 24, 2013, accessed February 16, 2016. http://www.newsweek.com/conde-nast-would-rather-abandon-unpaid-labor-pay-interns-840.

Banet-Weiser, Sarah. *Authentic: The Politics of Ambivalence in a Brand Culture.* New York: New York University Press, 2012.

——. "Keynote Address: Media, Markets, Gender: Economies of Visibility in a Neoliberal Moment." *Communication Review* 18, no. 1 (2015): 53–70.

——. "Rate Your Knowledge: The Branded University." In *The Routledge Companion to Advertising and Promotional Culture,* edited by Matthew P. McAllister and Emily West, 298–312. New York: Routledge, 2013.

Banet-Weiser, Sarah, and Inna Arzumanova. "Creative Authorship: Self-Actualizing Individuals and the Self-Brand." In *Media Authorship,* edited by Cynthia Chris and David A. Gerstner, 163–69. New York: Routledge, 2013.

Banet-Weiser, Sarah, and Alexandra Juhasz. "Feminist Labor in Media Studies/Communication: Is Self-Branding Feminist Practice?" *International Journal of Communication* 5 (2011): 1768–75.

Banks, John, and Sal Humphreys. "The Labour of User Co-Creators: Emergent Social Network Markets?" *Convergence* 14, no. 4 (2008): 401–18.

Banks, Mark, and Katie Milestone. "Individualization, Gender and Cultural Work." *Gender, Work & Organization* 18, no. 1 (2011): 73–89.

Baym, Nancy K. "Connect with Your Audience!: The Relational Labor of Connection." *Communication Review* 18, no. 1 (2015): 14–22.

Beck, Ulrich. *The Brave New World of Work.* Cambridge: Polity Press, 2000.

Becker, Holly. "Can Full-Time Bloggers Live Off of Rainbows and Hugs?" *Decor 8,* July 18, 2014, accessed February 21, 2016. http://decor8blog. com/2014/07/18/can-full-time-bloggers-live-off-of-rainbows-hugs.

Bentley University. "The Millennial Mind Goes to Work: How Millennial Preferences Will Shape the Future of the Modern Workplace." November 11, 2014, accessed December 3, 2014. http://www.bentley.edu/ newsroom/latest-headlines/mind-of-millennial.

Berlant, Lauren. *The Female Complaint: The Unfinished Business of Sentimentality in American Culture.* Durham, NC: Duke University Press, 2008.

Blair, Helen. "'You're Only as Good as Your Last Job': The Labour Process and Labour Market in the British Film Industry." *Work, Employment & Society* 15, no. 1 (2001): 149–69.

Bobila, Maria. "Susie Bubble and Bryanboy Respond to Vogue.com Criticism on Fashion Bloggers." *Fashionista,* September 26, 2016, accessed September 26, 2016. http://fashionista.com/2016/09/vogue-criticism-bryanboy-susie-bubble.

Bourdieu, Pierre. *Distinction: A Social Critique of the Judgement of Taste.* Cambridge, MA: Harvard University Press, 1984.

boyd, danah. "Taken Out of Context: American Teen Sociality in Networked Publics." PhD diss., University of California–Berkeley, School of Information. ProQuest, 2008.

Brabham, Daren C. "The Myth of Amateur Crowds: A Critical Discourse Analysis of Crowdsourcing Coverage." *Information, Communication & Society* 15, no. 3 (2012): 394–410.

Braitwaite, Brian. *Women's Magazines: The First 300 Years.* London: Peter Owen, 1994.

Brienza, Casey. "Degrees of (Self-)Exploitation: Learning to Labour in the Neoliberal University." *Journal of Historical Sociology* 29, no. 1 (2016): 92–111.

Brooke, Eliza. "Could Former Condé Nast Interns Jeopardize Their Careers by Filing a Payment Claim?" *Fashionista,* March 23, 2015, accessed February 17, 2016. http://fashionista.com/2015/03/conde-nast-interns-payment.

Brown, Caitlin. "Viewpoint: Amateur Fashionistas Blog Their Way to the Top." *Centretown News Online,* March 25, 2011, accessed January 1, 2013. http://centretownnesonline.ca/index.php?option=com_content&task=view&id=2272&Itemid=1.

Bruns, Axel. *Blogs, Wikipedia, Second Life, and Beyond: From Production to Produsage.* New York: Peter Lang, 2008.

Bryant, Miranda. "Plus-Size Designer Slams Lack of Diversity in the Fashion Industry, Insisting It 'Shouldn't Be a Headline' When Curvier Models like Size 14 Ashley Graham Land Major Campaigns." *Daily Mail,* March 7, 2016, accessed April 3, 2016. http://www.dailymail.co.uk/femail/article-3476658/Plus-size-designer-slams-lack-diversity-fashion-industry-insisting-shouldn-t-headline-curvier-models-like-size-14-Ashley-Graham-land-major-campaigns.html.

Bucher, Taina. "Want to Be on the Top?: Algorithmic Power and the Threat of Invisibility on Facebook." *New Media & Society* 14, no. 7 (2012): 1164–80.

Buckley, Cara. "Sued Over Pay, Condé Nast Ends Internship Program." *New York Times,* October 23, 2013, accessed February 17, 2016. http://www.nytimes.com/2013/10/24/business/media/sued-over-pay-conde-nast-ends-internship-program.html.

Bullas, Jeff. "Blogging Statistics, Facts and Figures in 2012." August 2, 2012, accessed April 3, 2014. http://www.jeffbullas.com/2012/08/02/blogging-statistics-facts-and-figures-in-2012-infographic/.

Burgess, Jean E., and Joshua B. Green. "The Entrepreneurial Vlogger: Participatory Culture beyond the Professional-Amateur Divide." In *The YouTube Reader,* edited by Pelle Snickars and Patrick Vonderau, 89–107. Stockholm: National Library of Sweden/Wallflower Press, 2009.

Byerly, Carolyn M. *Global Report on the Status of Women in the News Media.* Washington, DC: International Women's Media Foundation, 2011. http://www.iwmf.org/wp-content/uploads/2013/09/IWMF-Global-Report-Summary.pdf.

Caldwell, John Thornton. *Production Culture: Industrial Reflexivity and Critical Practice in Film and Television.* Durham, NC: Duke University Press, 2008.

Campbell, John Edward. "It Takes an iVillage: Gender, Labor, and Community in the Age of Television-Internet Convergence." *International Journal of Communication* 5 (2011): 492–510.

Cannon, Mike. "Yahoo Admits Workforce Is Mostly White Males: Where's the Diversity?" *Tech Times*, June 19, 2014. http://www.techtimes.com/articles/8770/20140619/yahoo-admits-workforce-is-mostly-white-males-wheres-the-diversity.htm.

Carnoy, Juliet. "Why Millennial Women Crave Authenticity." *The Huffington Post*, December 18, 2015, accessed February 4, 2016. http://www.huffingtonpost.com/juliet-carnoy/why-millennial-women-crav_b_8832614.html.

Chayka, Kyle. "Instagram's Creepy New Ads Look like Posts from Your Friends." *Atlantic*, September 22, 2016, accessed September 26, 2016. http://www.theatlantic.com/technology/archive/2016/09/the-uncanny-valley-of-instagram-ads/501077/.

Chen, Adrian. "The Laborers Who Keep Dick Pics and Beheadings out of Your Facebook Feed." *Wired*, October 23, 2014, accessed February 17, 2016. http://www.wired.com/2014/10/content-moderation.

Chen, Eva. "Editor's Letter: Who's That Girl?" *Lucky* (February 2015): 16.

Chen, Gina Masullo. "Don't Call Me That: A Techno-Feminist Critique of the Term Mommy Blogger." *Mass Communication and Society* 16, no. 4 (2013): 510–32.

Chess, Shira, and Adrienne Shaw. "A Conspiracy of Fishes, or, How We Learned to Stop Worrying about #GamerGate and Embrace Hegemonic Masculinity." *Journal of Broadcasting & Electronic Media* 59, no. 1 (2015): 208–20.

Chia, Aleena. "Welcome to Me-Mart: The Politics of User-Generated Content in Personal Blogs." *American Behavioral Scientist* 56, no. 4 (2012): 421–38.

Chittenden, Tara. "Digital Dressing Up: Modelling Female Teen Identity in the Discursive Spaces of the Fashion Blogosphere." *Journal of Youth Studies* 13, no. 4 (2010): 505–20.

Cho, Joy Deangdeelert. *Blog, Inc.: Blogging for Passion, Profit, and to Create Community.* San Francisco: Chronicle Books, 2012.

Cirucci, Angela M. "The Structured Self: Authenticity, Agency, and Anonymity in Social Networking Sites." PhD diss., Temple University, 2014.

Cisneros, Darby. "Instagram: Socality Barbie on Instagram." Instagram, November 4, 2015, accessed March 6, 2016. https://www.instagram.com/p/9rFl36HjIc/?hl=en.

Clark, Doug Block. "The Bot Bubble: How Click Farms Have Inflated Social Media Currency." New Republic, April 20, 2015, accessed February 17, 2016. https://newrepublic.com/article/121551/bot-bubble-click-farms-have-inflated-social-media-currency.

Clifford, Catherine. "Women Dominate Every Social Media Network—Except One." Entrepreneur, March 4, 2014, accessed February 21, 2016. http://www.entrepreneur.com/article/231970.

Clough, Patricia Ticineto. "Introduction." In The Affective Turn: Theorizing the Social, edited by Patricia Ticineto Clough and Jean Halley, 1–33. Durham, NC: Duke University Press, 2007.

Cohen, Nicole S. "Cultural Work as a Site of Struggle: Freelancers and Exploitation." tripleC: Communication, Capitalism & Critique 10, no. 2 (2012): 141–55.

———. Writers' Rights: Freelance Journalism in a Digital Age. Montreal, Canada: McGill–Queen's University Press, 2016.

Conor, Bridget, Rosalind Gill, and Stephanie Taylor. "Gender and Creative Labour." In Gender and Creative Labour, edited by Bridget Conor, Rosalind Gill, and Stephanie Taylor, 1–22. Hoboken, NJ: Wiley-Blackwell, 2015.

Consalvo, Mia. "Selling the Internet to Women: The Early Years." In Women and Everyday Uses of the Internet: Agency and Identity, edited by Mia Consalvo and Susanna Paasonen, 111–38. New York: Peter Lang, 2002.

Corrigan, Thomas. "Media and Cultural Industries Internships: A Thematic Review and Digital Labor Parallels." tripleC: Communication, Capitalism & Critique 13, no. 2 (2015): 336–50.

Covert, Bryce. "The Gender Wage Gap Is a Chasm for Women of Color, in One Chart." Think Progress, September 18, 2014, accessed March 23,

2016. https://thinkprogress.org/the-gender-wage-gap-is-a-chasm-for-women-of-color-in-one-chart-1e8824ee6707#.k2b9k94p8.

Crain, Matthew. "Financial Markets and Online Advertising: Reevaluating the Dotcom Investment Bubble." *Information, Communication & Society* 17, no. 3 (2014): 371–84.

Cranfeld School of Management and Working Families. *Flexible Working and Performance*. London: Working Families, 2008. http://www.som.cranfield.ac.uk/som/dinamic-content/media/WF-DA%20Flex%20Working%20Report.pdf.

Crenshaw, Kimberlé. "Mapping the Margins: Intersectionality, Identity Politics, and Violence against Women of Color." *Stanford Law Review* 43 (1991): 1241–99.

Cronin, A. M. "Regimes of Mediation: Advertising Practitioners as Cultural Intermediaries?" *Consumption Markets & Culture* 7, no. 4 (2004): 349–69.

Cross, Gary S. *An All-Consuming Century: Why Commercialism Won in Modern America*. New York: Columbia University Press, 2000.

Damon-Moore, Helen. *Magazines for the Millions: Gender and Commerce in the* Ladies' Home Journal *and the* Saturday Evening Post, *1880–1910*. Albany: State University of New York Press, 1994.

De Grazia, Victoria. "Introduction." In *The Sex of Things: Gender and Consumption in Historical Perspective,* edited by Victoria De Grazia and Ellen Furlough, 11–24. Berkeley: University of California Press, 1996.

DeMeré, Nichole Elizabeth. "The Problem with Influencer Marketing." *Medium,* February 26, 2016, accessed September 26, 2016. https://medium.com/@NikkiElizDemere/the-problem-with-influencer-marketing-dca36712ea33#.ynfoqp3gv.

Deuze, Mark. *Media Work*. Cambridge, UK: Polity, 2007.

Discko, Amber. "The Harsh Realities of Being a Woman on Social Media." *Teen Vogue,* March 8, 2016. http://www.teenvogue.com/story/female-online-harassment-femsplain.

D'Onfro, Jillian. "Meet the Snapchat Stars Who Quit Their Day Jobs and Now Make Eye-Popping Amounts of Money." *Business Insider*, April 1,

2016, accessed May 23, 2016. http://www.businessinsider.com/top-snapchat-stars-2016-3.

Duff, Michelle. "The Gap between Us and Our Online Selves." *Stuff,* September 25, 2016, accessed September 26, 2016. http://www.stuff.co.nz/life-style/life/84592726/the-gap-between-us-and-our-online-selves.

Duffy, Brooke Erin. "Amateur, Autonomous, Collaborative: Myths of Aspiring Female Cultural Producers in Web 2.0." *Critical Studies in Media Communication* 32, no. 1 (2015): 48–64.

———. "Empowerment through Endorsement?: Polysemic Meaning in Dove's User-Generated Advertising." *Communication, Culture & Critique* 3, no. 1 (2010): 26–43.

———. "Link Love and Comment Karma: Norms and Politics of Evaluation in the Fashion Blogosphere." In *Online Evaluation of Creativity and the Arts,* edited by Hiesun Cecilia Suhr, 41–59. New York: Routledge, 2014.

———. "Manufacturing Authenticity: The Rhetoric of 'Real' in Women's Magazines." *Communication Review* 16, no. 3 (2013): 132–54.

———. "The New 'Real Women' of Advertising: Subjects, Experts and Producers in the Interactive Era." In *The Routledge Companion to Advertising and Promotional Culture,* edited by M. McAllister and E. West, 223-36. New York: Routledge, 2013.

———. *Remake, Remodel: Women's Magazines in the Digital Age.* Champaign: University of Illinois Press, 2013.

———. "The Romance of Work: Gender and Aspirational Labour in the Digital Culture Industries." *International Journal of Cultural Studies* 19, no. 4 (2016): 441-57.

Duffy, Brooke Erin, and Emily Hund. "'Having It All' on Social Media: Entrepreneurial Femininity and Self-Branding among Fashion Bloggers." *Social Media + Society* 1, no. 2 (2015): 1–11.

Du Gay, Paul, ed. *Production of Culture/Cultures of Production.* London: Sage, 1997.

Dunn, Gaby. "Get Rich or Die Vlogging: The Sad Economics of Internet Fame." *Fusion,* December 15, 2014, accessed February 17, 2016. http://

fusion.net/story/244545/famous-and-broke-on-youtube-instagram-social-media.

———. "Making Split Ends Meet: The Hustle of Being a Beauty Vlogger." *Broadly*, February 1, 2016. https://broadly.vice.com/en_us/article/making-split-ends-meet-the-hustle-of-being-a-beauty-vlogger.

Duggan, Maeve, and Joanna Brenner. "The Demographics of Social Media Users—2012." Pew Internet & American Life Project, February 14, 2013, accessed September 4, 2015. http://www.pewinternet.org/Reports/2013/Social-media-users.aspx, accessed 6 March 2013.

Dvorak, Petula. "Addicted to a Web Site Called Pinterest: Digital Crack for Women." *Washington Post*, February 20, 2012, accessed February 21, 2016. http://www.washingtonpost.com/local/addicted-to-a-web-site-called-pinterest-digital-crack-for-women/2012/02/20/gIQAP3wAQR_story.html.

Dwyer, Liz. "Briefcase in Hand, Entrepreneur Barbie Wants to Help Girls Break the 'Plastic Ceiling.'" *Take Part*, June 19, 2014, accessed December 3, 2014. http://www.takepart.com/article/2014/06/19/entrepreneur-barbie-wants-help-girls-break-the-plastic-ceiling.

Edelman Digital. "Friday Five: How Fashion (and Other) Brands Can Leverage Instagram." *Edelman Digital*, August 17, 2012, accessed February 21, 2016. http://www.edelmandigital.com/2012/08/17/friday-five-fashion-brands-instagram.

Einstein, Mara. *Black Ops Advertising: Native Ads, Content Marketing and the Covert World of the Digital Sell*. New York: OR Books, 2016.

Ellison, Nicole, Rebecca Heino, and Jennifer Gibbs. "Managing Impressions Online: Self-Presentation Processes in the Online Dating Environment." *Journal of Computer-Mediated Communication* 11, no. 2 (2006): 415–41.

Ewen, Stuart. *Captains of Consciousness: Advertising and the Social Roots of Consumer Culture*. New York: Basic Books, 2001.

Fantozzi, Sienna. "Guess and Marc Jacobs Used Instagram to Cast Models, So It's Definitely Time to Build Up Those Selfie Portfolios." *Bustle*, October 3, 2014, accessed February 17, 2016. http://www.bustle.com/articles/42724-guess-and-marc-jacobs-used-instagram-to-cast-models-so-its-definitely-time-to-build-up.

Farzan, Antonia. "Meet the 22-Year-Old Blogger Who Gets Paid up to $15,000 for a Single Instagram Post." *Business Insider*, May 21, 2015, accessed May 21, 2015. http://www.businessinsider.com/fashion-blogger-who-gets-paid-15000-for-a-single-instagram-post-2015-5.

Featherstone, Michael. *Consumer Culture and Postmodernism*. 2nd edition. London: Sage, 2007.

Federici, Silvia. "Precarious Labor: A Feminist Viewpoint." Lecture at Bluestockings Radical Bookstore, New York, October 28, 2006, accessed February 17, 2016. https://inthemiddleofthewhirlwind.wordpress.com/precarious-labor-a-feminist-viewpoint/.

Fortunati, Leopoldina. *The Arcane of Reproduction: Housework, Prostitution, Labor and Capital*. New York: Autonomedia, 1995.

Frank, Thomas. *The Conquest of Cool: Business Culture, Counterculture, and the Rise of Hip Consumerism*. Chicago: University of Chicago Press, 1997.

Friedman, Ann. "Why Do We Treat PR like a Pink Ghetto?" *New York Magazine*, July 18, 2014, accessed February 17, 2016. http://nymag.com/thecut/2014/07/why-do-we-treat-pr-like-a-pink-ghetto.html.

Fuchs, Christian. "Labor in Informational Capitalism and on the Internet." *The Information Society* 26, no. 3 (2010): 179–96.

Gandy, Oscar H., Jr. "Information in Health: Subsidized News?" *Media, Culture & Society* 2, no. 2 (1980): 101–15.

Garber, Megan. "Barbie Leans In." *Atlantic*, June 18, 2014, accessed February 17, 2016. http://www.theatlantic.com/business/archive/2014/06/entrepreneur-barbie-is-ready-to-lean-in/373004.

——. "The Digital (Gender) Divide: Women Are More Likely Than Men to Have a Blog (and a Facebook Profile)." *Atlantic*, April 27, 2012, accessed May 12, 2014. http://www.theatlantic.com/technology/archive/2012/04/the-digital-gender-divide-women-are-more-likely-than-men-to-have-a-blog-and-a-facebook-profile/256466/.

Garcia, Alana. "Life: The Diary of a D-List Blogger at NYFW." *YUPNYC*, September 21, 2015, accessed February 21, 2016. http://www.yupnyc.com/2015/09/the-diary-of-d-list-blogger-at-nyfw.html.

Gaudeul, Alexia, and Chiara Peroni. "Reciprocal Attention and Norm of Reciprocity in Blogging Networks." *Economics Bulletin* 30, no. 3 (2010): 1–18. http://www.accessecon.com/Pubs/EB/2010/Volume30/EB-10-V30-I3-P205.pdf.

Genz, Stéphanie. "My Job Is Me: Postfeminist Celebrity Culture and the Gendering of Authenticity." *Feminist Media Studies* 15, no. 4 (2015): 545–61.

Gibson, Rebecca. "The 14 Best Instagram Campaigns of 2014." *Postano,* December 9, 2014, accessed February 21, 2016. http://www.postano.com/blog/the-14-best-instagram-campaigns-of-2014.

Gill, Rosalind. "Academics, Cultural Workers and Critical Labour Studies." *Journal of Cultural Economy* 7, no. 1 (2014): 12–30.

———. "Cool, Creative and Egalitarian?: Exploring Gender in Project-Based New Media Work in Europe." *Information, Communication & Society* 5, no. 1 (2002): 70–89.

———. "Life Is a Pitch: Managing the Self in New Media Work." In *Managing Media Work,* edited by Mark Deuze, 249–62. Los Angeles: Sage, 2010.

Gill, Rosalind, and Andy Pratt. "In the Social Factory?: Immaterial Labour, Precariousness and Cultural Work." *Theory, Culture & Society* 25, no. 7–8 (2008): 1–30.

Givhan, Robin. "Everyone's a Fashion Critic." *Harper's Bazaar,* August 9, 2007, accessed February 17, 2016. http://www.harpersbazaar.com/fashion/trends/a183/fashion-critic-givhan-0907.

———. "The Golden Era of Fashion Blogging Is Over." *New York Magazine,* April 21, 2014, accessed February 17, 2016. http://nymag.com/thecut/2014/04/golden-era-of-fashion-blogging-is-over.html.

Gleam Futures. "Tanya Burr." *Gleam Futures,* n.d., accessed February 21, 2016. http://www.gleamfutures.com/talent/tanya-burr.

Goffman, Erving. *Gender Advertisements.* London: Macmillan Education UK, 1976.

———. *The Presentation of Self in Everyday Life.* Harmondsworth, UK: Penguin, 1978.

Goldman, Robert, Deborah Heath, and Sharon L. Smith. "Commodity Feminism." *Critical Studies in Media Communication* 8, no. 3 (1991): 333–51.

Gottlieb, Jenna, and Maleri, Jayna. "New Girls." *Lucky Magazine,* February 2015, 69–75.

Gough-Yates, Anna. *Understanding Women's Magazines: Publishing, Markets and Readerships in Late-Twentieth Century Britain.* New York: Routledge, 2003.

Gray, Ann. "Enterprising Femininity: New Modes of Work and Subjectivity." *European Journal of Cultural Studies* 6, no. 4 (2003): 489–506.

Grazian, David. *Blue Chicago: The Search for Authenticity in Urban Blues Clubs.* Chicago: University of Chicago Press, 2003.

Gregg, Melissa. "Feeling Ordinary: Blogging as Conversational Scholarship." *Continuum: Journal of Media & Cultural Studies* 20, no. 2 (2006): 147–60.

———. "The Normalisation of Flexible Female Labour in the Information Economy." *Feminist Media Studies* 8, no. 3 (2008): 285–99.

———. "On Friday Night Drinks: Workplace Affects in the Age of the Cubicle." In *The Affect Theory Reader,* edited by Melissa Gregg and Gregory J. Seigworth, 250–68. Durham, NC: Duke University Press, 2010.

———. *Work's Intimacy.* New York: Polity, 2011.

Grey, Sarah. "Between a Boss and a Hard Place: Why More Women Are Freelancing." *Bitch Media,* August 2, 2016, accessed September 1, 2016. https://bitchmedia.org/article/between-boss-and-hard-place-why-more-women-are-freelancing.

Grindstaff, Laura. *The Money Shot: Trash, Class, and the Making of TV Talk Shows.* Chicago: University of Chicago Press, 2002.

Grit & Glamour. "Fashion, Beauty & Lifestyle Blogger Survey Results." October 29, 2013, accessed March 8, 2015. http://www.gritandglamour.com/2013/10/29/fashion-beauty-lifestyle-blogger-survey-results/.

———. "Photography for the Amateur, Stagefright-Afflicted Blogger." June 22, 2010, accessed January 7, 2013. http://www.gritandglamour.com/2010/06/22/photography-for-the-amateur-stagefright-afflicted-blogger/.

Grose, Jessica. "How Did I, a Woman, End Up in Women's Media?" *Slate,* March 19, 2014, accessed February 22, 2016. http://www.slate.com/

blogs/xx_factor/2014/03/19/journalism_s_pink_ghetto_a_resident_speaks_out.html.

Gutelle, Sam. "Are the Economics of Internet Fame Really So Sad?" *Tube Filter,* December 17, 2015, accessed February 21, 2016. http://www.tubefilter.com/2015/12/17/jared-polin-fro-knows-photo-youtube.

Halpern, Megan, and Lee Humphreys. "Iphoneography as an Emergent Art World." *New Media & Society* 18, no. 1 (2016): 62–81.

Hardt, Michael, and Antonio Negri. *Empire.* Cambridge, MA: Harvard University Press, 2000.

Harris, Anita. *Future Girl: Young Women in the Twenty-First Century.* New York: Routledge, 2004.

Harvey, Alison, and Stephanie Fisher. "Making a Name in Games." *Information, Communication and Society* 16, no. 3 (2012): 362–80.

Haughney, Christine. "Condé Nast Faces Suit from Interns over Wages." *New York Times,* June 13, 2013, accessed February 17, 2016. http://www.nytimes.com/2013/06/14/business/media/two-ex-interns-sue-conde-nast-over-wages.html.

Haynes, Monica. "Advertisers Model Campaigns on 'Real' Women." *Pittsburgh Post-Gazette*, August 30, 2005, accessed April 14, 2016. http://www.post-gazette.com/business/businessnews/2005/08/30/Advertisers-model-campaigns-on-real-women/stories/200508300179.

Hearn, Alison. "Meat, Mask, Burden: Probing the Contours of the Branded Self." *Journal of Consumer Culture* 8, no. 2 (2008): 197–217.

———. "Through the Looking Glass: The Promotional University 2.0." In *Blowing up the Brand: Critical Perspectives on Promotional Culture,* edited by M. Aronczyk and D. Powers, 197–219. New York: Peter Lang, 2010.

Herring, Susan. "Gender and Power in Online Communication." In *The Handbook of Language and Gender,* edited by Janet Holmes and Miriam Meyerhoff, 202–28. Oxford, UK: Blackwell, 2003.

Herring, Susan C., Inna Kouper, Lois Ann Scheidt, and Elijah Wright. "Women and Children Last: The Discursive Construction of Weblogs." In *Into the Blogosphere: Rhetoric, Community, and Culture of Weblogs,* ed-

ited by Laura Gurak, Smiljana Antonijevic, Laurie Johnson, Clancy
Ratliff, and Jessica Reyman. Minneapolis: University of Minnesota,
2004. http://conservancy.umn.edu/handle/11299/172825.

Hesmondhalgh, David, and Sarah Baker. *Creative Labour: Media Work in
Three Cultural Industries.* London: Routledge, 2011.

———. "Sex, Gender and Work Segregation in the Cultural Industries." *Sociological Review* 63, no. 51 (2015): 23–36.

Hochschild, Arlie Russell. *The Managed Heart: Commercialization of Human
Feeling.* Berkeley: University of California Press, 1983.

Hochschild, Arlie Russell, and Anne Machung. *The Second Shift.* New York:
Penguin, 2003.

Hoffman, Ashley. "Stop Calling Us 'Real Women' Just Because We're Not
Victoria's Secret Models." *Huffington Post,* December 9, 2014, accessed
February 17, 2016. http://www.huffingtonpost.com/2014/12/09/stop-
calling-us-real-wome_n_6294174.html.

Holmes, Elizabeth. "How Style Bloggers Earn Sales Commissions One Click
at a Time." *Wall Street Journal,* February 11, 2015, accessed February 21,
2016. http://www.wsj.com/articles/how-style-bloggers-earn-sales-
commissions-one-click-at-a-time-1423693911.

Horowitz, Sara. "The Freelance Surge Is the Industrial Revolution of Our
Time." *Atlantic,* September 1, 2011, accessed February 17, 2016. http://
www.theatlantic.com/business/archive/2011/09/the-freelance-surge-is-
the-industrial-revolution-of-our-time/244229.

Huntemann, Nina B. "Introduction: Digital Labor behind the Screen." *Critical Studies in Media Communication* 32, no. 3 (2015): 158–60.

Illouz, Eva. *Cold Intimacies: The Making of Emotional Capitalism.* New York:
Polity, 2007.

Infante, David. "The Hipster Is Dead and You Might Not Like Who Comes
Next." *Mashable,* June 9, 2015, accessed February 17, 2016. http://mash-
able.com/2015/06/09/post-hipster-yuccie.

Jackson, Nancy Mann. "After Recession, Wave of 'Accidental' Entrepreneurs." *CNBC,* November 20, 2014, accessed February 21, 2016. http://
www.cnbc.com/id/102200095.

Jacob, Jennine. "Daily Inspiration: Every Artist Was First an Amateur." *IFB: Independent Fashion Bloggers,* May 3, 2013, accessed February 17, 2016. http://heartifb.com/2013/05/03/daily-inspiration-every-artist-was-first-an-amateur.

———. "Stop the Presses! For the First Time Ever, Fashion Bloggers Are on the Cover of *Lucky* Magazine." *IFB: Independent Fashion Bloggers,* January 2, 2015. https://heartifb.com/2015/01/02/stop-the-presses-for-the-first-time-ever-fashion-bloggers-are-on-the-cover-of-lucky-magazine.

Jane, E. A. "'Your a Ugly, Whorish, Slut': Understanding E-bile." *Feminist Media Studies* 14, no. 4 (2014): 531–46.

Jarrett, Kylie. *Feminism, Labour and Digital Media: The Digital Housewife.* Vol. 33. New York: Routledge, 2015.

———. "The Relevance of 'Women's Work': Social Reproduction and Immaterial Labour in Digital Media." *Television & New Media* 15, no. 1 (2014): 14–29.

Jenkins, Henry, Sam Ford, and Joshua Green. *Spreadable Media: Creating Value and Meaning in a Networked Culture.* New York: New York University Press, 2013.

Jobs, Steve. "Find What You Love." *Wall Street Journal,* October 6, 2011, accessed February 21, 2016. http://www.wsj.com/articles/SB10001424052970203388804576613572842080228.

Kaplan, Sarah. "How Ellen Pao, who oversaw the effort to rid Reddit of harassment, became its Latest Victim." *The Washington Post,* July 13, 2015, accessed July 24, 2016. https://www.washingtonpost.com/news/morning-mix/wp/2015/07/13/how-ellen-pao-who-oversaw-the-effort-to-rid-reddit-of-harassment-became-its-latest-victim/.

Kay, Karen. "The Fashion Blog Stars." *Daily Mail,* January 15, 2007, accessed February 17, 2016. http://www.dailymail.co.uk/femail/article-428821/The-fashion-blog-stars.html.

Keen, Andrew. *The Cult of the Amateur: How Today's Internet Is Killing Our Culture and Assaulting Our Economy.* New York: Doubleday, 2007.

Keinan, Anat, Kristina Maslauskaite, Sandrine Crener, and Vincent Dessain. "The Blonde Salad." Harvard Business School Case 515–074, January 2015. http://www.hbs.edu/faculty/Pages/item.aspx?num=48520.

Kerr, Aphra, and John D. Kelleher. "The Recruitment of Passion and Community in the Service of Capital: Community Managers in the Digital Games Industry." *Critical Studies in Media Communication* 32, no. 3 (2015): 177–92.

King, Molly M., Shelley J. Correll, Jennifer Jacquet, Carl T. Bergstrom, and Jevin D. West. "Men Set Their Own Cites High: Gender and Self-Citation across Fields and over Time." Working paper. https://www.insidehighered.com/news/2015/08/25/study-finds-men-are-more-likely-women-engage-self, 2015.

Klein, Bethany, Leslie M. Meier, and Devon Powers. "Selling Out: Musicians, Autonomy, and Compromise in the Digital Age." *Popular Music and Society* (2016): 1–17. http://dx.doi.org/10.1080/03007766.2015.1120101.

Korobka, Tanya. "'Instagrammer' Is Now a Six-Figure Job." *Social Media Week,* February 26, 2015, accessed February 17, 2016. http://socialmediaweek.org/blog/2015/02/instagrammer-now-six-figure-job.

Kuehn, Kathleen Mary. "'There's Got to Be a Review Democracy': Communicative Capitalism, Neoliberal Citizenship and the Politics of Participation on the Consumer Evaluation Website Yelp.com." *International Journal of Communication* 7 (2013): 607–25.

Kuehn, Kathleen, and Thomas F. Corrigan. "Hope Labor: The Role of Employment Prospects in Online Social Production." *The Political Economy of Communication* 1, no. 1 (2013): 9–25.

La Ferla, Ruth. "Who Am I Wearing? Funny You Should Ask." *New York Times,* September 12, 2012, accessed February 21, 2016. http://www.nytimes.com/2012/09/13/fashion/new-york-fashion-week-street-style-is-often-a-billboard-for-brands.html.

Lazarsfeld, Paul. "Remarks on Administrative and Critical Communications Research." *Studies in Philosophy and Social Science* 9 (1941): 2–16.

Lazauskas, Joseph. "The Anatomy of a Killer Content Marketing Strategy." *Mashable,* July 27, 2012, accessed February 21, 2016. http://mashable.com/2012/07/27/refinery29-marketing.

Lazzarato, Maurizio. "Immaterial Labour." In *Radical Thought in Italy: A Potential Politics,* edited by Paolo Virno and Michael Hardt, 133–50. Minneapolis: University of Minnesota Press, 1996.

Leach, William R. *Land of Desire: Merchants, Power, and the Rise of a New American Culture.* New York: Vintage, 1994.

Leadbeater, Charles, and Paul Miller. *The Pro-Am Revolution: How Enthusiasts Are Changing Our Society and Economy.* London: Demos, 2004. http://www.demos.co.uk/files/proamrevolutionfinal.pdf.

Lears, T. J. Jackson. *Fables of Abundance: A Cultural History of Advertising in America.* New York: Basic Books, 1994.

Lee, Aileen. "Why Women Rule the Internet." *Tech Crunch,* March 20, 2011, accessed February 21, 2016. http://techcrunch.com/2011/03/20/why-women-rule-the-internet.

Leighton, Patricia, and Duncan Brown. *Future Working: The Rise of Europe's Independent Professionals.* London: Professional Contractors Group, 2013. http://www.um.es/prinum/uploaded/files/Future_Working_Full_Report-2%20final%20subir%20web.pdf.

Letchford, Adrian, Helen Susannah Moat, and Tobias Preis. "The Advantage of Short Paper Titles." *Royal Society Open Science* 2, no. 8 (2015): 150266.

Levine, Elana. "Toward a Paradigm for Media Production Research: Behind the Scenes at *General Hospital.*" *Critical Studies in Media Communication* 18, no. 1 (2001): 66–82.

Levinson, Alana Hope. "The Pink Ghetto of Social Media." *Medium,* July 16, 2015, accessed February 17, 2016. https://medium.com/matter/the-pink-ghetto-of-social-media-39bf7f2fdbe1.

Lewine, Ari. "Outside Voices: The Visual Web is Changing Everything in Media and Advertising." *Wall Street Journal,* June 24, 2014, accessed February 21, 2016. http://blogs.wsj.com/cmo/2014/06/24/outside-voices-the-visual-web-is-changing-everything-in-media-and-advertising.

Lewis, Casey. "How to Make It as a Fashion Blogger." *Teen Vogue,* November 2, 2012, accessed February 17, 2016. http://www.teenvogue.com/careers/fashion-careers/2012–10/fashion-blogger-tips.

Lieber, Chavie. "The Dirty Business of Buying Instagram Followers." *Racked,* September 11, 2014, accessed February 21, 2016. http://www.racked.com/2014/9/11/7577585/buy-instagram-followers-bloggers.

———. "Inside the Internet's Craziest Destination for Blogger Hate." *Racked,* July 30, 2014, accessed February 18, 2016. http://www.racked. com/2014/7/30/7584149/gomi-get-off-my-internets-fashion-bloggers-style-blogs-mom-blogs.

Lien, Tracey. "Why Are Women Leaving the Tech Industry in Droves?" *Los Angeles Times,* February 22, 2015, accessed March 23, 2016. http://www. latimes.com/business/la-fi-women-tech-20150222-story.html.

Liss-Mariño, Tara. "Sell (It) Yourself: Marketing Pleasure in Digital DIY." PhD diss., University of Pennsylvania, 2014. Retrieved from: http://repository.upenn.edu/edissertations/1347/.

Little, Danyelle. "Forever 21 'Meet Our Bloggers' Lacks a Woman of Color." *The Cubicle Chick,* October 12, 2010, accessed February, 21, 2016. http:// www.thecubiclechick.com/2010/10/12/forever-21-meet-our-bloggers-lacks-a-woman-of-color.

Lopez, Lori Kiddo. "The Radical Act of 'Mommy Blogging': Redefining Motherhood through the Blogosphere." *New Media & Society* 11, no. 5 (2009): 729–47.

Lord, Audra E. "Blog Lovin'? Do Brands Really Support Bloggers of Color?" *Clutch,* November 2010, accessed April 2, 2015. http://www.clutchmagonline.com/2010/11/blog-lovin-do-brands-really-support-bloggers-of-color/.

Luckman, Susan. "The Aura of the Analogue in a Digital Age: Women's Crafts, Creative Markets and Home-Based Labour after Etsy." *Cultural Studies Review* 19, no. 1 (2013): 249–70.

Luvaas, Brent. "Indonesian Fashion Blogs: On the Promotional Subject of Personal Style." *Fashion Theory: The Journal of Dress, Body & Culture* 17, no. 1 (2013): 55–76.

———. *Street Style: An Anthropology of Fashion Blogging.* London: Bloomsbury, 2016.

Manjoo, Farhad. "ThinkUp Helps the Social Network User See the Online Self." *New York Times,* December 31, 2014, accessed February 18, 2016. http://mobile.nytimes.com/2015/01/01/technology/personaltech/thinkup-helps-the-social-network-user-see-the-online-self.html.

Manko, Katina L. " 'Now You Are in Business for Yourself': The Independent Contractors of the California Perfume Company, 1886–1938." *Business and Economic History* 26, no. 1 (1997): 5–26.

Marchand, Roland. *Advertising the American Dream: Making Way for Modernity, 1920–1940.* Berkeley: University of California Press, 1986.

Mari, Francesca. "The Click Clique." *Texas Monthly,* September 2014, accessed February 18, 2016. http://www.texasmonthly.com/articles/the-click-clique.

Marikar, Sheila. "Sundance Courts a New Celebrity Crowd." *New York Times,* January 30, 2015, accessed February 21, 2016. http://www.nytimes.com/2015/02/01/style/sundance-courts-a-new-celebrity-crowd.html.

———. "Turning 'Likes' into a Career: Social Media Stars Use Instagram, Twitter and Tumblr to Build Their Career." *New York Times,* July 11, 2014, accessed February 21, 2016. http://www.nytimes.com/2014/07/13/fashion/social-media-stars-use-instagram-twitter-and-tumblr-to-build-their-career.html.

Marvin, Carolyn. *When Old Technologies Were New.* Oxford: Oxford University Press, 1997.

Marwick, Alice E. "Silicon Valley Isn't a Meritocracy. And It's Dangerous to Hero-Worship Entrepreneurs." *Wired,* November 25, 2013, accessed February 18, 2016. http://www.wired.com/2013/11/silicon-valley-isnt-a-meritocracy-and-the-cult-of-the-entrepreneur-holds-people-back.

———. *Status Update: Celebrity, Publicity, and Branding in the Social Media Age.* New Haven, CT: Yale University Press, 2013.

Marwick, Alice E., and danah boyd. "I Tweet Honestly, I Tweet Passionately: Twitter Users, Context Collapse, and the Imagined Audience." *New Media & Society* 13, no. 1 (2011): 114–33.

———. "To See and Be Seen: Celebrity Practice on Twitter." *Convergence: The International Journal of Research into New Media Technologies* 17, no. 2 (2011): 139–58.

Mattel. Barbie website, n.d., accessed February 18, 2016. http://www.barbie.com.

Mayer, Vicki. *Below the Line: Producers and Production Studies in the New Television Economy.* Durham, NC: Duke University Press, 2011.

———. "To Communicate Is Human; To Chat Is Female: The Feminization of U.S. Media Work." *Routledge Companion to Media and Gender*, edited by Cindy Carter, Lisa McLaughlin, and Linda Steiner, 51–60. New York: Routledge, 2013.

Mazzarella, William. *Shoveling Smoke: Advertising and Globalization in Contemporary India*. Durham, NC: Duke University Press, 2003.

MBO Partners. *The State of Independence in America*. Herndon, VA: MBO Partners, 2013. http://info.mbopartners.com/rs/mbo/images/2013-MBO_Partners_State_of_Independence_Report.pdf.

McAllister, Matthew P., Tanner R. Cooke, and Catherine Buckley. "Fetishizing Flo: Constructing Retail Space and Flexible Gendered Labor in Digital-Era Insurance Advertising." *Critical Studies in Media Communication* 32, no. 5 (2015): 347–62.

McCall, Tyler. " 'Lucky' Puts Three Bloggers on Its February Cover." *Fashionista*, January 2, 2015, accessed February 18, 2016. http://fashionista.com/2015/01/lucky-blogger-cover.

McClusky, Megan. "Teen Instagram Star Speaks Out about the Ugly Truth behind Social Media Fame." *Time*, November 2, 2015, accessed February 18, 2016. http://time.com/4096988/teen-instagram-star-essena-oneill-quitting-social-media.

———. "The 30 Most Influential People on the Internet: Essena O'Neill." *Time*, March 16, 2016, accessed September 2, 2016. http://time.com/4258291/30-most-influential-people-on-the-internet-2016/.

McPherson, Tara. *Digital Youth, Innovation, and the Unexpected*. Cambridge, MA: MIT Press, 2008.

McQuarrie, Edward F., Jessica Miller, and Barbara J. Phillips. "The Megaphone Effect: Taste and Audience in Fashion Blogging." *Journal of Consumer Research* 40, no. 1 (2013): 136–58.

McRobbie, Angela. *The Aftermath of Feminism: Gender, Culture and Social Change*. London: Sage, 2008.

———. *Be Creative: Making a Living in the New Culture Industries*. London: Polity, 2016.

——. *British Fashion Design: Rag Trade or Image Industry?* New York: Routledge, 1998.

——. "Clubs to Companies: Notes on the Decline of Political Culture in Speeded Up Creative Worlds." *Cultural Studies* 16, no. 4 (2002): 516–31.

——. "Reflections on Feminism, Immaterial Labour and the Post-Fordist Regime." *New Formations* 70, no. 1 (2011): 60–76.

Meece, Mickey. "On to Plan B: Starting a Business." *New York Times,* August 22, 2009, accessed February 21, 2016. http://www.nytimes.com/2009/08/23/business/smallbusiness/23venture.html.

Menkes, Suzy. "The Circus of Fashion." *New York Times,* February 10, 2013, accessed February 18, 2016. http://www.nytimes.com/2013/02/10/t-magazine/the-circus-of-fashion.html.

Miller, Clare Cain. "Technology's Man Problem." *New York Times,* April 5, 2014, accessed February 18, 2016. http://www.nytimes.com/2014/04/06/technology/technologys-man-problem.html.

Molla, Rani, and Renee Lightner. "Diversity in Tech." *Wall Street Journal,* December 30, 2014, accessed April 10, 2016. http://graphics.wsj.com/diversity-in-tech-companies/.

Morahan-Martin, Janet. "The Gender Gap in Internet Use: Why Men Use the Internet More Than Women—A Literature Review." *CyberPsychology and Behavior* 1, no. 1 (2009): 3–10.

Moss-Racusin, C. A., and L. A. Rudman. "Disruptions in Women's Self-Promotion: The Backlash Avoidance Model." *Psychology of Women Quarterly* 34, no. 2 (2010): 186–202.

Murdock, Graham. "Political Economies as Moral Economies: Commodities, Gifts, and Public Goods." In *The Handbook of Political Economy of Communication,* edited by Janet Wasko, Graham Murdock, and Helena Sousa, 13–40. Oxford, UK: Wiley-Blackwell, 2011.

Murray, Alex. "Fashion Week: The Ordinary People Who Stole the Show." *BBC News,* September 11, 2009, accessed February 18, 2016. http://www.bbc.co.uk/news/mobile/magazine-14813053.

Murray, Dara Persis. "Branding 'Real' Social Change in Dove's Campaign for Real Beauty." *Feminist Media Studies* 13, no. 1 (2013): 83–101.

Murray, Susan, and Laurie Ouellette. *Reality TV: Remaking Television Culture*. New York: New York University Press, 2004.

Nathanson, Elizabeth. "Dressed for Economic Distress: Blogging and the 'New' Pleasures of Fashion." In *Gendering the Recession: Media and Culture in an Age of Austerity*, edited by Diane Negra and Yvonne Tasker, 136–60. Durham, NC: Duke University Press, 2014.

Nathanson, Hannah. "Meet the Slashies . . . The Savvy Londoners Holding Down More Than One Job." *London Evening Standard,* September 7, 2012, accessed February 18, 2016. http://www.standard.co.uk/lifestyle/ esmagazine/meet-the-slashies-the-savvy-londoners-holding-down-more-than-one-job-8113327.html.

Nava, Mica. "Modernity's Disavowal: Women, the City, and the Department Store." In *Modern Times: Reflections on a Century of English Modernity*, edited by Mica Nava and Alan O'Shea, 38–76. New York: Routledge 1996.

Neff, Gina. *Venture Labor: Work and the Burden of Risk in Innovative Industries*. Cambridge, MA: MIT Press, 2012.

Neff, Gina, Elizabeth Wissinger, and Sharon Zukin. 2005. "Entrepreneurial Labor among Cultural Producers: 'Cool' Jobs in 'Hot' Industries." *Social Semiotics* 15, no. 3 (2005): 307–34.

Negra, Diane, and Yvonne Tasker. "Introduction: Gender and Recessionary Culture." In *Gendering the Recession: Media and Culture in an Age of Austerity*, edited by Diane Negra and Yvonne Tasker, 1–30. Durham, NC: Duke University Press, 2014.

Neilson, Brett, and Mark Coté. "Introduction: Are We All Cultural Workers Now?" *Journal of Cultural Economy* 7, no. 1 (2014): 2–11.

Newsinger, Jack. "Bullshit Jobs in the Creative Industries." *Antenna,* April 23, 2015, accessed February 18, 2016. http://blog.commarts.wisc. edu/2015/04/23/bullshit-jobs-in-the-creative-industries.

Nielsen Media Research. *CommerceNet/ Nielsen Media Research Survey.* New York: Cognizant Corporation, 1997.

Nixon, Sean, and Ben Crewe. "Pleasure at Work?: Gender, Consumption and Work-Based Identities in the Creative Industries." *Consumption Markets & Culture* 7, no. 2 (2004): 129–47.

Noricks, Crosby. "How a Personal Brand Pyramid Can Help Define Your Blog's Direction." *IFB: Independent Fashion Bloggers,* November 13, 2013, accessed February 21, 2016. http://heartifb.com/2013/11/13/how-a-personal-brand-pyramid-can-help-define-your-blogs-direction.

O'Neill, Essena. Instagram post, November 4, 2015. https://www.instagram.com/p/9poYKgOWk4.

———. "Why I REALLY Am Quitting Social Media." YouTube, November 3, 2015. Retrieved from: https://www.youtube.com/watch?v=Xe1Qyks8QEM.

Pan, Jennifer. "Pink Collar." *Jacobin,* June 2014, accessed February 22, 2016. https://www.jacobinmag.com/2014/06/pink-collar.

Pao, Ellen. "Silicon Valley Sexism IS Getting Better." *Lenny Letter,* November 11, 2015, accessed January 3, 2106. http://www.lennyletter.com/work/a151/ellen-pao-silicon-valley-sexism-is-getting-better/.

Pathak, Shareen. "Confessions of a Social Media Exec on Influencer Marketing: 'We Threw Too Much Money at Them.'" *Huffington Post,* May 12, 2016, accessed May 31, 2016. http://digiday.com/agencies/confessions-social-media-exec-no-idea-pay-influencers/.

Peck, Emily. "The Stats on Women in Tech Are Actually Getting Worse." *Huffington Post,* March 27, 2015, accessed March 29, 2016. http://www.huffingtonpost.com/2015/03/27/women-in-tech_n_6955940.html.

Peiss, Kathy. *Hope in a Jar: The Making of America's Beauty Culture.* Philadelphia: University of Pennsylvania Press, 1998.

———. "'Vital Industry' and 'Women's Ventures': Conceptualizing Gender in Twentieth Century Business History." *Business History Review* 72, no. 2 (1998): 219–41.

Perlin, Ross. *Intern Nation: How to Earn Nothing and Learn Little in the Brave New Economy.* New York: Verso, 2012.

Perlroth, Nicole. "Researchers Call Out Twitter Celebrities with Suspicious Followings." *New York Times,* April 25, 2013, accessed February 17, 2016. http://bits.blogs.nytimes.com/2013/04/25/researchers-call-out-twitter-celebrities-with-suspicious-followings.

Perrons, Diane. "The New Economy and the Work-Life Balance: Conceptual Explorations and a Case Study of New Media." *Gender, Work & Organization* 10, no. 1 (2003): 65–93.

Peters, Tom. *The Brand You 50: Or, 50 Ways to Transform Yourself from an 'Employee' into a Brand That Shouts Distinction, Commitment, and Passion!* New York: Alfred A. Knopf, 1999.

Pew Research Center. *Teens, Social Media, and Technology: Overview 2015: Smartphones Facilitate Shifts in Communication Landscape for Teens.* Washington, DC: Pew Research Center, 2015. http://www.pewinternet. org/files/2015/04/PI_TeensandTech_Update2015_0409151.pdf.

Pham, Minh-Ha T. "'Susie Bubble Is a Sign of the Times': The Embodiment of Success in the Web 2.0 Economy." *Feminist Media Studies* 13, no. 2 (2013): 245–67.

Phelan, Hayley. "How to Brand Yourself in Fashion: A Guide." *Fashionista,* May 31, 2013, accessed February 21, 2016. http://fashionista.com/2013/05/ how-to-brand-yourself-fashion-guide.

Phillips, Whitney. *This Is Why We Can't Have Nice Things: Mapping the Relationship between Online Trolling and Mainstream Culture.* Cambridge, MA: MIT Press, 2015.

Pooley, Jefferson. "The Consuming Self: From Flappers to Facebook." In *Blowing Up the Brand: Critical Perspectives on Promotional Culture,* edited by Melissa Aronczyk and Devon Powers, 71–92. New York: Peter Lang, 2010.

———. "Open Media Scholarship: The Case for Open Access in Media Studies." *International Journal of Communication* 10.

Postigo, Hector. "America Online Volunteers: Lessons from an Early Co-Production Community." *International Journal of Cultural Studies* 12, no. 5 (2009): 451–69.

Pous, Terri. "The Democratization of Fashion: A Brief History." *Time,* February 6, 2013, accessed February 18, 2016. http://style.time.com/ 2013/02/06/the-democratization-of-fashion-a-brief-history.

Pratt, Andy C. "Creative Cities: The Cultural Industries and the Creative Class." *Geografiska Annaler: Series B, Human Geography* 90, no. 2 (2008): 107–17.

Proctor-Thomson, Sarah B. "Gender Disruptions in the Digital Industries?" *Culture and Organization* 19, no. 2 (2013): 85–104.

Rappaport, Erika Diane. *Shopping for Pleasure: Women in the Making of London's West End.* Princeton, NJ: Princeton University Press, 2000.

Reed, Barbara Straus. " 'Be Somebody': Ruth Whitney of *Glamour.*" In *Women and Media: Content/Careers/Criticism,* edited by Cynthia Lont, 87–97. Belmont, CA: Wadsworth, 1995.

RICHES. "Creative Industries." *RICHES,* November 27, 2014, accessed February 22, 2016. http://resources.riches-project.eu/glossary/creative-industries.

Ritzer, George, and Nathan Jungenson. "Production, Consumption, Prosumption: The Nature of Capitalism in the Age of the Digital 'Prosumer.'" *Journal of Consumer Culture* 10, no. 1 (2010): 13–36.

Rocamora, Agnès. "Hypertextuality and Remediation in the Fashion Media: The Case of Fashion Blogs." *Journalism Practice* 6, no. 1 (2012): 92–106.

———. 2011. "Personal Fashion Blogs: Screens and Mirrors in Digital Self-Portraits." *Fashion Theory: The Journal of Dress, Body & Culture* 15, no. 4: 407–24.

Rodino-Colocino, Michelle, and Stephanie N. Berberick. " 'You Kind of Have to Bite the Bullet and Do Bitch Work': How Internships Teach Students to Unthink Exploitation in Public Relations." *tripleC: Communication, Capitalism & Critique* 13, no. 2 (2015): 486–500.

Rose, Nikolas. *Governing the Soul: The Shaping of the Private Self.* London: Free Association Press, 1999.

Rosen, Jay. "The People Formerly Known as the Audience." *Press Think,* June 27, 2006, accessed February, 18, 2016. http://archive.pressthink.org/2006/06/27/ppl_frmr.html.

Rosenbloom, Stephanie. "Sorry Boys, This Is Our Domain." *New York Times,* February 1, 2008, accessed February, 21 2016. http://www.nytimes.com/2008/02/21/fashion/21webgirls.html.

Ross, Andrew. *Nice Work If You Can Get It: Life and Labor in Precarious Times.* New York: New York University Press, 2009.

———. *No-Collar: The Humane Workplace and Its Hidden Costs.* Philadelphia: Temple University Press, 2004.

Roy, Jessica. "New 'Entrepreneur Barbie' Proves That the Perfect Work/Life Balance Is Just a Tiny Tablet Away." *Time,* February 18, 2014, accessed February 18, 2016. http://newsfeed.time.com/2014/02/18/new-entrepreneur-barbie-proves-that-the-perfect-worklife-balance-is-just-a-tiny-tablet-away.

Sabra, Ponn. "The 6 Marketing Principles Every Fashion Blogger Needs in 2015." *IFB: Independent Fashion Bloggers,* May 4, 2015, accessed February 18, 2016. http://heartifb.com/2015/05/04/the-6-marketing-principles-every-fashion-blogger-needs-in-2015.

Sandberg, Sheryl, and Nell Scovell. *Lean In: Women, Work, and the Will to Lead.* New York: Alfred A. Knopf, 2013.

Sandlin, Jennifer A., and Julie G. Maudlin. "Consuming Pedagogies: Controlling Images of Women as Consumers in Popular Culture." *Journal of Consumer Culture* 12, no. 2 (2012): 175–94.

Saul, Heather. "Instafamous: Meet the Social Media Influencers Redefining Celebrity." *Independent* (UK), March 27, 2016, accessed April 4, 2016. http://www.independent.co.uk/news/people/instagram-model-natasha-oakley-iskra-lawrence-kayla-itsines-kendall-jenner-jordyn-woods-a6907551.html.

Scanlon, Jennifer. "Advertising Women: The J. Walter Thompson Company Women's Editorial Department." In *Gender and Consumer Culture,* edited by Jennifer Scanlon, 208–16. New York: New York University Press, 2000.

Schaefer, Kayleen. "How Bloggers Make Money on Instagram." *Harpers Bazaar,* May 20, 2015, accessed February 17, 2016. http://www.harpersbazaar.com/fashion/trends/a10949/how-bloggers-make-money-on-instagram.

Scharff, Christina. "Blowing Your Own Trumpet: Exploring the Gendered Dynamics of Self-Promotion in the Classical Music Profession." *Sociological Review* 63, no. S1 (2015): 97–112.

Scholz, Trebor, ed. *Digital Labor: The Internet as Playground and Factory.* New York: Routledge, 2013.

Schor, Juliet B. "In Defense of Consumer Critique: Revisiting the Consumption Debates of the Twentieth Century." *Annals of the American Academy of Political and Social Science* 611, no. 1 (2007): 16–30.

Schultz, Colin. "The Unpaid Intern Economy Rides on the Backs of Young Women." *Smithsonian,* March 22, 2014. http://www.smithsonianmag. com/ist/?next=/smart-news/unpaid-intern-economy-rides-backs-young-women-1-180951540/.

Schwartz, Madeleine. "Opportunity Costs: The True Costs of Internships." *Dissent,* Winter 2013, accessed February 18, 2016. http://www.dissent-magazine.org/article/opportunity-costs-the-true-price-of-internships.

Segrave, Kerry. *Shoplifting: A Social History.* Jefferson, NC: McFarland, 2001.

Sender, Katherine. *Business, Not Politics: The Making of the Gay Market.* New York: Columbia University Press, 2004.

———. *The Makeover: Reality Television and Reflexive Audiences.* New York: New York University Press, 2012.

Senft, Theresa M. *Camgirls: Celebrity and Community in the Age of Social Networks.* New York: Peter Lang, 2008.

———. "Microcelebrity and the Branded Self." In *A Companion to New Media Dynamics,* edited by John Hartley, Jean Burgess, and Axel Bruns, 346–54. West Sussex, UK: Wiley-Blackwell, 2013.

Sennett, Richard. *The Culture of the New Capitalism.* New Haven, CT: Yale University Press, 2007.

Serazio, Michael. "Selling (Digital) Millennials: The Social Construction and Technological Bias of a Consumer Generation." *Television & New Media* (2013): 1527476413491015.

———. *Your Ad Here: The Cool Sell of Guerrilla Marketing.* New York: New York University Press, 2013.

Serazio, Michael, and Brooke Erin Duffy. "Social Media Marketing." In *The Sage Handbook of Social Media,* edited by J. Burgess, A. Marwick, and T. Poell. Thousand Oaks, CA: Sage Publications, in press.

Shade, Leslie Regan. *Gender and Community in the Social Construction of the Internet.* New York: Peter Lang, 2002.

———. "'Give Us Bread, but Give Us Roses': Gender and Labour in the Digital Economy." *International Journal of Media & Cultural Politics* 10, no. 2 (2014): 129–44.

Shade, Leslie Regan, and Jenna Jacobson. "Hungry for the Job: Gender, Unpaid Internships, and the Creative Industries." *Sociological Review* 63, no. S1 (2015): 188–205.

Sherman, Lauren. "Desperate Measures?: Bloggers Faking VIP Status by Paying for Their Own Swag." *Fashionista*, January 31, 2013, accessed February 21, 2016. http://fashionista.com/2013/01/bloggers-fake-free-swag.

———. "The Unexpected Costs of Being a Fashion Blogger." *Fashionista*, January 14 2014, accessed April 28, 2015. http://fashionista.com/2014/01/fashion-blogger-expenses.

Shirky, Clay. *Here Comes Everybody: The Power of Organizing without Organizations.* New York: Penguin, 2008.

Sieghart, M. A. "Real Women, Real Beauty: It's Time to Start the Fightback." *Times of Malta*, August 2, 2008, accessed February 18, 2016. http://www.timesofmalta.com/articles/view/20080802/life-features/real-women-real-beauty-its-time-for-the-fightback.219196.

Sivulka, Juliann. *Soap, Sex, and Cigarettes: A Cultural History of American Advertising.* Boston: Wadsworth, 2012.

Skeggs, Beverley. "The Moral Economy of Person Production: The Class Relations of Self-Performance on 'Reality' Television." *Sociological Review* 57, no. 4 (2009): 626–44.

Slater, Don. *Consumer Culture and Modernity.* Cambridge, UK: Polity, 1997.

Smith, Aaron. "Searching for Work in the Digital Era." Pew Research Center, November, 2015, accessed January 7, 2016. http://www.pewinternet.org/files/2015/11/PI_2015-11-19-Internet-and-Job-Seeking_FINAL.pdf.

Smith, Katlyn. "Scholar Speaks on Feminism." *Observer*, March 19, 2008, accessed January 18, 2016. http://ndsmcobserver.com/2008/03/scholar-speaks-on-feminism.

Smythe, Dallas W. "Communications: Blindspot of Western Marxism." *Canadian Journal of Political and Social Theory* 1, no. 3 (1977): 1–27.

Sozzani, Franca. "Editor's Blog: Bloggers—A Cultural Phenomenon or an Epidemic Issue?" *Vogue (Italia)*, January 28, 2011, accessed March 23, 2013. http://www.vogue.it/en/magazine/editor-s-blog/2011/01/january-28th.

Spigel, Lynn. "Designing the Smart House: Posthuman Domesticity and Conspicuous Production." *European Journal of Cultural Studies* 8, no. 4 (2005): 403–26.

Steedman, P. H. "On the Relations between Seeing, Interpreting and Knowing." In *Research and Reflexivity*, edited by Frederick Steir, 53–62. London: Sage, 1991.

Strugatz, Rachel. "The Blonde Salad at Harvard." *WWD*, February 12, 2015, accessed February 21, 2016. http://wwd.com/globe-news/digital/the-blonde-salad-at-harvard-8172610.

Swant, Marty. "Twitter Says Users Now Trust Influencers Nearly as Much as Their Friends." *Adweek*, May 10, 2016, accessed on May 15, 2016. http://www.adweek.com/news/technology/twitter-says-users-now-trust-influencers-nearly-much-their-friends-171367.

Technorati Media. *Technorati Media: 2013 Digital Influence Report*. San Francisco: Technorati Media, 2013. http://technorati.com/wp-content/uploads/2013/06/tm2013DIR1.pdf.

Terranova, Tiziana. "Free Labor: Producing Culture for the Digital Economy. *Social Text* 18, no. 2 (2000): 33–58.

Thompson, Piers, Dylan Jones-Evans, and Caleb Kwong. "Women and Home-Based Entrepreneurship: Evidence from the United Kingdom." *International Small Business Journal* 27, no. 2 (2009): 227–39.

Tokumitsu, M. "In the Name of Love." *Jacobin Magazine*, January 2014, accessed February 18, 2016. https://www.jacobinmag.com/2014/01/in-the-name-of-love.

Tuchman, Gaye. *Making News: A Study in the Construction of Reality*. New York: Free Press, 1978.

———. "Making News by Doing Work: Routinizing the Unexpected." *American Journal of Sociology* 79, no. 1 (1973): 110–31.

Turner, Graeme. "The Mass Production of Celebrity 'Celetoids,' Reality TV and the 'Demotic Turn.'" *International Journal of Cultural Studies* 9, no. 2 (2006): 153–65.

Turow, Joseph. *Breaking Up America: Advertisers and the New Media World.* Chicago: University of Chicago Press, 2007.

———. *The Daily You: How the New Advertising Industry Is Defining Your Identity and Your Worth.* New Haven, CT: Yale University Press, 2012.

VanderBeek, Emily. "Why Instagram Captions Matter." *IFB: Independent Fashion Bloggers,* November 27, 2012, accessed February 21, 2016. http://heartifb.com/2012/11/27/why-instagram-captions-matter.

Van Dijck, José. *The Culture of Connectivity: A Critical History of Social Media.* Oxford, UK: Oxford University Press, 2013.

———. "'You Have One Identity': Performing the Self on Facebook and LinkedIn." *Media, Culture & Society* 35, no. 2 (2013): 199–215.

Van Natten, Amber. "50% of Millennials Read Buzzfeed: Why Marketers Should Care." *NewsCred,* n.d., accessed February 21, 2016. http://blog.newscred.com/50-of-millennials-read-buzzfeed-why-marketers-should-care.

Veblen, Thorstein. *The Theory of the Leisure Class.* Oxford, UK: Oxford University Press, 2007.

Veselinovic, Milena. "Cash a la Mode: How Style Bloggers Are Turning Social Savvy into Six-Figure Salaries." *CNN,* October 5, 2014, accessed February 18, 2016. http://www.cnn.com/2014/10/01/world/europe/bloggers-six-figure-salaries.

Vitak, Jessica. "The Impact of Context Collapse and Privacy on Social Network Site Disclosures." *Journal of Broadcasting & Electronic Media* 56 (2012): 451–70.

Walker, Nancy A. *Shaping Our Mothers' Worlds: American Women's Magazines.* Jackson: University Press of Mississippi, 2000.

Waller-Zuckerman, Ellen. "'Old Homes, in a City of Perpetual Change': Women's Magazines, 1890–1916." *Business History Review* 63, no. 4 (1989): 715–56.

Weeks, Kathi. *The Problem with Work: Feminism, Marxism, Antiwork Politics, and Postwork Imaginaries*. Durham, NC: Duke University Press, 2011.

Weissman, Jordan. "Entrepreneurship: The Ultimate White Privilege?" *Atlantic*, August 16, 2013, accessed February 18, 2016. http://www.theatlantic.com/business/archive/2013/08/entrepreneurship-the-ultimate-white-privilege/278727.

Wicker, Alan. "You Need to Know This about Your Favorite Fashion Blogger." *Ecocult*, September 10, 2014, accessed February 21, 2016. http://ecocult.com/2014/you-need-to-know-this-about-your-favorite-fashion-blogger.

Williamson, Harriet. "Are Ultra-Thin Fashion Bloggers Encouraging Young Women to Starve Themselves?" *New Statesman*, March 14, 2014, accessed February 18, 2016. http://www.newstatesman.com/lifestyle/2014/03/are-ultra-thin-fashion-bloggers-encouraging-young-women-starve-themselves.

Wissinger, Elizabeth. "Modelling a Way of Life: Immaterial and Affective Labour in the Fashion Modelling Industry." *Ephemera: Theory and Politics in Organization* 7, no. 1 (2007): 250–69.

———. *This Year's Model: Fashion, Media, and the Making of Glamour*. New York: New York University Press, 2015.

Wittel, Andreas. "Toward a Network Sociality." *Theory, Culture & Society* 18, no. 6 (2001): 51–76.

Women's Media Center. *The Status of Women in the U.S. Media, 2014*. New York: Women's Media Center, 2014. http://wmc.3cdn.net/2e85f9517dc2bf164e_htm62xgan.pdf.

Wright, Erik Olin. "Social Class." In *The Encyclopedia of Social Theory*, edited by George Ritzer. Thousand Oaks, CA: Sage Publications, 2003.

Zaino, Gene. "The Independent Work Boom: Why It's Good for the U.S. Economy." *Huffington Post*, October 1, 2015, accessed February 22, 2016. http://www.huffingtonpost.com/gene-zaino/the-independent-work-boom_b_8213714.html.

Ziv, Yuli. *Fashion 2.0: Blogging Your Way to the Front Row; the Insider's Guide to Turning Your Fashion Blog into a Profitable Business and Launching a New Career*. n.c.: CreateSpace, 2012.

Zobl, Elke. "About: The Global Grrrl Zine Network: Grrrl, Lady, Queer, and Trans Folk Zines, Distros and Do-It-Yourself Projects from All over the World." *Grrrl Zines,* 2016, accessed February 21, 2016. http://grrrlzines.net/about.htm.

Zola, Émile. *The Ladies' Paradise.* Oxford, UK: Oxford University Press, 1995.

Zukin, Sharon, and Jennifer Smith Maguire. "Consumers and Consumption." *Annual Review of Sociology* 30 (2004): 173–97.

Zwick, Detlev, Samule K. Bonsu, and Aron Darmody. "Putting Consumers to Work: 'Co-Creation' and New Marketing Govern-mentality." *Journal of Consumer Culture* 8, no. 2 (2008): 163–96.

Acknowledgments

Producing a monograph is an uneven endeavor with moments of solitary reflection and writing punctuated by intensely social experiences—from formal interviews and research presentations to convivial exchanges at field sites and chats with colleagues over coffee or cocktails. Undoubtedly, it was the latter sort that animated and sustained the former. As such, I want to extend my sincere gratitude to those who helped make this book possible.

First and foremost, I am indebted to the (current and former) content creators and technology specialists who graciously shared their time, insight, and experiences. They include: Hunter Abrams, Crystal Anderson, Heather Armstrong, Danielle Audain, Daneen Baird, Lauren Bath, Olivia Brenman, Christina Brown, Tess Candell, Alice Chan, Sarah Chipps, Megan Collins, Jenn Coyle, Brittany Cozzens, Ian Michael Crumm, Erika Marie de Palol, Julia DiNardo, Ana Divinagracia, Gaby Dunn, Kristy Eléna, Sophie Elkus, Alana Garcia, Sarah Greene, Hélène Heath, Kat Henry, Julianne Higgins, Jessie Holeva, Sissi Johnson, Amber Katz, Yolanda Keil, Nishita Lulla, Chrisi Lydon, Rachel Lynch, Madeline McCallum, Jen Morgan, Siobhan Murphy, Tanya Pham, Marissa Pina, Hillary Puckett, Thomas Rankin, Ana Redmond, Kelly Reid, Emily Rhodes, Jennifer Sikic, Dom Smales, Kimberly Smith, Lauren Snyder, Maeve Stier, Caitlin Sweeney, Emily Ulrich, Jason Wagenheim, Rachel Whitehurst, Alissa Wilson, and

Deirdre Zahl. My research also benefited from the collective knowledge of the organizers, presenters, and fellow participants at a wide range of fashion, branding, and social media events, including Bloggy Boot Camp: Women Get Social Philadelphia; FashionForward; the *Cosmopolitan* Fun, Fearless, Life Weekend; Philly Tech Week; the Fashion & Business Club of Temple University; and New York Fashion Week 2014.

Interviews and fieldwork were supported by research grants from the Organization for Research on Women and Communication and the Waterhouse Family Institute for the Study of Communication and Society at Villanova University, and I am grateful to these institutions for their generosity. Thanks as well to the Temple University Office of the Provost for awarding me a yearlong sabbatical to conduct research for this book. Several passages from Chapter 3 were published in an edited collection, *Online Evaluation of Creativity and the Arts* (2014), so I wish to express my appreciation to Routledge.

Working with Yale University Press senior editor Joseph Calamia has been an absolute pleasure, and I appreciate his enthusiasm, reassurance, and the painstaking care he took to edit the book's first draft. Thanks as well to editorial assistant Samantha Ostrowski, production editor Margaret Otzel, and copyeditor Susan Donoghue. In addition, the constructive feedback of the anonymous reviewers provided crucial clarity and purpose as I undertook revisions. I also wish to extend my gratitude to the University of North Carolina Press's Joseph Parsons along with Leslie Regan Shade for their support during the early stages of this project. Thanks are also owed to Bobby Mercadante for his research assistance and to Cathy Hannabach for providing editorial support with eagle-eye attention to detail.

The incisive feedback I received at numerous academic conferences was crucial to the development and refinement of this book's contents, including the annual meetings of the Association of Internet Researchers, the National Communication Association, Theorizing the Web, and the International Communication Association, the latter of which included a thought-provoking panel on "Feminist Approaches to Social Media Research," organized by Laura Portwood-Stacer. Additionally, I had the great fortune to present portions of this research at a number of academic institutions, including Boston College, Columbia University, Drexel University, Muhlenberg College, The Pennsylvania State University, Temple University, The University of Georgia, and The University of North Carolina at Chapel Hill. I am incredibly grateful for the compelling questions and insightful commentary that I received from faculty and students alike. Let me extend a special thanks to my brand new colleagues in Cornell University's Department of Communication for their enthusiasm for the project; I'm delighted to join such a superb intellectual community.

My former academic advisor, Joseph Turow, has been a steadfast source of encouragement for more than a decade (!), and I feel fortunate that I can continue to count on him for advice and inspiration. Many others have provided support and mentorship over the course of this project, including Osei Appiah, Sarah Banet-Weiser, Michael X. Delli Carpini, Mara Einstein, Laura Grindstaff, Jay Hamilton, David Hesmondhalgh, Lee Humphreys, Carolyn Kitch, Matt McAllister, Gina Neff, Sharrona Pearl, Stephanie Schulte, and Katherine Sender. Temple University faculty members John Campbell, Brian Creech, Lauren Kogen, Tony Liao, Wazhmah Osman, Hector Postigo, and Adrienne Shaw were terrific colleagues, and I'm grateful for their support and camaraderie.

The undergraduate and graduate students I worked with at Temple University both challenged and energized me, and this book has no doubt benefited from their insight and limitless curiosity. The

Ph.D. students in my "Cultural Production in the Digital Age" seminar deserve special mention for motivating me to think through the many similarities between academic labor and aspirational labor. I'm also deeply grateful for the support, spirit, and friendship of my former advisees: Angela Cirucci, Justin Dowdall, and Susannah McMonagle.

Working with two all-star collaborators—Emily Hund and Michael Serazio—on separate writing projects helped me to refine the ideas put forth in this monograph, and I'm grateful for their insight, cooperation, and friendship. Thanks as well to Brent Luvaas for fruitful conversations about the blogging profession, and for letting me tag along during his street-style photography adventures. Brent was one of a number of photographers who gave me permission to use their images, and I'm delighted that I can bring ideas to life through these photos.

Many others helped to shape the book, by exchanging ideas, providing support or welcome distraction, and cheering me to the finish line; they include Shira Chess, Jeff Gottfriend, Devon Powers, Piotr Szpunar, Katie Brown, Katie Greiner, Matt Crain, Kate Miltner, and Mario Rodriguez. My friends from "back home"—Megan Graham, Mike Perestock, and Jackie Krymski—supported me in a time of tragedy, and I feel lucky to still count on them from hundreds of miles away. Thanks as well to the Greiner family for the support and encouragement over the years. Lauren Anderson, Bruce Hardy, Urszula Pruchniewska, and Betsy Wissinger deserve my special, heartfelt thanks for their encouragement, friendship, and routine hilarity.

The contribution of Jeff Pooley to this book cannot be overstated; he has read (and re-read) the entire contents of this manuscript, providing meticulous comments, spot-on advice, and superb wordsmithery, all of which make him something of a co-author. Beyond that, he has provided unflagging support, and I'm so fortunate to have him as a mentor, advocate, collaborator, and friend. A million "thank you's" could never be enough.

I owe my deepest gratitude to my small-yet-wonderful family. My mother, Leslie Pilszak, has a love that knows no bounds and feelings of pride that are interminable. Her unconditional support has helped me to get where I am today, and I'm grateful that she is my mom, my friend, and undoubtedly my biggest fan. The strength she has shown in recent years is truly remarkable. My husband, Michael, is my lifeline: he has provided encouragement and relief, companionship and laughter. He's listened patiently to every single presentation; motivated me through feelings of self-defeat; borne the brunt of stress; and picked up the slack when deadlines loomed large. Most recently, he moved a couple hundred miles away from our longtime home to support this exciting new stage of my career. I thank him for being part of my fantastically weird world, and I look forward to our future adventures in Ithaca, and always.

Finally, I wish to thank my late father, Daniel Lee Pilszak, for inspiring me through his infinite compassion, playful humor, and unfaltering work ethic. His repeated reassurance to me—"If it was that easy, everyone would do it"—takes on added significance in the context of this project. I miss him terribly and know he would be beaming with pride to hold this book in his hands. I couldn't have asked for a more loving father, and I dedicate this book to his memory.

Lansing, New York

Index

Page numbers in **boldface** refer to figures.

INDEX

Fortunati, Leopoldina, 24

Frank, Thomas, 142

freelancers, 10, 186, 191, 231. *See also* gig economy; iPro; political economy of insecurity

Freelancers Union, 190, 229

Friedman, Ann, 33

Fuchs, Christian, 46, 249n2

Fusion, 211, 217

Gaby, 115, 130, 180, 211, 229; brand relationships, 168, 176–77; compensation, 217–18, 217–19. See also *Just Between Us*

Gal Meets Glam, 138

#Gamergate, 38. *See also* trolls

Garber, Megan, 8

Gary Pepper Girl, 98

gender, 121, 126–27, 134, 248n102, 248n104, 249n105; advertising and, 30, 31, 39, 100–101, 204–5, 217, 224; consumption and, xii, 9–10, 12, 16–22, 24–26, 30–31, 38, 41, 43, 48, 72, 91, 130, 142–43, 225, 244n11, 244n12, 246n34; empowerment and, 1, 43–44, 47, 101, 122, 207–9, 214, 222; entrepreneurship and, 1, 2, 36, 40, 106–13, 187, 204–5, 208; exploitation and, 21, 24–29, 33–39, 93, 142, 204–5, 207–8, 222–24, 244n12; flexibility and, 28–29, 38–39, 189–90, 207–14, 258n31; gendered labor, xii, 8–10, 15, 18–44, 72, 93, 119, 159, 171, 179–83, 204–14, 219–24, 234, 237; gendered violence, 130–32, 220–22; social media use and, 40–44, 48, 72, 91, 201. *See also* femininity; feminism; masculinity; misogyny; patriarchy; pink ghetto

Genz, Stéphanie, 106

Get Off My Internets (GOMI), 131

Gevison, Tavi, 102

gig economy, xi, 3, 10, 190, 225. *See also* freelancers; iPro; neoliberalism; political economy of insecurity

Gill, Rosalind, 68, 226, 231, 250n26, 251n47, 253n28

Girls Who Code, 1

Glam, 144, 147

Glamour, 13, 31–32

Gleam Futures, 145

"Global Report on the Status of Women in the News Media," 32

Godin, Seth, 140

Goffman, Erving, 200, 217

Google, 35, 222, 247n82; Googleplex, 225

Google Analytics, 149

GQ, 13

GrapeStory, 145

Green, Joshua, 8

Gregg, Melissa, 29, 202, 250n34, 253n28, 258n31

Grey, Sarah, 29, 209

Grindstaff, Laura, 106, 254n49

Grit & Glamour, 16, 107

Groth, Aimee, 223

grrrl zinesters, 40

Grrrl Zone, 40

Guardian, 148, 165

Gucci, 20, 174

Halpern, Megan, 257n25

Hardt, Michael, 25

Harper's Bazaar, 12, 23, 146

Julianne, xi, 98–99, 108; blogging/social media labor, 62–63, 65–66, 69–70, 96, 118–21, 149, 157–58
Just Between Us, 217
J. Walter Thompson (agency), 30

Kardashians, 150, 201
Kat, 81, 83, 108, 146
Kay, Karen, 102
Kayture, 117
Keen, Andrew, 51
Kelly, 35
Kimberly, 92, 107–8, 120–21, 125, 208–9; brand relationships, 118, 175; creative self-expression, 52–53. *See also* Penny Pincher Fashion
Kleiner Perkins, 37
Korobka, Tanya, 45
Kristy, 68, 85–86, 102; critiques of blogging, 92–93, 112–13, 129, 170–71, 178, 206
Kuehn, Kathleen, 9–10, 47, 251n59

labor (types of): affective, 25, 38, 73, 77–79, 90, 96, 224, 227, 248n89; domestic, 9, 24–25, 27, 29, 164, 207–8; emotional, 9, 25–26, 38, 43–44, 134, 159, 164, 183, 210, 248n89; glamour, 92, 201; hope, 9–10, 47–48; reproductive, 9, 24–25; unpaid, ix, 4, 7, 9, 13–15, 24–25, 34–35, 47, 72, 88, 93, 114, 156–58, 163–66, 182, 190, 221, 224, 231; venture, 9, 58. *See also* class; gig economy
Ladies' Home Journal, 20, 31
La Ferla, Ruth, 155, 157
Lau, Susanna, 103. *See also* Susie Bubble
Lauren B., 123, 161, 163, 199, 202
Lauren S., 34–35, 75, 104–5, 166
Leach, William, 21

leisure, 18–19, 21, 39, 95, 225; blurring with labor, 4, 7, 15, 46, 48, 52, 62, 80, 116, 201, 219, 226–27, 232
Lenny, 37
Levin, Amy, 113
Levinson, Alana Hope, 33–34
Linda Farrow (brand), 115
LinkedIn, 11, 237, 255n29
Liss-Mariño, Tara, 213, 252n61
Live Journal, 40
London Fashion Week, 45, 86, 102
Lookbook, 74
Louis Vuitton (brand), 149, 174
LoveBrownSugar, 103, 126, 194
Lucky, 59, 80–81, 98–99, 104–5, 118. *See also* Fashion and Beauty Blog (FABB) conference
Luvaas, Brent, 104, 152, 161, 221

Madeline, 120
Madewell, 156, 162
Maeve, **42,** 61, 74, 126
magazines, xi, 1, 63, 100, 107–8, 133, 228, 245n27; fashion, 59–60, 67, 98–99, 104–5, 118, 156, 180; industry, 6, 13–14, 19–20, 30–32, 41, 57, 61, 94, 185–86, 238, 247n68, 257n7; women's, ix, 6, 19–20, 30–32, 37, 40, 50, 72, 102, 141, 255n13. *See also individual publications*
Maguire, Jennifer Smith, 244n11
Man Repeller, 132
Marikar, Sheila, 159
Marissa, 60–61, 91, 105, 153
marketing, 1, 47, 79, 117–18, 155, 160, 175, 210, 238; affiliate, 6, 78, 84, 138–39, 144, 146–48, 165, 172, 182–83, 237; content, 155, 172, 179; gender politics of, 30–31, 33, 39, 100–101, 179–83, 204–5, 217, 224, 248n102; guerrilla, 140–41; for

Old Navy, 22, 109

Olivia, 111–12, 126, 170

O'Neill, Essena, 216–18, 220, 229

#OOTD (outfit of the day), 89–90

Palermo, Olivia, 117–18

Pao, Ellen, 37–38

Parkins, John, 2

participatory culture, 40–41

passion projects, ix, xi–xii, 46, 113, 171, 198, 223, 227. *See also* "do what you love" mantra; slash generation/slashies

patriarchy, 9, 16, 29, 43, 209. *See also* misogyny

peacocking, 50, 87, 90

Peg's Paper, 255n13

Peiss, Kathy, 142, 247n61,

Penny Pincher Fashion, 52

performativity, 85, 200–202, 206, 217–18

Perlin, Ross, 34

Perrons, Diane, 208, 257n26

Peters, Tom, x, 69

Pew Internet and American Life Project, 248n104, 249n105

Pham, Minh-Ha T., 103

Phelps, Nicole, 51

Phillips, Barbara J., 243n11

Phillips, Whitney, 254n43

Philly Tech Week Fashion Blogger's event, xi, 239, 294

pink ghetto, 33–34, 43. *See also* public relations (PR)

Pinterest, 42, 70, 83, 144, 150, 200, 205, 207, 228

playbour. *See* pro-sumption

podcasting, 40, 116, 195, 211

Polin, Jared, 218

political economy of insecurity, 10, 190–91. *See also* freelancers; gig economy

Pooley, Jefferson, 69, 120, 235, 254n51

Pope, Alexander, 19

Postano, 156–57

Postigo, Hector, 249n8

Prada, 88

presence bleed, 29, 205–6

Price, Katie, 106

Printers' Ink, 19

pro-am. *See* pro-sumption

Proctor & Gamble, 81

produsage. *See* pro-sumption

pro-sumption, 46

public relations (PR), xi, 33–35, 59, 62, 82–83, 118, 139–40, 155, 158, 160, 163–64, 238. *See also* pink ghetto

race, 39, 106, 140; racialized labor, 27, 32, 37, 103, 110, 180–81, 184, 222–23, 237

Rachel L., 52–53, 123–24; blogging/social media labor, 67, 71, 114, 151, **153**–54, 162, 168–69. *See also* I Hate Blonde

Rachel W., 54, 131–32, 167–68, 179–80, 188, 204; blogging/social media labor, 68, 115–16, 195, 211–12

Rankin, Thomas, 75, 147

realness. *See* authenticity

Reddit, 37

Refinery29, 89; Next Big Style Blogger contest, 157

relatability, 73, 100, 106–13, 119, 133, 134, 218–19. *See also* authenticity

Rent the Runway, 1

ResearchGate, 235

rewardStyle, 138, 144–45, 147

Riot Grrrl, 40

risk, 9–10, 44, 58, 191, 194, 213, 223, 226, 259n15

Rocamora, Agnès, 51, 252n15, 253n32